Study Guide

to accompany

Life-Span Development

Seventh Edition

John W. Santrock

University of Texas-Dallas

Prepared by

Anita Rosenfield

Chaffey Community College

McGraw-Hill College

Boston   Burr Ridge, IL   Dubuque, IA   Madison, WI   New York   San Francisco   St. Louis
Bangkok   Bogotá   Caracas   Lisbon   London   Madrid
Mexico City   Milan   New Delhi   Seoul   Singapore   Sydney   Taipei   Toronto

McGraw-Hill College

A Division of The McGraw·Hill Companies

Study Guide to accompany
LIFE-SPAN DEVELOPMENT

2 3 4 5 6 7 8 9 0 QPD/QPD 9 0 9

ISBN 0-697-36513-1

www.mhhe.com

Contents

A Letter to You, the Student

Dear Student,

I am writing this letter to you to offer some thoughts on how you can use this Study Guide to help you learn the material contained in *Life-Span Development, 7ᵗʰ edition*, by John W. Santrock. Although these ideas come from many years of being a student (*many years*) and a psychology professor, they are not particularly new, and you may already know many of them-- but sometimes we need to be reminded about how helpful these tips can be. I hope you will find this Study Guide and my suggestions to be useful.

First and foremost, let me tell you that *the most effective way to use this material is to apply it to your life!!!!* What my students tell me at the end of the semester are things like: "This course really helped me to understand the things I did as a teenager--now I have better insight about how to live a more productive life as an adult"; "By taking this class, I have come to terms with some things in my life. I am getting divorced and am now better able to prepare for this stage in my life. . . . I have also seen what went wrong in my marriage. . . . I can see where things went wrong and I can now try to work them out"; "Now, when I think about middle age and late adulthood, I feel I have something to look forward to rather than be afraid. I can go through these stages with open arms now"; "The most important thing I learned in this class is a better understanding of people of all ages. I understand my son's feisty temperament and deal with him much more effectively." "I thought that some of the things my two-year-old was doing were problem behaviors; now I see how they are typical of two-year-olds and I can work with her more effectively. It's amazing how this has improved our relationship and *her* behavior!"

This is just a sampling, but you can get the idea of how you, as a consumer of information, can use the information in the text and your class for your own life, whatever your major in college.

Now, let me tell you how the Study Guide is set up. The first section is *Learning Objectives*, a set of approximately ten to twelve statements of the ideas and material you should understand after having read the chapter. You may wish to read the learning objectives *before* you read the chapter, so you can have an idea of what you're trying to learn as you read; then again, after having read the chapter, by going through the learning objectives you can see if you did, indeed, "get it all."

The second section is a set of approximately 24 *Study Cards*. Throughout my undergraduate, graduate, and doctoral studies my friends and I made our own study cards because we found them to be so helpful. All key terms in the chapters are contained on the study cards; you may note as you go through the text that sometimes there are fewer (or more) than 24 key terms--I have consolidated some of the related terms onto one card, and have added questions about other key ideas throughout the chapters onto other cards. By cutting out the cards and going through each of them, you can test yourself on the terms and ideas they contain; you can sort through them as you go, putting the ones you answer easily aside, and repeating the ones with which you have difficulty until you have remembered all of the information.

The third section contains *Self Tests. Self-Test A: Multiple Choice* contains a set of 30-40 multiple-choice questions covering most of the material in each chapter so you can be sure you are not only memorizing terms (Heaven forbid!), but are actually understanding the concepts contained in the text. There are many "applied" questions that require you to think about how these ideas would work if you were looking at real people (well, okay, in this case they are hypothetical, but use your imagination). The answers to all the questions, and the page numbers where the information is located in the text, are included at the end of the self test sections. Depending on how much the content of the material in the text suggested matching tests to me, there are anywhere from one to three self tests that require you to match certain categories (e.g., researchers, stages of development) with a descriptive statement. I will admit that not only my students, but sometimes I, too, have difficulty remembering what all those different stages are (when you look at all the theories and all the stages in each one, it sometimes gets confusing!), and what all the different researchers said and did. This is a way for you to connect the ideas with the people, stages, etc. Answers to these matching tests are at the end of the self test section.

Also in the *Self Test* section you will find self essay tests (most chapters have two, occasionally, you will see three of them). In these questions, I tried to tie the material from the entire chapter together so you can see how all of the research, ideas, facts, and theories tie together. My answers to these questions are merely skeletal, and, should you choose to answer them, you will have to expand on what is in there by drawing on the material in the chapter. To be honest, if I were to give these essay questions in my own classes (which I sometimes do), I would want my students to be able to put together information from more than one chapter to answer the questions fully--so you may want to think about how to do that.

Finally, each chapter has at least one suggested *Research Activity* (although most have two, and some have three). The best way to learn the course material of any class is to use it, to think about its application to your own life. These activities will force you to do just that. You may ask your professor if you may choose one of these as a class project or for extra credit, or just do them for the fun of it to see how they work. Go through all of the activities in the beginning of the term because you may see one in later chapters that you might have wanted to work on throughout the term, and if you wait until the last week or two you may not have enough time to get it done.

Okay, so that's the structure of the chapters in the Study Guide. Now, let's talk about effective ways to study. As I mentioned earlier, you may already know some of these ideas, but oftentimes they can bear repeating because you say to yourself, "Oh, yeah, I knew that. I tried it before and it worked, but then for some reason I stopped. I think I'll try it again." Other ideas may be new to you, so you may want to give them a try. Remember that we are all unique, so some strategies work better for some people than for others--try out a suggestion for a fair period of time (only you can decide what "fair" is), and if it works, great--if it doesn't try something else.

BEING AN EXCELLENT STUDENT[1]

Most students who are in college want to be good students, and most students have some particular goal in mind, which is probably why they chose the particular college or university they are attending. As you chose your college or university, and perhaps even an area of major

---

[1]Much of the information on "Being an Excellent Student," including formulating the plan, establishing goals, attending classes, benefitting from lectures, reading for learning, the SQ3R method of studying, taking tests, and parts of the section on dealing with test anxiety have been adapted from the 6th edition of the Student Study Guide, which was prepared by Blaine Peden, John W. Santrock, and Allen Keniston. I would like to thank them for sharing those ideas with me for incorporation into this 7th edition of the Student Study Guide.

interest or concentration, you had certain goals in mind, which likely include doing well in school, earning good grades, and graduating.

Unfortunately, many students do not do as well in college as they had hoped and expected. Let's examine some of the reasons for this disappointing outcome to see how to avoid them and to learn, instead, how to be a good student and guide your behavior to improve your chances of achieving your goals.

A common definition of education is that it is "how people learn stuff." For most of our history, educators have focused on the "stuff." Teachers were required to be masters of their respective academic fields. Even today, some states have requirements that speak only to the need to be qualified in the subject matter one teaches, not in the teaching methods themselves.

In the 1960s, we became more interested in the "people" part of the definition, which was evidenced by moving to strategies like open classrooms and free universities. The idea was that, given the opportunity to do so, people will naturally learn. Although these experiments were dismal failures, they taught us something.

The key to the definition of education is the word *how*. Today, thanks to a wealth of research on the principles that guide the phenomenon of learning, and on the nature of learning and memory, we know much more about how learning occurs and how we can make it better. By using these principles, we can become better students.

Formulating the Plan

Anything worth having is worth planning for. Whether you hope to learn to teach, to fly, to write for profit, or to change diapers correctly, you have in mind a goal. An everyday question from the first days in elementary school is, "What do you want to be when you grow up?" The answer to this question is one way of formulating a goal. Now that you are a college student, many people will expect you to know what you want to do for a profession or career. Yet you may not have the foggiest notion, or you might have an idea that is still slightly foggy. That is OK. What is clear, however, is that you want to succeed in your college courses. This is a relatively long-range goal, and as such can serve a purpose in keeping you on track.

But our day-to-day behavior is often hard to connect to our long-range goals. We need short-term goals to keep us organized and to be sure that the flow of our activities is in the direction we want to be going. To accomplish our long-range goals, we need to focus on three types of short-term goals. First, we need goals for the day; second, we need goals for the week; and third, we need goals for the semester or term. Let's look at each of these separately.

Goals for Today

It is helpful to keep a daily checklist, diary, or schedule as a reminder of what must be done each day. Check off the things as you accomplish them. A pocket calendar is particularly helpful for this task.

Goals for the Week

Students who are successful in college also schedule their time weekly. Sometime during the course of registration, you made up a schedule showing your classes for the whole week. If you have a job, you must allow time for that, too. Also, many college or university students have family obligations that need to be considered as well. Finally, everyone needs some time for relaxing, eating, sleeping, and playing (even in graduate school we were advised that we needed to find some time to have fun in order to keep our balance). With all these things in mind, it is no wonder many students find little time to study.

But good students do all these things, too, yet they study. Do they have more time? No, we all have the same amount of time. But successful students schedule their time carefully. So, make up a weekly schedule and block off time for all these necessary events: classes, work, relaxation, eating, sleeping, playing, family, and studying. Students who actually schedule their time and keep to their schedules are amazed at how much time they find they have!

As you make up your weekly schedule, you may find your study time in a large block. If this is true, please remember to take a short break every twenty to thirty minutes. This is called distributed practice and is far more efficient than studying for hours on end. After the first twenty or thirty minutes, most of us become much less efficient anyway. When you take that break, reward yourself somehow; then get back to your studying. Something I always tell my students is never to try to read a whole chapter in one sitting--in fact, when I am preparing for a new class, or have changed texts in a class I have been teaching, I take that advice myself!

Goals for the Semester

At the beginning of each semester, we find ourselves immersed in many new courses. Often, you will be confronted by several new professors with whom you have never worked before. It is difficult to sort out the expectations and demands of these several courses. However, it is important to organize the information that will be needed for completing all of the course requirements in order to be successful in the courses.

If you can, obtain a large wall calendar, and mark on it all the dates of tests, exams, and term paper due dates, being sure to write on the calendar the course for which each date applies. Now, estimate how long it will take you to make final preparations for those exams, and mark those dates as warning or alert dates. Look over the dates on which papers are due, and see if they are bunched together. If your college is typical, they are. You can help yourself to avoid the last-minute all-nighters if you simply determine a spread of due dates for yourself, and mark those on the calendar too. As you do this step, please be sure to avoid any days that have personal significance for you, such as birthdays, anniversaries, and so on. This calendar gives you an overview of major dates in your semester.

If you have followed this carefully, you now have a large semester calendar plastered on your wall, a weekly schedule of major life events, classes, and study times taped over your desk, and a daily checklist of must-do items in your pocket or purse. So, your scheduling is on its way. Let's look now at other important strategies.

Attending Classes

Many students believe that, since they are in college, they can decide whether to go to class at all. This is true. Some students also believe that attendance in class is not important to their grade. This is not true! Some colleges or universities have attendance requirements, so that if students miss a given number of classes it will either lower their grade a full letter grade, or the instructor may drop the student from the course; some instructors have in-class activities that count toward students' grades, so if students are not in class, they do not get credit for participating. Even without such strategies, students who do not attend class sessions almost always do more poorly on the tests and exams. Perhaps they were absent when a crucial item was discussed, or when the instructor lectured over the material this examination requires. Remember, that more often than not, instructors will include information in their lectures that is not in your textbook, and that information (whether from class lecture, videos shown in class, guest lectures, and so on) is fair game for tests. Moreover, if you are not there, the instructor cannot get to know you, and therefore cannot give you the benefit of the doubt on your answers. It should come as no surprise that in study after research study, the data clearly show that those students who attend class regularly receive the highest grades and actually learn more, too! So, the first rule of being an effective student is to attend classes. Besides, how else can you get your money's worth?

But okay, now that you've determined you will go to every class, what will you do?

Benefitting from Lectures

Sometimes students think that if they come to class and "pay attention," they will remember what the instructor talked about; they think that if they take notes, they will miss much of what the instructor says. But sitting and paying attention is difficult. For one thing, most people can think much faster than they can speak. While the instructor lectures at 80 words per minute, the student thinks at about 350 words per minute! If the student is using this extra "thinking capacity" to focus on what the instructor is saying, it is fine. This rarely lasts more than five minutes at a time, however. Most of the time, this extra "thinking capacity" is used in daydreaming!

Daydreaming can be helpful in resolving our emotional problems, planning the course of our lives, and avoiding work. Often, it is motivated by the desire to avoid work. For whatever motive, however, daydreaming is not compatible with attending a lecture. Human beings simply cannot attend to more than one stimulus at one time. And you have to admit, your daydreams can be ever so much more interesting than your professor's lectures.

Attending lectures is best done while taking notes. Use plenty of paper, and leave blank lines at regular intervals, or leave wide side margins. You will use these spaces later (they are not wasted!). If the instructor permits it, be brave and interrupt with questions if you do not understand what is being said. One thing I try to stress to my students is that I may know what I am talking about, but it may be unclear to them--and if it's unclear to one student, it may well be unclear to other students. So, for the sake of the other students who didn't understand what I was talking about, each student should take on the responsibility of asking me to clarify what I said, or to expand in a way that will help them understand. Remember that lectures have a way of progressing and building on earlier information. It is important to understand each point, or later points will be lost. (But please, DO NOT ask the person sitting next to you what the professor said--it disrupts the class, disturbs your neighbor, and you are likely NOT to get an accurate response!)

When you take notes, write out the major points, and try to just make simple notes on the supporting minor points. If you miss something, and you cannot ask a question about it, approach the instructor immediately afterward, when it is likely to still be fresh in both your minds. DO NOT try to write down every word, and DO try to use abbreviations or symbols (the Greek symbols Ψ and Φ are a lot shorter to write than the words "psychology" and "physiology"!); or, you could do what I did--learn shorthand! (Or, make up your own.)

Often my students will ask if they may tape record my lectures. Personally, I have no objection to having students do this. In fact, I did this my first term back in college (I had dropped out of college for sixteen years), but found it was terribly tedious trying to transcribe the lecture. The students for whom this may be particularly helpful is those who have visual, auditory, or motor impairments. However, do not ever tape record a lecture without first asking for and obtaining the professor's permission.

Within one or two hours after the lecture, but for sure on the same day, go back over your notes, and do two things. First, fill in the rest of the minor points. This often amounts to completing the sentence or other element. Second, write brief summaries and any questions that you now have in the blank spaces (lines or margins) you left earlier (clever of you to leave those spaces!). These few minutes spent reviewing and organizing your notes will pay off in greatly improved memory. The questions you have you can ask in class, or during the instructor's office hours, and reap two benefits. First, you will get the answers. Second, you will demonstrate that you are a serious student, and that will impress your instructor.

One other thing about going to class. While this is not always true, I have found that typically my best students sit in front. And most students seem to have a need to have "their seat," while a few students have a need to move around, sitting in one seat one day and a different seat the next. It wasn't until my graduate school days that I realized why I needed "my seat"--as a student, we are being overwhelmed with new information, a stressful experience; we need some structure we can count on to reduce that stress. So, if you are one of those who likes to wander, be considerate of your classmates' needs for stress reduction.

By the way, to get the most out of the lectures, do complete the assigned reading BEFORE the class begins so you are familiar with the material. This will help you keep up with what the instructor is talking about, will reduce the amount of information you do not understand, but may also bring up important questions for you to ask in class if the instructor does not talk about them.

Reading for Learning

We all know how to read. You are proving it by reading these words. Hopefully, you are also realizing some ideas as a result of reading. If you are only reading words, please WAKE UP! STOP DAYDREAMING!

We can read a variety of things: newspapers, movie reviews, novels, magazines, and textbooks. Textbooks are unlike all the others, and must be read with a strategy all their own.

There are many reading and studying strategies, and all of them work to an extent. Perhaps you learned one or more in the course of going to high school. Perhaps you even took a how-to-study course when you entered college. If so, you probably learned one or two of these systems. If you have one you like, that works for you, keep it. If you are interested in learning a new one, read on.

The SQ3R Method

One of the most successful and most widely used methods of studying written material is the SQ3R method, first developed at The Ohio State University. Researchers had noted that students who were more successful were more active readers. This method teaches you the same skills that have made many thousands of students successful. If you use this method when you read and study, you will be more successful, too.

The S stands for SURVEY. After you have read the overview or chapter outline, and the list of learning objectives, you should survey the chapter in the text. This is also called skimming. Look at the headings and subheadings, and get the gist of the major points in this chapter. If you have an outline of the chapter (some books provide them), check off each point as you pass it in the pages of the text.

The Q stands for QUESTION. Reading is greatly enhanced if you are searching for the answers to questions. For this text, the Student Study Guide provides learning objectives that can serve as questions. For other texts, make up questions for yourself, based on the chapter overview or on your own survey of the chapter. Be sure that you have at least one question for each major unit in the chapter; you will be less efficient at studying those units for which you do not have questions.

The first of the three Rs is for READ. As you read, look for the answers to the questions you posed, or to the study or learning objectives furnished for you. When you find material that answers these questions, put a mark (X) or a "post-it" note in the margin next to that material. This will help now, since you are actively involved, and later, when you review. It is a good idea to wait to underline or highlight lines of text until after you have read the entire chapter at least once, so you will know what is and what is not most important. (In fact, while some "authorities" suggest you underline or highlight no more than 10% of what you are reading, I find that when most of us begin to underline or highlight, we wind up doing it to most of the chapter--I suggest not doing it at all because it becomes too passive, which counteracts your attempts to read "actively.")

The second R is for RECITE. One of the oldest classroom techniques in the world (Aristotle used it) is recitation. In the classroom version, the teacher asks the questions and the students answer them. Unless you can get your teacher to study with you regularly, you'll have to play both roles. Periodically stop in your reading and say aloud (if possible) what the author is telling you. Try to put it in your own words, but be sure to use technical terms as you learn them. If you are not in a situation where you can recite out loud, do it in writing. Just thinking it is not enough. When should you pause to recite? A good rule of thumb is that each time you come to the end of a major subheading, you should recite. One professor encourages his students to recite at least one sentence at the end of each paragraph, and two or three or more sentences at the end of each subunit (when you come to a new heading).

People who do not use recitation usually forget half of what they read in one hour, and another half of the half they remembered by the end of the day. People who use recitation often remember from 75 to 90 percent of what they studied. This technique pays off. By the way, if anyone questions why you are talking to yourself, tell them that a psychologist recommended it.

The third R is for REVIEW. You should review a chapter soon after you have studied it (using the SQ and first 2Rs). You should review it again the day or evening before a test. It is not usually helpful to cram the night before a test, and particularly not the day of the test! That type of studying does not produce good memory, and is likely to make you more anxious during the test itself.

Taking Tests

One of the things students fear most is failure. Failure signifies that things are not going well, and alerts us to the possibility that we may not achieve our goals. Unfortunately, many students see tests and exams as opportunities to fail. They prepare by becoming anxious and fearful, and trying to cram as much as possible right before the exam. These students rarely do well on the exam. They often fail, thus accomplishing just what they feared.

Taking tests requires strategy and planning. First, it is helpful to know what type of tests you will have. Your instructor probably told you during the first class meeting, or perhaps is waiting for you to ask, or it may be in the class syllabus or course outline. If you do not know, ask.

If you are going to be taking essay exams, the best way to prepare is by writing essays. Before you do this, it is a good idea to find out what types of questions the instructor asks, and what is expected in a response. Again, it is helpful to ask the instructor for this material. Perhaps you can even see some examples of essay questions from previous years--some instructors at some colleges have copies of their exams on file in the department office or in the library, although many do not do this. By finding out what is expected, you can formulate a model against which you can evaluate your answers.

Now, using the learning objectives, or some essay questions you wrote, actually sit down and write out the answers. I have prepared at least two essay questions for each chapter in this text, and have provided the basic ideas you need for answering those essays. Use those to practice writing answers to essay questions. HINT: If you usually feel more anxious during a test, it may help you to practice writing your essays in the room in which the test will be given. Simply find a time when the room is vacant, and make yourself at home.

If your instructor gives multiple-choice tests, then you should practice taking multiple-choice tests. For each chapter, either use questions provided in the Student Study Guide, or make up your own. You may find it helpful to work out an arrangement to pool questions with other students, thereby reducing the amount of work you have to do, and developing a network of friends. Or, you may ask your professor if he or she would entertain the idea of having students write some of the exam questions--some of my professors did that in my undergraduate classes, and it is something I sometimes have my students do (my rationale is not that it makes things easier for me--it doesn't--but that it gets my students to study!).

Whichever way you do it, the important thing is to prepare for tests and exams. Preparation is about 95 percent of the secret to getting a good grade. (Yes, there is some actual luck or chance involved in test scores, as even your instructor will admit!) Preparation is not only a good study and review technique, but also helps to reduce anxiety.

Dealing with Test Anxiety

Some students find that the prospect of a test or an examination produces a set of responses that leave them feeling helpless, very anxious, and certain of failure. They find it hard to read the questions, often leave the examination incomplete, have stomach pains and other somatic problems, and contemplate drastic measures, such as dropping out. Other students are less severely affected. For some, a little anxiety gives them the "edge" they need to do well. In fact, anxiety can be a helpful response when it occurs at low levels. In 1908, Yerkes and Dodson showed that the amount of anxiety that could benefit performance was a function of the difficulty and complexity of the task. As the difficulty of the task rose, anxiety became less helpful and more likely to interfere with performance.

If you have ever been so anxious in a test situation that you were unable to do well, even though you knew the information, you have test anxiety. If you get your exams back, and are surprised that you marked wrong answers when you knew the correct answers, or if you can only remember the correct answers after you leave the examination room, you too may have test anxiety. Short of dropping out of college, or seeing a professional counselor, what can you do? Well, here are some suggested strategies:

Strategy Number One: Effective Study

Use study habits that promote learning and make the best use of time. Strategies, such as scheduling your time and using the SQ3R system, reduce anxiety by increasing confidence. As you come to realize that you know the material, your confidence rises and anxiety retreats.

Strategy Number Two: Relaxation

Each of us develops a unique pattern of relaxation. Some people relax by going to a specific place, either in person or mentally. Others relax by playing music, by being with friends, by using autogenic relaxation phrases, or by meditating. Whatever you do, be aware of it, and try to practice relaxation techniques. If you are good at relaxing, try thinking about those situations that make you anxious, and relax while you think of them. To do this, allow yourself to think only briefly (fifteen to thirty seconds at a time) of the situation that makes you anxious, and then relax again. After a number of such pairings, you will find that thinking about that situation no longer makes you anxious. At this point, you may be surprised to find that the situation itself also no longer produces anxiety. You may find that it is helpful to think about these anxiety-provoking situations in a sequence from those that produce very little anxiety to those that are more anxiety-evoking. Such a list, from low to high anxiety, might look something like this:

1.   Your instructor announces that there will be a test in four weeks.
2.   Your instructor reminds you of the test next week.
3.   As you study, you see on the course outline the word *test*, and remember next week's test.
4.   One of your friends asks you if you want to study together for the test, which is the day after tomorrow.
5.   You choose not to go out with your friends because of the test tomorrow.
6.   As you get up in the morning, you remember that today is the day of the test.
7.   You are walking down the hall toward the classroom, thinking about what questions might be on the test.
8.   The instructor enters the classroom, carrying a sheaf of papers in hand.
9.   The instructor distributes the papers, and you see the word *test* or *exam* at the top.
10.   After reading the first five questions, you have not been able to think of the answer to any of them.

If you work at it gradually and consistently, pairing these types of thoughts (briefly) with relaxation and remembering to let go and relax after each one, this will dispel test anxiety and make test taking a more productive and successful experience.

Strategy Number Three: Thinking Clearly

Most students who have test anxiety think in unclear and unproductive ways. They say to themselves things like: "I can't get these answers correct . . . I don't know this stuff . . . I don't know anything at all . . . I'm going to fail this test . . . I'm probably going to flunk out of school . . . I'm just a dumb nerd." These thoughts share two unfortunate characteristics: they are negative and they are absolute. They should be replaced.

When we tell ourselves absolute and negative thoughts, we find it impossible to focus on the test material. The result is that we miss questions even when we know the answers. Our thinking prevents us from doing well.

A good strategy for replacing these negative and absolute thoughts is to practice thinking positive and honest thoughts, such as: "I may not know all the answers, but I know some of them . . . I don't know the answer to that right now, so I will go on to the next one and come back to that . . . I don't have to get them all right . . . I studied hard and carefully, and I can get some of them correct . . . I am a serious student, and have some abilities . . . I am prepared for this test, and know many of the answers . . . This test is important, but it is not going to determine the course of my entire life and if I don't do well, it doesn't mean I'm a horrible person or a dummy."

By thinking clearly, honestly, and positively, we quiet the flood of anxiety and focus on the task at hand. Students who use this technique invariably do better on the tests. It takes practice to think clearly, but it is worth the effort. After a while, you will find that it becomes natural and does not take any noticeable effort. And as anxiety is reduced, more energy is available for studying and for doing well on examinations. The eventual outcome is more enjoyment with learning, better learning, more success in college, and the achievement of your goals.

Strategy Number Four: Guided Imagery

Something I often do with my students before a test is to have them relax (see strategy Two), close their eyes, and visualize themselves walking into a tall building. They go into the elevator in the building and take it to the top floor, which is fifty-six stories up. They walk out of the elevator, and go to the stairwell, then climb to the top of the building. There is no railing on the top of the building. I direct them to walk over to the very edge of the building and put their toes at the very edge, then look down. I ask them to think about how they are feeling as they are looking down onto the street from the top of this building. I then tell them to back up, have the realization that they can fly--just spread out their arms and they can fly. Then they are directed back to the edge of the building, knowing that they can fly. They put their toes on the edge, look down, then spread their arms and fly, eventually flying down to land safely on the ground below. Next I have them visualize themselves in the classroom; on the desk before them is their test. They look at the test and see themselves reading the questions, saying "I know that answer. Yes, I remember learning that." They visualize themselves being successful, answering all the questions correctly, feeling good about themselves. Then I have them visualize getting their tests back, with a big "A" on the test.

Some students are much better able to visualize than others. You can try combining strategy two with this strategy to help you improve your visualization, since it can be an effective success strategy.

Strategy Number Five: Do the Easy Ones First

One technique I learned while studying for the GRE (Graduate Record Exam) was to read each question and answer the ones I knew, then go back to the harder ones. Two things to watch out for on this: first, be sure you get the answers in the right place--sometimes when we skip a question or two, we wind up marking the wrong space, so check that your answer to question 10 is in space 10; second, you may find you're stumped by the first several questions--don't let that throw you, just keep going because there is bound to be one you jump on and say, "Yes! I know that one." Answer the easy ones first, then go back to the others after you've built up your confidence seeing you DO know "stuff." Then, always go back over the whole test to be sure you answered every question (the exception here is if you have a professor who takes more than one point off for wrong answers--in that case, it's better not to answer than to answer wrong, but I don't know anyone who does that). I'm always upset to see that a student has gotten an answer marked wrong because no answer was provided.

Strategy Number Six: State Dependent Learning

Research has found that we remember information best when we are in the same "state" we were in when we first learned the information. So, for example, you might remember a certain song when prompted by a specific stimulus (seeing someone who reminds you of your "first true love"); or, we will remember things we learned when we were particularly happy if we are again in that mood. This goes for physical contexts as well--so that we have an advantage if we take an exam in the same room where we learned the information in the first place. But it also goes to physical context in terms of our bodies--if you drink coffee or caffeine-laden sodas when you study, try to do the same before your exam. On the other hand, if you don't consume caffeine when you study, by all means, DO NOT suddenly have a cup of coffee before your exam. Because of the power of this phenomenon, you may want to create a particular mental context for yourself when you study so that you can put yourself into the same mental context when you take your exams.

Strategy Number Seven: Take a Break

If you find yourself getting stressed out during the test, take a break. Put your pencil down, breath deeply, you may even want to put your head down on the desk (please, do not fall asleep!). Use the relaxation techniques or the guided imagery strategy; visualize yourself looking at the test and suddenly realizing that you DO know the answers to at least most of the questions. Then go back to taking the test.

Do remember, that with all of these strategies, if you don't do the first one, none of the others will help! Passing the course requires that you actively study the material.

Memory Techniques

No matter how much you read, it won't help you if you don't remember *what* you read. The most critical factor in remembering is being able to apply what you have learned. Of course, some things such as people's names, or certain dates, or statistical information are not easily applied to your life, so you'll have to use other techniques. But first, let's talk about the "easy way."

Apply It to Your Life

If you can take the material you are learning and use it in your everyday life, you will remember it without any problem. If you have a two-year-old child, then you read about what Piaget said about how two-year-olds think, or what Erikson said about the need for children to gain a sense of autonomy over their bodies, or what the information-processing theorists say about how much a two-year-old can remember, you can see how (and if) these theories apply to your child. Of course, not everyone has a two-year-old child, but we all were two years old at some point in our lives, or we may know children who are that age. Watch children, see how the theories work by observing what these children do. The same goes for observing infants, teenagers, adults--and particularly yourself!

Another method of applying the material to your life is to connect it with what you already know, either from life experience or other courses you have taken. Sometimes what you are learning fits nicely with what you already knew; sometimes it will contradict what you learned before. This is an opportunity to look at how the new information fits in with the old--were there new research findings? Or, is it merely a difference of opinion? Make these associations--don't keep the information for any class neatly compartmentalized--if you do, you'll have a hard time trying to find it when you need it.

Teach It to Someone Else!

In graduate school, I was having problems learning statistics. My advisor told me that the best way for me to learn it would be to teach it. When we start teaching something to someone else, we find we HAVE TO learn it, and by trying to explain the material to another person, we examine it and think about it differently. So, take the material you are learning in this class (or any class) and teach it to someone else. When they ask you questions, you can look them up and find the answers, or think them out together, or ask someone else. As you explain these concepts to someone else (your children, your friends, or even your dog), you will suddenly see them in a totally different light.

Mnemonic Techniques

Some things are just really difficult to apply to your own life. Dates, names, places, statistics, and such may not have a great deal of meaning for you. In that event, use the tricks that memory specialists use--mnemonics. There are many different types. For example, one famous mnemonic is an acronym for remembering the Great Lakes: HOMES=Huron, Ontario, Michigan, Erie, and Superior; or the colors of the rainbow is a man's name: ROY G. BIV=Red, Orange, Yellow, Green, Blue, Indigo, and Violet (if not for this "man," I'd never remember indigo!) You can make up your own acronyms by taking the first initial of any term, person, etc. It's easiest, though, if it's something that makes sense to you.

Another mnemonic technique is called the "method of loci," and I've been told it's one that medical students use to remember body parts. You list the things you need to remember, then visualize yourself walking around a familiar place (like your living room), putting one item on a particular piece of furniture. Then, when you need to remember that item, you go through your "living room" to see where it is. Say, for example, you need to remember the theorists in Chapter 2 of this text. You might put Piaget on the piano, Freud on the floor, Skinner on the sofa, and so on. (They don't have to be on the object that starts with their name, but it might help when you CAN do that.) Now, you also need to associate the theorists with their theories. So, you might imagine Piaget is thinking about how to play the piano; Freud has hidden unacceptable thoughts under the carpet on the floor; Skinner has been reinforced for sitting so nicely on the sofa, etc.

One other mnemonic technique is the story method. Take the information you need to remember and put it into a story. So, you may make up a story about how Piaget came up with his four stages of development (since he relied so heavily on his own three children, you might want to incorporate them into the story, but it's your story--do it the way you want).

Be an "Information Dropper"

This is similar to the suggestion to teach, but less formal. Ask your friends to "indulge" you by listening to what you learned in your Life Span Development class (or any other class). Then *tell* them what you are learning. You may, in fact, find that you have managed to help one of your friends by sharing this information!

Rote Memory

If you can remember back to grade school, when you learned to multiply, somehow the only way that seems to happen is by repeating the multiplication tables over and over and over again. Personally, I think this is about the worst way to learn most anything, but for some things (like multiplication tables) it works. The Study Cards that are included in each chapter of this Study Guide are a way to help you learn through repeating the material you don't know until you are able to answer the questions posed without looking at the reverse side of the cards. Hopefully you will then go further, and apply the information to other areas of your life.

Most Important

Remember this: professors don't actually "teach" their students, rather, they facilitate learning so students end up teaching themselves. While we try really hard to motivate our students, keep them interested, and present information in a way that helps students to understand, the ultimate responsibility for learning rests with the student. Some students have learned *despite* their professors, others don't learn even with the very best of professors. So, keep your goals in mind, study hard, ask questions, and aim for success.

If you have thoughts you'd like to share with me--other ideas for how to learn/study, things that worked for you or didn't work for you--you may reach me through my e-mail address: arosenfield@eee.org.

With good thoughts for your continued success,

Anita Rosenfield, Ph.D.

Two Important Notes About Getting Permission

In each chapter of this Study Guide you will find suggested Research Activities. Some of these involve working with children, many involve requesting participation by persons (children, adolescents, and/or adults) who are not members of your Life-Span Development class. Whenever you work with persons under the age of 18, you should obtain written permission from a parent or guardian (even if that is not specifically mentioned in the particular Research Activity); also, **always** ask the person assisting you if he or she is willing to help you with your project, despite that person's age. (A sample form is included below.) If the parent, guardian, or participant indicates a reluctance to participate, thank them anyway and move on to someone else. Participation in research is **always** voluntary; no one should ever be coerced into involvement, and once having begun, participants **always** have the right to discontinue their participation should they so desire.

Further, each institution (college, university, etc.) has its own standards for conducting research. Before engaging in any of the suggested Research Activities, check with your instructor to determine whether you need to obtain approval from your school's Institutional Review Board (IRB). If approval is necessary, be sure to plan sufficient time for completing your project that includes time for getting your proposal reviewed.

SAMPLE CONSENT FORM

Psychology_____   Life-Span Development

In partial fulfillment of the requirements of this course, I will need to *[fill in what you will need to do, for example: observe a child who is between five and ten years of age. I will need to have this child perform three tasks and answer questions about _____ . During the observations I will assess the child's ability to complete various tasks, including:*

     *   *Discussing whether various items (such as a car or an egg) are alive*
     *   *Telling me if certain shapes look like boys or girls to the child)*

I will compile a summary report based on these observations, and I will submit this report to my Psychology Professor, _____. In my report, I will include information about the child's age and gender, but I will not disclose the child's identity. The child's performance on these tasks cannot be used to speculate about the child's potential, and I will make no speculations about the child based on these observations. I will read the above statements to the parents of the child I will observe.

_____   _____

Date   Student's Signature

_____   _____ / _____

Parent's Name Printed   Child's Name   Age

The above statements were read to me, and I understand that my child will be observed in the manner described. I agree to allow my child to participate in these observations. I understand that I can withdraw this agreement at any time. If I have any further questions I understand that I may contact _____, Professor of Psychology at _____ (phone #:   ).

                                                               _____Date

_____
Parent's Signature

Life-Span Development

Section I   The Life-Span Developmental Perspective

Chapter 1   Introduction

Learning Objectives

1. Explain the importance of studying life-span development.

2. Describe the history of interest in children and adolescents and indicate how contemporary concerns have arisen from previous views.

3. Describe the seven basic characteristics of the life-span perspective.

4. List and describe the three interacting systems of contextualism.

5. Describe the role that experts in developmental psychology have regarding health and well-being, parenting and education, sociocultural contexts, and social policy.

6. Define and distinguish among biological processes, cognitive processes, and socioemotional processes.

7. Understand the major developmental periods from conception to death.

8. Define and distinguish among chronological age, biological age, psychological age, and social age.

9. Understand the three major developmental issues (nature and nurture, continuity and discontinuity, stability and change).

10. Identify several options that are available to individuals who are interested in careers in life-span development.

Define the notions of
original sin,
tabula rasa,
and innate goodness.

What are
cross-cultural studies?

What are
the storm-and-stress view
and
the interventionist view?

Explain the issue of
social policy.

Define gerontology.

Explain generational inequity.

State the seven basic characteristics
of the life-span perspective.

Define development.

Compare
normative age-graded influences,
normative history-graded influences,
and nonnormative life events.

Explain these processes:
biological,
cognitive,
and socioemotional

What are
context, culture, and ethnicity?

Describe the prenatal period.

Cross-cultural studies involve a comparison of a culture with one or more other cultures and provide information about the degree to which development is similar (universal) across cultures or is culture-specific.

Original sin: children are born evil
Tabula rasa: children are like a "blank tablet" and learn through experience (Locke)
Innate goodness: children are inherently good (Rousseau)

Social policy is a national government's course of action designed to influence the welfare of its citizens.

Storm-and-stress: adolescence is a turbulent time of conflict & mood swings (G. Stanley Hall)
Inventionist: sociohistorical conditions contributed to the emergence of the concept of adolescence, "inflicted" this status on young people, & kept them dependent

---

Generational inequity is the condition in which an aging society is being unfair to its younger members.

Gerontology is the study of aging and its biological, cognitive, & socioemotional dimensions (from the Greek word *gerant*, "old man").

Development is the pattern of movement or change that begins at conception and continues through the life span.

Development is lifelong, multidimensional, multidirectional, plastic, historically embedded, multidisciplinary, & contextual. (Baltes)

Biological: involve changes in the individual's physical nature (e.g., genes)
Cognitive: involve changes in the individual's thought, intelligence, language
Socioemotional: involve changes in the individual's relationships with other people, changes in emotions, & changes in personality

Normative age-graded: similar biological & environmental influences for individuals of a particular age group
Normative history-graded: biological & environmental influences associated with history
Nonnormative life events: unusual occurrences having a major impact on a person's life, not applicable to many persons

---

The prenatal period is the time from conception to birth.

Context: the setting in which development occurs (influenced by historical, economic, social & cultural factors)
Culture: behavior patterns, beliefs, other products a group passes on from generation to generation
Ethnicity: based on cultural heritage, race, nationality, characteristics, religion, language

Name the three developmental periods extending from birth to puberty.

Define maturation.

What is adolescence and when does it occur?

Explain the nature-nurture controversy.

Define the three developmental periods of adulthood.

Explain the concept of continuity of development.

What is biological age?

What does the notion of discontinuity of development state?

Explain the concept of psychological age.

Explain the stability-change issue.

Define social age.

Define the dialectical model.

Maturation is the orderly sequence of changes dictated by an individual's genetic blueprint.

Infancy: from birth to 18 or 24 months
Early childhood: from the end of infancy to about 5 or 6 years of age (also called the "preschool years")
Middle & late childhood: from about 6 to 11 years of age (also called the "elementary school years)

The nature-nurture controversy involves the debate about whether development is primarily influenced by maturation or by experience; this debate has been part of psychology since its beginning.
Nature refers to biological inheritance.
Nurture refers to environmental experiences.

Adolescence is the developmental period of transition from childhood to early adulthood; it begins at approximately 10 to 12 years of age and ends at 18 to 22 years of age.

Continuity of development: development involves gradual, cumulative change from conception to death (e.g., from practice) (This is "quantitative" change--there is "more of something" such as language)

Early adulthood: begins in late teens/early 20s & lasts through the 30s
Middle adulthood: begins approximately at 35-45 & extends to the 60s
Late adulthood: begins in 60s or 70s & lasts until death (young old: 65-74; old old: 75+; oldest old: 85+)

Discontinuity of development: development involves distinct stages in the life span, such as a caterpillar changing into a butterfly (This is "qualitative" change--the butterfly is a different kind of organism from the caterpillar)

Biological age: a person's age in terms of biological health--the younger a person's biological age, the longer the person is expected to live, regardless of chronological age (the number of years that have elapsed since a person's birth)

Stability-change issue: addresses whether development is best described by stability or by change; involves the degree to which we become older renditions of our early experience or someone different from who we were earlier in our development

Psychological age: an individual's adaptive capacities compared to those of other individuals of the same chronological age--persons who adapt more effectively than their chronological agemates are considered "psychologically young"; those who do not adapt as effectively are "psychologically old"

Dialectical model: each individual is continually changing because of various forces that push & pull development forward' each person is viewed as acting on & reacting to social & historical conditions (Riegel)

Social age refers to social roles an expectations related to a person's age, such as the role of "mother" or "father.

Self-Test A: Multiple Choice

1. Which of the following *is not* a reason the text gave to study life-span development?
   a. The more you learn about children, the better you can deal with them.
   b. You may gain insight into your own history.
   c. It is a requirement for such fields as nursing, psychology and child development.
   d. As a parent or teacher, you may have responsibility for children.

2. During medieval times, European artists often depicted children as:
   a. beggars.
   b. satanic.
   c. angelic.
   d. miniature adults.

3. Parents who believe their children are basically good and need little discipline have adopted which philosophical view?
   a. original sin
   b. *tabula rasa*
   c. innate goodness
   d. experiential

4. From the viewpoint of the 1990s, the most representative description of childhood is that it is a period:
   a. of preparing to become an adult.
   b. requiring much discipline to shape proper behavior.
   c. to be tolerated until adult behavior emerges.
   d. of growth and change requiring special care.

5. What does it mean when it is stated that "American society may have 'inflicted' the status of adolescence on its youth"?
   a. American society has recognized the innate biological nature of adolescence.
   b. We have laws for youth that put them in submissive, dependent positions and keep them out of the workforce.
   c. American youth are pressured into becoming adults too early.
   d. Adolescence is an arbitrary designation created by legislators and educators.

6. Parents adhering to the fundamental premise of Jean-Jacques Rousseau's "innate goodness" argument would:
   a. reject the need to "teach" language since speech is inherited.
   b. provide their children with little monitoring or constraints.
   c. view their child as intellectually indistinguishable from themselves.
   d. argue that their newborn's brain is like a "blank slate."

7. According to G. Stanley Hall, the life of a typical teenager would best be described in terms of:
   a. storm and stress.
   b. trust and mistrust.
   c. love and sex.
   d. an Oedipal or Electra conflict.

8. The life-span perspective emphasizes:
   a. extreme change from birth to adolescence, little in adulthood.
   b. much change in childhood, stability in adolescence and adulthood.
   c. little change in adulthood, decline in older years.
   d. change during adulthood as well as childhood.

9. Which of the following is true concerning the maximum life span of humans?
   a. It has increased dramatically over the past 100 years.
   b. It has increased gradually over the past 100 years.
   c. It has increased dramatically since the beginning of recorded history.
   d. It has not changed since the beginning of recorded history.

10. A psychologist adhering to the traditional approach in development would most likely describe change during middle age using the term:
    a. crisis.
    b. gradual.
    c. negative.
    d. stagnant.

11. Many older persons become wiser with age, yet perform more poorly on cognitive speed tests. This supports the life-span perspective notion that development is:
    a. multidirectional.
    b. multidimensional.
    c. lifelong.
    d. plastic.

12. Researchers have demonstrated that an older adult can learn to improve cognitive skills. This would demonstrate Baltes' notion that development is:
    a. multidimensional.
    b. multidirectional.
    c. plastic.
    d. embedded in history.

13. The onset of puberty is an example of:
    a. normative age-graded influences.
    b. normative history-graded influences.
    c. nonnormative life events.
    d. storm-and-stress events.

14. The AIDS epidemic in the United States would be an example of a:
    a. normative age-graded influence.
    b. normative history-graded influence.
    c. nonnormative life event.
    d. storm-and-stress event.

15. Experts on family policy are concerned about families that are at high risk for having their children placed in foster care, but whose problems are not sufficiently extreme to qualify for public services. These experts believe:
    a. the children should be removed before the problems become too great.
    b. these families need to be monitored to determine when the problems erupt.
    c. the parents need to take parenting classes to ensure the welfare of their children.
    d. more attention should be given to preventing family problems.

16. The studies designed to provide information about the degree to which development is universal across cultures or is culture-specific are referred to as:
    a. cross-cultural.
    b. life span.
    c. counter-cultural.
    d. inter-cultural.

17. The behavior patterns, beliefs, and all other products of a particular group of people that are passed on from generation to generation are called:
    a. nationality.
    b. religion.
    c. culture.
    d. ethnicity.

18. A nation's course of action adopted by government to influence the welfare of its citizens is called:
    a. social policy.
    b. social slate.
    c. national policy.
    d. policy agenda.

19. Marian Wright Edelman, president of the Children's Defense Fund, states that with respect to how well children are treated in industrialized nations, the United States:
    a. is the highest ranking.
    b. ranks amongst the highest.
    c. ranks around the middle.
    d. is at or near the lowest ranking.

20. The concept of generational inequity describes:
    a. the situation in which older individuals receive more of the resources than younger individuals.
    b. differences in values, and is commonly called the "generation gap."
    c. differences in years of education between older and less educated individuals and younger and better educated individuals.
    d. family power patterns in which older individuals typically have more decision-making power.

21. Development is defined as the pattern of movement or _____ across the life cycle.
    a. growth
    b. change
    c. decline
    d. stability

22. Which of the following would involve a cognitive process?
    a. hormonal changes at puberty
    b. putting together a two-word sentence
    c. an infant responding to her mother's touch with a smile
    d. an elderly couple's affection for each other

23. What is true concerning the biological, cognitive, and socioemotional processes?
    a. Each is distinct from the others.
    b. The cognitive and biological are more closely related than the cognitive.
    c. They are intricately interwoven.
    d. They are more obvious in the early years of life.

24. _____ typically marks the end of the early childhood period of development.
    a. Walking without assistance
    b. The emergence of the first word
    c. First grade
    d. The onset of puberty

25. Penny is just beginning to use language and other symbols. If she is developing normally, we would expect her to be in which developmental period?
    a. perinatal
    b. prenatal
    c. infancy
    d. early childhood

26. Which period of development is characterized by establishing independence, developing an identity, and thinking more abstractly?
    a. middle childhood
    b. late childhood
    c. adolescence
    d. early adulthood

27. People in the middle adulthood period of development would most likely spend their time in which of the following activities?
    a. developing a new career
    b. joining groups concerned with the environment
    c. going to the doctor
    d. writing an autobiography

28. Bernice Neugarten has emphasized reemerging life themes in development. Her observations have led her to conclude that:
    a. life stages are important for understanding development.
    b. each person relives his or her childhood during later development.
    c. we must focus on the later developmental periods.
    d. age is becoming less important for understanding development.

29. Researchers who are proponents of the nurture perspective would argue that:
    a. genetics determines all behavior.
    b. the environment a person is raised in determines that individual's longevity.
    c. how long an individual's parents lived is the best predictor of that individual's longevity.
    d. genetics and the environment in which an individual is raised will jointly determine that person's longevity.

30. In studying changes in the way we think as we age, Dr. Long notes a child moves from not being able to think abstractly about the world to being able to, which is a qualitative change in processing information. Dr. Long emphasizes:
    a. continuity.
    b. discontinuity.
    c. stability.
    d. maturation.

31. As men get older, their personalities tend to mellow out and they become more in touch with their feminine side. This would demonstrate the issue of:
    a. nature versus nurture.
    b. continuity versus discontinuity.
    c. stability versus change.
    d. the power of contexts.

32. According to the dialectical model, the key to understanding development is:
    a. change.
    b. stability.
    c. continuity.
    d. discontinuity.

33. Most life-span developmentalists recognize that:
    a. nature, continuity, and stability are the primary determinants of behavior.
    b. nurture, discontinuity, and change are the primary determinants of behavior.
    c. the key to development is in the interaction of nature and nurture, continuity and discontinuity, and stability and change.
    d. while nurture (the environment) is important, nature (heredity) plays the stronger role.

34. With regard to improving health in the later years, researchers have found that:
    a. if you had bad health habits during adolescence and young adulthood, you will be in poor health in old age.
    b. if your parents did not take care of your health needs when you were a child, you will be in poor health in old age.
    c. even in late adulthood exercise can significantly improve your health.
    d. exercising in late adulthood will cause serious damage to your health.

35. Ian is a health professional who studies the aging process, as well as the impact of aging on government programs, social policy, and service delivery. He has a masters degree and is currently working on his Ph.D. Ian is most likely a:
    a. college professor.
    b. gerontologist.
    c. geropsychologist.
    d. medical social worker.

Self-Test B: Matching

Match the following persons with the statement or theory that most closely reflects their perspective:

f   1. Marian Wright Edelman
c   2. John Locke
e   3. Jean-Jacques Rousseau
g   4. Bernice Neugarten
a   5. Paul Baltes
d   6. G. Stanley Hall
h   7. Klaus Riegel
b   8. Maggie Kuhn

a. The life-span perspective has 7 fundamental contentions
b. The elderly need a political voice such as Gray Panthers
c. Children are like blank slates & grow through experience
d. Adolescence is a time of storm and stress
e. Children are innately good
f. The U.S. ranks very low in the treatment of children
g. Our society is increasingly age-irrelevant
h. Change is the key to understanding development

Essay Questions:

1. After hearing that you are taking this class in Life-Span Development, your roommate says, "Life span development? Everyone knows that we are pretty much complete by the time we're six, and *nothing* much changes after adolescence--except, of course, becoming senile in old age!" Bring this less educated person up to date on today's life-span perspective, being sure to include in your response Baltes' seven factors of development (and any others that you consider relevant).

2. The "nature-nurture controversy" has been around for a long time. At coffee in the cafeteria you get into a discussion about this with two of your friends. One of them stubbornly states that nature is the only thing that matters; the other one just as stubbornly argues that nurture is the only thing that is important in terms of who we are, how we develop, and what our lives will be like. Knowing you are taking this class in Life-Span Development, they turn to you to tell them who is right. Discuss this issue with them, being sure to incorporate into your answer all you know about the biological, cognitive, and socioemotional processes.

Key to Self-Test A:

1.	c	p.	6					
2.	d	p.	6	19.	d	p.	15	
3.	c	p.	6	20.	a	p.	16	
4.	d	p.	7	21.	b	p.	16	
5.	b	p.	7	22.	c	p.	16	*should be b*
6.	b	p.	7	23.	c	p.	16-17	
7.	a	p.	7	24.	c	p.	18	
8.	d	p.	8	25.	c	p.	18	
9.	d	p.	8	26.	c	p.	18	
10.	d	p.	8	27.	b	p.	18	
11.	a	p.	10	28.	d	p.	19	
12.	c	p.	10	29.	b	p.	20-21	
13.	a	p.	11	30.	b	p.	21	
14.	b	p.	11	31.	c	p.	21	
15.	d	p.	12	32.	a	p.	22	
16.	a	p.	13	33.	c	p.	22	
17.	c	p.	13	34.	c	p.	23	
18.	a	p.	15	35.	b	p.	26	

Key to Self-Test B:

1.	f	5.	a	
2.	c	6.	d	
3.	e	7.	h	
4.	g	8.	b	

Key to Essay Questions:

1. A proper answer should describe the seven factors that Baltes states are important to understanding life-span development, that development is: lifelong, multidimensional, multidirectional, plastic, embedded in history, interdisciplinary, and contextual (being sure to discuss what each of these means). You would also want to mention the different periods of development (e.g., prenatal, infancy, etc.), and some reference to the work of Bernice Neugarten, who raises issues concerning how age should be conceptualized (i.e., chronological, biological, psychological, and social).

2. A proper answer should first explain what "nature" and "nurture" are in terms of biological predisposition and environmental influence, then look at the interaction between the two.

Research Project 1:   Issues in the Media

Review the learning objectives for this chapter and notice the issues that Santrock discusses. Then monitor the media (newspapers, talk/news radio, television) for a week and keep track of when and in what context these issues are raised. Calculate how often each specific issue is discussed and note which issue was raised most often, how it was presented (did you notice biased reporting, was it presented in terms of the life-span perspective, was it fully covered, etc.), and what additional information you would need to understand the issue (or story presented in the media) better. Discuss your findings in class.

Research Project 2:   Playground Observation of Social Interaction*

This exercise will help you hone your skills of observation and will help you learn the process of systematic observation. With a classmate, go to a place where children are present, such as a park, the children's center on your campus, a nursery school, etc. Pick two same-sex children to observe, one about 3 or 4 years old, the other about 8 or 9, then observe the social interactions of these children for five minutes. For each 30 seconds during the five minutes, as one of you observes the other records whether the child interacted with another person and whether that other person was a child (C) or an adult (A).

Time		Child 1: Sex _____ Age _____			Child 2: Sex _____ Age _____		
1.	0-30	N	C	A	N	C	A
2.	31-60	N	C	A	N	C	A
3.	61-90	N	C	A	N	C	A
4.	91-120	N	C	A	N	C	A
5.	121-150	N	C	A	N	C	A
6.	151-180	N	C	A	N	C	A
7.	181-210	N	C	A	N	C	A
8.	211-240	N	C	A	N	C	A
9.	241-270	N	C	A	N	C	A
10.	271-300	N	C	A	N	C	A

N = No interaction C = Interaction with child   A = Interaction with adult

Questions:

1. How often did each child interact with only one other child? With more than one other child? With an adult? With no one else?
2. Did you observe differences in the total number of time periods in which these two children interacted with other children and/or adults? Describe these differences.
3. Based solely on these observations, which of these two children engaged in more social interaction with children? With adults? Overall?
4. What factors do you think would explain these differences?
5. Why do you think you were instructed to observe same-sex children?

*Adapted from Simons, J. A. (1994). *Student Study Guide for Child Development*, 6th ed. (Santrock, J. W.)

Personal Application

After you have read each chapter in the text, take a moment to ask yourself the following questions. This will help you retain the information you are learning, and you will be able to make it a part of your life.

1. What information in this chapter did you already know?

2. How can/do you use that information in your own life?

3. What information in this chapter was totally new to you?

4. How can you use that new information in your own life?

5. What information in this chapter was different from what you previously believed?

6. How was this information different?

7. How do you account for the differences between what you believed and what you learned in the chapter?

Chapter 2   The Science of Life-Span Development

Learning Objectives

1.   Define and distinguish among theory, hypotheses, and the scientific method.

2.   Compare and contrast Freud's psychoanalytic theory with Erikson's psychoanalytic theory.

3.   Describe Piaget's theory of cognitive development and explain how it differs from an information-processing approach.

4.   Understand how social learning theory has been modified in recent years.

5.   Describe the basic concepts from ethological theories.

6.   Compare and contrast Bronfenbrenner's ecological theory with Elder's life-course theory.

7.   Describe what is meant by an eclectic theoretical orientation.

8.   Describe the different research measures used by developmental psychologists.

9.   Compare and contrast the experimental and correlational strategies for collecting information scientifically.

10.   Define dependent variable, independent variable, and random assignment, and explain why causal conclusions cannot be made from correlational studies.

11.   Describe cross-sectional, longitudinal, and sequential approaches to research.

12.   Understand the standard ethics of developmental research.

Explain what a theory is, then explain what a hypothesis is and how theories differ from hypotheses.

What are the primary underlying beliefs of psychoanalytic theory?

What is the scientific method?

What is the Oedipus complex?

Name and describe the three parts of the personality according to Freud's psychoanalytic theory.

What are the specific crises in each of Erikson's eight stages of development?
Match each stage with its age group.

What are defense mechanisms?
Name and describe what Freud said was the most powerful defense mechanism.

How does assimilation differ from accommodation?
Which theory do these processes fit?

What are erogenous zones?

Describe Piaget's four stages of cognitive development and state what happens in each.

Describe the five stages of development according to psychoanalytic theory including approximate age spans & erogenous zone focus.

What is the information-processing approach?

According to **psychoanalytic theory**, development is primarily unconscious & heavily colored by emotion; behavior is a surface characteristic & is symbolic of the deep inner workings of the mind; early experiences with parents shape our development.

Theory: a coherent set of ideas that helps explain data and make predictions
Hypothesis: an assumption that can be tested to determine its accuracy
Theories are broader explanations that need to be narrowed down into testable hypotheses.

The **Oedipus complex** is the Freudian concept that the young child develops an intense desire to replace the same-sex parent and enjoy the affections of the opposite-sex parent (based on the Greek myth).

The **scientific method** attempts to discover accurate information about behavior and development, which includes: identifying & analyzing the problem, collecting data, drawing conclusions, & revising theories.

Trust/Mistrust: 1st year; trust requires physical comfort; minimal fear
Autonomy/Shame & Doubt: 1-3; independence
Initiative/Guilt: 3-5; purposeful behavior
Industry/Inferiority: 6-puberty; master intellect
Identity/Identity Confusion: adolescence
Intimacy/Isolation: early adult; intimate relations
Generativity/Stagnation: middle adult; productivity
Integrity/Despair: older adult; evaluate one's life

Id: the Freudian structure of personality that consists of instincts (it is the reservoir of psychic energy)
Ego: the Freudian structure of personality that deals with the demands of reality
Superego: the Freudian structure of personality that is the moral branch

Assimilation: occurs when new information is incorporated into existing knowledge
Accommodation: occurs when new information does not fit into existing information, so individuals must adjust to the new information
These are part of Piaget's theory of cognitive development.

Defense mechanisms: psychoanalytic term for unconscious methods through which the ego distorts reality to protect against anxiety
Repression, the most powerful of these, works by pushing unacceptable id impulses out of awareness and back into the unconscious mind.

Sensorimotor: birth-2; infants coordinate sensory experiences with physical motoric actions to understand the world
Preoperational: 2-7; represent the world symbolically (words, images, drawings)
Concrete operational: 7-11; perform operations; (concrete) logic replaces intuition
Formal operational: 11+; ability to think abstractly & more logically

Erogenous zones: parts of the body that have especially strong pleasure-giving qualities at each stage of development
(Freud)

Information-processing approach: Concerned with how individuals process information about their world; how information enters the mind, is stored & transformed, & is retrieved to perform complex activities (e.g., problem solving, & reasoning).

Oral: first 18 months; pleasure centers around the mouth
Anal: 1½-3; pleasure involves anus or eliminative functions
Phallic: 3-6; focus on genitalia
Latency: 6-puberty; sexuality repressed; social/intellectual skills develop
Genital stage: puberty on; sexual reawakening; adult sexuality focus on genitalia

What are the basic beliefs of behaviorism?

Name the different scientific techniques researchers use to gather information about developmental issues.

What are the three key factors of social learning theory?
What is its primary difference from behaviorism?
What is self-efficacy?

How is the emic approach different from the etic approach?
What is ethnic gloss?

What does ethological theory say about development?
Explain imprinting and critical periods (of maximum plasticity).

Explain how correlational strategies differ from experimental strategies.

Describe the five systems of ecological theory.

Why do we need random assignment?
How does the independent variable differ from the dependent variable?

How does life-course theory differ from ecological theory?

Compare and contrast cross-sectional, longitudinal, and sequential approaches.

What is an eclectic theoretical orientation?

What are cohort effects?

Techniques: Laboratory observation; Naturalistic observation; Interviews; Questionnaires; Case studies; Standardized tests; Cross-cultural research; Life-history records; Physiological research & research with animals; Multimeasure/multisource/ multicontext approach; Correlational strategies; Experimental strategies

Behaviorism emphasizes scientific study of observable behavioral responses & their environmental determinants (rewards/punishments); rearranging experiences can change development (behavior is learned & therefore can be unlearned).

Emic approach: goal is to describe behavior of one culture/ethnic group in terms meaningful & important to the people in that group
Etic approach: goal is to describe behavior so generalizations can be made across cultures

Social learning theory emphasizes behavior, environment, and cognition; its emphasis on cognition differentiates it from strict behaviorism.
Self-efficacy is the expectation that one can master a situation and produce positive outcomes.

Correlational strategy: goal is to describe the strength of the relation between two or more events/characteristics
Experimental strategy: precisely determines behavior's causes via an experiment--a carefully regulated setting in which factors believed to influence the behavior studied are manipulated while other factors are held constant

Ethology: behavior strongly influenced by biology, tied to evolution, & characterized by critical or sensitive periods
Imprinting: rapid, innate learning within a critical period of time involving attachment to the first moving object seen
Critical period: fixed time period early in development during which certain behaviors optimally emerge

Random assignment reduces the likelihood that experimental results are due to preexisting differences between experimental & control group
Independent variable: manipulated, influential, experimental factor in the experiment
Dependent variable: the factor (outcome) measured in an experiment (it depends on what happens to the subjects in the experiment)

Microsystem: setting in which individual lives (e.g., family, school, peers, neighborhood)
Mesosystem: involves relations between microsystem or connections between contexts
Exosystem: social setting where person is not active influences person's immediate experiences
Macrosystem: the culture in which person lives
Chronosystem: patterns of environmental events & transitions over lifecourse; sociohistorical circumstances

All three are time span inquiries.
Cross-sectional: individuals of different ages are compared at one time
Longitudinal: the same individuals are studied over a period of time, usually several years
Sequential: starts with cross-sectional study of people of different ages; at next testing of these individuals, a new group is added for each age

Elder's life-course theory is an ecological, contextual theory that has a strong life-span developmental orientation; the human life span can be best understood in terms of historical time and place, the timing of lives, linked or interdependent lives, and human agency and social constraints.

Cohort effects: effects that are due to a subject's time of birth or generation, but not to actual age (e.g., cohorts may differ in years of education); cohort effects can powerfully affect the dependent measures in a study concerned with age (i.e., our findings may be from cohort effects, not from manipulation of independent variable).

An eclectic theoretical orientation selects and uses from each theory whatever is considered the best in it; since no single theory can entirely explain the complexity of development.

Self-Test A: Multiple Choice

1. The science of life-span development is a:
    a. systematic body of testable theories that can be verified or refuted.
    b. set of specific, testable world views that describe life-span development.
    c. descriptive catalogue of methods used to collect information about life-span development.
    d. chronological identification of the stages of socioemotional, cognitive, and physical changes in children.

2. An assumption or prediction that can be tested to determine its accuracy is:
    a. a theory.
    b. an hypothesis.
    c. a scientific fact.
    d. an independent variable.

3. Persons who will not take illegal drugs because they believe that any law breaking is immoral are relying on the _____ in the decision-making process.
    a. id
    b. superid
    c. ego
    d. superego

4. Freud believed defense mechanisms reduce:
    a. anxiety.
    b. dependence on others.
    c. pleasure.
    d. schizophrenia.

5. During the _____ stage, Freud believed that pleasure centers on the genital area and resolution of the Oedipus complex occurs.
    a. oral
    b. anal
    c. phallic
    d. genital

6. Erik Erikson's theory emphasized:
    a. repeated resolutions of unconscious conflicts about sexual energy.
    b. success in confronting specific conflicts at particular ages in life.
    c. changes in children's thinking as they mature.
    d. the influence of sensitive periods in the various stages of biological maturation.

7. Karen Horney's criticism of Freud's theory was based on:
    a. the finding that women find meaning in their emotions.
    b. the notion that women are more likely than men to define themselves in terms of relationships.
    c. Malinowski's observations that the Oedipus complex is not universal.
    d. her model of women with positive feminine qualities and self-evaluation.

8. Bobby is interested in school. He reads a lot and likes to do experiments. Bobby is likely in Erik Erikson's _____ stage.
    a. autonomy versus shame and doubt
    b. initiative versus guilt
    c. industry versus inferiority
    d. identity versus identity confusion

9. _____ occurs when a person is able to fit new information into an existing schema.
    a. Assimilation
    b. Accommodation
    c. Organization
    d. Disequilibrium

10. The key to formal operational thinking is the ability to think about _____ concepts.
    a. concrete
    b. sensory
    c. symbolic
    d. abstract

11. The information-processing approach to development emphasizes:
    a. the quality of thinking among children of different ages.
    b. overcoming certain age-related problems or crises.
    c. age appropriate expressions of sexual energy.
    d. perception, memory, reasoning ability, and problem solving.

12. From B. F. Skinner's point of view, behavior is explained by paying attention to:
    a. external consequences of that behavior.
    b. the self-produced consequences of that behavior.
    c. individuals' cognitive interpretations of their environmental experiences.
    d. the biological processes that determine maturation.

13. The frequent finding that adults who abuse their children typically come from families in which they were abused would support which theory of life-span development?
    a. Freudian psychoanalytic theory
    b. information-processing theory
    c. ecological theory
    d. social learning theory

14. The three factors that reciprocally influence development according to Bandura's social learning theory are:
    a. personal, behavioral, & environmental.
    b. punishment, reward, & reinforcement.
    c. memory, problem solving, and reasoning.
    d. cognition, reward, & observation.

15. Individuals' beliefs that they can master their environment and produce positive outcomes refers to their sense of:
    a. self-esteem.
    b. self-efficacy.
    c. self-concept.
    d. self-centeredness.

16. Findings that children who are deprived of speech during the first five years of life will have difficulty learning to use language effectively is an example of which concept?
    a. imprinting
    b. critical periods
    c. linguistic relativity
    d. sensitive periods

17. Konrad Lorenz discovered that baby geese imprint to:
    a. only their mother.
    b. any adult female bird.
    c. any adult bird.
    d. any large moving object.

18. According to Bronfenbrenner's ecological theory, growing up in a particular culture would be a part of an individual's:
    a. microsystem.
    b. exosystem.
    c. macrosystem.
    d. chronosystem.

19. A major strength of ecological theory is its framework for explaining:
    a. environmental influences on development.
    b. biological influences on development.
    c. cognitive development.
    d. affective processes in development.

20. Growing up as a member of Generation-X would be part of your:
    a. microsystem.
    b. mesosystem.
    c. exosystem.
    d. chronosystem.

21. The notion that human lives are usually embedded in family relationships, friendships, and other social relationships throughout the life span is central to Elder's notion of:
    a. the timing of lives.
    b. human agency.
    c. linked lives.
    d. social constraints.

22. The term _____ is used to describe an approach simultaneously consisting of several different theoretical perspectives.
    a. nondescript
    b. eclectic
    c. quasi-experimental
    d. pseudoscientific

23. One difficulty of doing life-span research in the laboratory setting is that:
    a. it is difficult to generalize findings to the real world.
    b. random assignment is impossible.
    c. extraneous factors are difficult to control.
    d. subjects tend to be unaware that they are in an experiment.

24. The main advantage of the naturalistic observation technique involves:
    a. real world validity.
    b. great control over extraneous variables.
    c. the ability to utilize inferential statistics.
    d. a lack of ethical concerns.

25. The method of gathering information that gives an in-depth look at one individual is the:
    a. interview.
    b. emic approach.
    c. participant observation.
    d. case study.

26. An advantage of using multiple materials in the life-history records approach is that:
    a. comparing sources and resolving discrepancies provides greater accuracy.
    b. archival data are easier to understand.
    c. it avoids the subjectivity of interviews.
    d. it avoids the subjectivity from a subject's written and oral reports.

27. An experimenter interested in the similarity between the pattern of language development in Brazilian, Cuban, and Australian children would most likely take an _____-based approach to this research.
    a. edic
    b. emic
    c. epic
    d. etic

28. _____ is a superficial description of a cultural or ethnic group that makes the members seem much more similar than they actually are.
    a. An emic approach
    b. An etic approach
    c. Ethnic gloss
    d. Standardization

29. Which of the following **is not** a reason the text gives for conducting research on animals?
    a. Some research is unethical to perform on humans.
    b. It is easy to generalize findings from animals to humans.
    c. It is easy to control subjects' genetic background, diet, and experience.
    d. It is often possible to track the subjects' entire life span over a short time period.

30. Many investigators use multiple measures to assess development because:
    a. virtually every method of gathering information has limitations.
    b. it is a more complex method that allows for greater intellectual challenge.
    c. most funding agencies require this method.
    d. it is one of the simplest ways of gathering information to administer and interpret.

31. Which of the following questions would best be answered using a correlational study?
    a. Does depression increase with age?
    b. Are people more depressed before or after retirement?
    c. Does exercise decrease depression?
    d. How depressed are 14-year-olds?

32. A _____ design compares individuals of different ages (e.g., 30-year-olds, 40-year-olds, and 50-year-olds) at one testing time.
    a. cross-sectional
    b. longitudinal
    c. Latin squares
    d. sequential

33. Experimental designs are superior to correlational approaches when dealing with:
    a. concepts that have not been studied in any great detail (e.g., dating behavior in the elderly).
    b. variables that are difficult to manipulate (e.g., factors that lead to suicide).
    c. variables that are unethical to manipulate (e.g., the relationship between alcohol consumption and birth defects).
    d. variables that can be controlled easily (e.g., the relationship between stimulus presentation time and item recall).

34. Effects due to a subject's time of birth or generation, but not to actual age are referred to as _____ effects:
    a. subjective
    b. cohort
    c. confounding
    d. historical

35. When psychologists are conducting research with children, once the parents have provided consent:
    a. the psychologist may continue to the end of the study unless the child becomes ill.
    b. if the child does not want to participate, the psychologist must not test the child.
    c. if the child does not want to participate, the psychologist must stop long enough to talk to the parents and calm the child down before proceeding.
    d. if the child does not want to participate, the psychologist will ask the parents to calm the child down so the testing may continue.

Self-Test B: Matching

Match the following persons in the left column with the theory they are associated with in the right column.

f 1. Albert Bandura   a. Feminist revision of psychoanalytic theory
e 2. Erik Erikson   b. Ecological theory
i 3. Glen Elder   c. Ethological theory
b 4. Urie Bronfenbrenner   d. Psychosexual theory
c 5. Konrad Lorenz   e. Psychosocial theory
h 6. Jean Piaget   f. Social learning theory
d 7. Sigmund Freud   g. Behaviorism
a 8. Nancy Chodorow   h. Cognitive development theory
g 9. B. F. Skinner   i. Life-course theory

Essay Questions:

1. Since your roommate's mother knows you are taking this class in Life Span Development, she has asked you to come talk to her local parents' group about what sorts of behaviors these parents might expect from their children as they develop. She told you they have many questions and concerns about Freud's theories and his emphasis on sexuality, but they have heard good things about Piaget's theories. How would you present both of these theories, and what others might you include as well?

2. Your best friend's father works at a Youth Center that offers after-school activities for school-aged children (kindergarten through 12th grade). He has noticed that while some older children have been teasing the younger children, other older children have been quite nurturing. He has asked you to come to the Center to assess the situation and then to design some type of intervention so that the children of all ages would have mutually beneficial relations. What research methods would you employ to accomplish these goals?

Key to Self-Test A:

1.	a	p.	32	19.	a	p. 42-44
2.	b	p.	32	20.	d	p. 44
3.	d	p.	33	21.	c	p. 44-45
4.	a	p.	33	22.	b	p. 47
5.	c	p.	34	23.	a	p. 50
6.	b	p.	34	24.	a	p. 50
7.	d	p.	35	25.	d	p. 51
8.	c	p.	35	26.	a	p. 52
9.	a	p.	37	27.	d	p. 52
10.	d	p.	38	28.	c	p. 52
11.	d	p.	38	29.	b	p. 53
12.	a	p.	39	30.	a	p. 53
13.	d	p.	39-40	31.	a	p. 53
14.	a	p.	39, 41	32.	a	p. 55
15.	b	p.	41	33.	d	p. 55
16.	b	p.	41	34.	b	p. 55
17.	d	p.	41-42	35.	b	p. 57
18.	c	p.	42-44			

Key to Self-Test B:

1.	f		6.	h
2.	e		7.	d
3.	i		8.	a
4.	b		9.	g
5.	c			

Key to Essay Questions:

1. A proper answer should describe the basic elements of Freud's and Piaget's respective theories. With regard to Freud, you would include the importance of unconscious motives to behavior, development of the three parts of the personality (id, ego, superego), and the five developmental stages, noting what types of behavior one might expect in each (e.g., toilet training would take place most easily in the anal stage when the child is focusing on the anal region as a source of pleasure). Note that Piaget was interested in the process of *how* children think, and saw children as little scientists who need a sufficiently stimulating environment to develop their cognitive abilities. Discuss his four stages of development and his concepts of assimilation, accommodation, and schemas. You might suggest how parents could see evidence of these theories (e.g., when a child begins to "identify" with the same sex parent by imitating that parent's behaviors) and how they can use the information for their child's healthy development (e.g., don't expect the child to be toilet trained until the child is ready). Then select one of the other theories to discuss that you think would be particularly helpful for parents in providing a healthy environment for their children.

2. The first thing to discuss is naturalistic observation and how you would do that. You might try a correlational strategy to explore relationships among certain variables that currently exist, particularly for what behaviors seem to go along with either teasing or nurturing younger children. You would then need to design an experimental intervention, being careful to discuss your independent and dependent variables, as well as random assignment to experimental and control groups.

Research Project 1: Child Observation and Theory

Go to a place, such as a park or the Children's Center on your campus, where you can "people watch" without seeming to be out of place. Choose a child between the ages of 2 and 6 to observe, then watch that child for half an hour. Record the various types of behaviors in which the child engages as well as how the child interacts with other children and adults. On the basis of these observations:

1. What theory do you think best explains development at this level? Explain your reasons for choosing this theory.
2. What hypothesis would you make that you could test concerning development at this level? How would you go about testing that hypothesis?
3. What other theories do you think fit the behaviors you observed? Explain how these fit.

Research Project 2: Adult Observation and Theory

Go to a place, such as a park or the cafeteria on your campus, where you can "people watch" without seeming to be out of place. Choose an adult to observe, then watch that individual for half an hour. Record the various types of behaviors in which that individual engages as well as how the individual interacts with others. On the basis of these observations:

1. What theory do you think best explains development at this level? Explain your reasons for choosing this theory.
2. What hypothesis would you make that you could test concerning development at this level? How would you go about testing that hypothesis?
3. What other theories do you think fit the behaviors you observed? Explain how these fit.

Research Project 3: Journal Article Critique*

Professor Santrock notes the importance of becoming familiar with research published in professional journals. This is how we keep up with current information in our field. Select a topic that will be covered in this course that is of particular interest to you (e.g., parenting practices, the functions of play, language development), then find and read an article about research on that topic in a related professional journal (*Child Development, Developmental Psychology, Marriage and the Family*). Write a report that summarizes the main points of the research and how you reacted to that research. As you read the article:

1. Were you able to identify the independent and dependent variables from the title of the article?
2. What theoretical explanations were emphasized in the introduction, and what hypothesis was tested by the research?
3. What did you learn from reading the methods section of this article? Describe the participants in the study and the procedures that were used.
4. What did you learn from reading the results section of this article? What statistical methods were used, and did you understand why those methods were chosen? Which results, if any, did the researchers state were statistically significant? How were (or weren't) the graphs, figures, tables, or charts helpful?
5. What did you learn from reading the discussion section of this article? How were the results interpreted? Did the authors discuss any limitations to the study or suggest further research based on the study?
6. Based on reading this article, what ideas do you have for research on this same topic? How would you design that research?

*Adapted from Simons, J. A. (1994). *Student Study Guide for Child Development*, 6th ed. (Santrock, J. W.)

Research Project 4: Analogies

Professor Santrock discusses three different analogies that have been used to describe development: "a staircase, a seedling in a greenhouse, and a strand of ivy in a forest." Consider each of these theories and note how they do or do not work for you in terms of understanding development.

Consider an analogy for understanding the development of theories themselves. One I use in my classes is bricks. If you were building a brick structure for developmental psychology today, which bricks would you put on the bottom? Would you place all of the bricks directly on top of each other, or would some of them straddle two different bricks? For example, Pavlov and Watson would likely go on the bottom for their work in classical conditioning, then Skinner's "brick" may be placed directly on top. However, would Bandura's Social Learning Theory go directly on top of Skinner's, or might it straddle Skinner and some other (e.g., cognitive) theory?

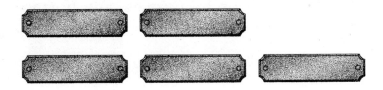

Chapter 3   Biological Beginnings

Learning Objectives

1. Discuss natural selection and the evolutionary perspective of human development.

2. Understand the relationship between chromosomes, genes, and human reproduction cells.

3. Describe the five most common techniques for helping infertile couples.

4. Discuss abnormalities in genes and chromosomes.

5. Describe the method and purpose for tests such as amniocentesis, ultrasound, sonography, the chorionic villus test, and the maternal blood test.

6. Explain why two brown-eyed parents can have a blue-eyed child, but two blue-eyed parents cannot have a brown-eyed child.

7. Compare and contrast adoption studies and twin studies, and explain why these studies do not show conclusively that a behavior or trait is inherited.

8. Define and distinguish among passive genotype→environment, evocative genotype→environment, and active genotype→environment interactions.

9. Distinguish shared environmental experiences from nonshared environmental experiences.

10. Explain Sandra Scarr's views that genotypes drive experience and explain criticisms of Scarr's views.

Explain the concepts of
natural selection
and adaptive behavior.

When does reproduction begin?
Explain the five most common "high-
tech" procedures for reproduction.

What is the basis of evolutionary
psychology?

Define infertility and explain possible
causes.

What are chromosomes?
How many do we (usually) have?
Where do we get our chromosomes?

What are the causes and results of
the following genetic abnormalities:
PKU, Down syndrome, and
sickle-cell anemia?

What are genes?
What is DNA?

Describe some disorders that are
caused by an irregularity in the
number of sex chromosomes (those
on the 23rd pair).

What are gametes?
What is a zygote?

What methods are commonly used
for prenatal testing to determine
abnormalities?

Explain meiosis.

What is a genome?

Reproduction begins with the fertilization of a female's gamete (ovum) by a male's gamete (sperm).
Five common **"high-tech" procedures** are: In vitro fertilization (IVF); Gamete intrafallopian transfer (GIFT); Intrauterine insemination (IUI); Zygote intrafallopian transfer (ZIFT); Intracytoplasmic sperm injection (CSI)

Natural selection is the evolutionary process that favors individuals of a species that are best adapted to survive & reproduce (Charles Darwin).
Adaptive behavior is behavior that promotes the organism's survival in the natural habitat (e.g., eagles' claws).

Infertility is the inability to conceive a child after 12 months of regular intercourse without contraception.
Common causes for women: not ovulating, blocked fallopian tubes, disease that prevents implantation in the ova; men: low sperm production, sperm lack motility, blocked passageways; both: use of drugs such as cocaine

Evolutionary psychology is a contemporary biological approach that emphasizes the roles of successful survival, reproduction, and psychological mechanisms in adaptive behavior. Per David Buss, psychological mechanisms evolve from successful solutions to adaptive problems faced by our ancestors.

Phenylketonuria (PKU): inability to metabolize protein properly; untreated, it results in mental retardation & hyperactivity
Down syndrome: genetically transmitted form of mental retardation, caused by an extra (third) chromosome on the 21st pair
Sickle cell anemia: affects red blood cells & occurs most often in African Americans

Chromosomes are threadlike structures that come in 23 pairs, one member of each pair coming from each parent.
Chromosomes contain the genetic substance deoxyribonucleic acid (DNA).
Chromosomes are subdivided into smaller segments called genes.

Klinefelter syndrome: males have an extra X chromosome (XXY); their testes are undeveloped & breasts are enlarged
Turner syndrome: females missing an X chromosome (XO); short stature, webbed neck
XYY syndrome: males have extra Y; was believed this contributed to violence/aggression; not so

Genes are the units of hereditary information; they are short segments, composed of DNA, that act as a blueprint for cells to reproduce themselves & manufacture the proteins that maintain life.
DNA (deoxyribonucleic acid) is a complex molecule containing hereditary information.

Amniocentesis: sample of amniotic fluid withdrawn by syringe (week 12-16)
Ultrasound sonography: high-frequency sound waves directed into pregnant woman's abdomen
Chorionic villus test (CVT): sample of placenta removed between weeks 8-11
Maternal blood test (alpha-fetoprotein test): assesses blood alphaprotein level associated with neural tube defects

Gametes are human reproduction cells that are created in the testes of males (sperm) & the ovaries of females (ovum)
A **zygote** is a single cell formed through fertilization (when the sperm reaches & fertilizes the ovum)

A **genome** is a complete set of genes.
Genes are mapped to help scientists reverse the course of genetic disorders.

Meiosis is the process of cell division in which each pair of chromosomes in the cell separates, with one member of each pair going into each gamete, or daughter cell.
(Each human gamete has 23 unpaired chromosomes.)

Explain the
dominant-recessive gene principle.

Compare identical twins with
fraternal twins.
Which are MZ and which are DZ?

Explain the concept of
polygenic inheritance.

Explain passive
genotype⇒environment interactions
evocative genotype⇒environment
interactions; &
active (niche-picking)
genotype⇒environment interactions.

What is the difference between
a genotype &
a phenotype?

Describe shared environmental
influences.

Compare and contrast a
reaction range with
canalization.

Describe nonshared environmental
influences.

What is behavior genetics?

What are genetic counselors &
what do they do?

Compare twin studies with
adoptive studies.

Identical (monozygotic or MZ) twins develop from a single fertilized egg that splits into two genetically identical replicas, each becoming a person.
Fraternal (dizygotic or DZ) twins develop from separate eggs and separate sperm.

Dominant-recessive gene principle: if one gene of the pair is dominant & one is recessive, the dominant gene exerts its effect, overriding the potential influence of the recessive gene. A recessive gene exerts its influence only if both genes of a pair are recessive.

Passive genotype⇒environment interactions occur when parents rear a genetically-related child.
Evocative genotype⇒environment interactions occur because a child's genotype elicits certain types of physical & social environments.
Active (niche-picking) genotype⇒environment interactions occur when children seek out environments they find compatible & stimulating.

Polygenic inheritance: a genetic principle describing the interaction of many genes to produce a particular characteristic (psychological disorders, for example, are not merely from one gene, but from several that interact)

Shared environmental influences: children's common experiences, such as parents' personalities & intellectual orientation, family's social class & the neighborhood in which they live

Genotype: the person's genetic heritage, the actual genetic material
Phenotype: the way an individual's genotype is expressed in observed & measurable characteristics
For each genotype, a range of pheontypes can be expressed.

Nonshared environmental influences: child's own unique experiences, both within the family & outside the family, that are not shared with another sibling; experiences that occur within the family can be part of the "nonshared" environment

Reaction range: describes the range of possible phenotypes for each genotype; suggests the importance of restricting/enriching environments
Canalization: describes the narrow path or developmental course certain characteristics take; preservative forces help protect or buffer a person from environmental extremes

Genetic counselors: Usually physicians or biologists well versed in medical genetics, familiar with the kinds of problems that can be inherited, odds for encountering them, & helpful measures for offsetting some of their effects in an effort to help parents decide to have children if the possibility exists for genetic abnormalities

Behavior genetics is concerned with the degree and nature of behavior's hereditary basis. (Behaviors are jointly determined by interaction of heredity & environment)

Twin studies compare behavior of identical twins with that of fraternal twins.
Adoption studies seek to discover whether, in behavior & psychological characteristics, adopted children are more like their biological or adoptive parents (nature vs. nurture); also look at adoptive & biological siblings.

Self-Test A: Multiple Choice

1. The key to survival in an environment based on natural selection involves:
   a. aggression.
   b. size.
   c. adaptation.
   d. mutation.

2. A major emphasis of evolutionary psychology is that:
   a. the roles that successful survival, reproduction, and psychological mechanisms play in adaptive behavior.
   b. cultural evolution is the dominant type of evolution among humans.
   c. genes are the most important determinant for survival.
   d. physical and psychological aspects of humans have different determinants.

3. According to David Buss (1995), _____ drives evolution.
   a. adaptation
   b. fear
   c. instinct
   d. reproduction

4. A major criticism of evolutionary psychology is that:
   a. it ignores evidence from animal behavior.
   b. its concepts can be used to justify existing social injustices.
   c. it is biased toward men, at the expense of women.
   d. it does not place enough emphasis on cultural diversity.

5. The principle of heredity explains how:
   a. culture is transmitted within a society.
   b. men are universally more aggressive than women.
   c. *Homo sapiens* are now able to live much longer than their ancestors.
   d. characteristics are transmitted from one generation to the next.

6. The nucleus of each human cell contains:
   a. 46 chromosomes.
   b. 23 chromosomes.
   c. 46 pairs of chromosomes.
   d. 46 genes.

7. The human reproduction cells that are created in the testes of males and the ovaries of females are called:
   a. chromosomes.
   b. genes.
   c. gametes.
   d. ova.

8. The typical female chromosome pattern is:
   a. YY.
   b. XX.
   c. XY.
   d. XXY.

9. In vitro fertilization is a possible solution to infertility that involves:
   a. having sperm and egg unite outside of a woman's body.
   b. implanting a fertilized egg into a substitute mother's womb.
   c. enhancing the possibility of conception by taking fertility drugs.
   d. incubating a zygote outside of a woman's body.

10. Which is a disadvantage of adoption in comparison to medical treatments for infertility?
   a. Adoptive parents tend not to try as hard as nonadoptive parents to care for their children.
   b. Adopted children are more likely than non-adopted children to have adjustment problems.
   c. Adoption is more likely to involve third parties than nonadoption.
   d. Biological parents find it easier to love their child than do adopting parents.

11. Which of the following *is not* a common cause of male infertility?
   a. a low sperm count
   b. a lack of motility in sperm
   c. damaged/blocked sperm ducts
   d. endometriosis

12. Which of these syndromes *is not* sex-linked?
   a. Down syndrome
   b. Klinefelter syndrome
   c. Turner syndrome
   d. XXY syndrome

13. A physician orders amniocentesis be performed to determine if a woman's fetus is genetically normal. This procedure will involve:
    a. taking a blood sample from the mother.
    b. drawing a sample of the fluid that surrounds the baby in the womb.
    c. taking a sample of the placenta between the eighth and eleventh week of pregnancy.
    d. taking a blood sample from the fetus.

14. _____ involves removal of a small sample of the placenta.
    a. The alpha-fetoprotein test
    b. An ultrasound
    c. Amniocentesis
    d. The chorionic villus test

15. The most practical way to use the technique of gene mapping is through:
    a. genetic screening.
    b. CT scans of the brain.
    c. amniocentesis.
    d. the chorionic villus test.

16. Traits that are produced by the interaction between two or more genes are calle
    a. dominant.
    b. recessive.
    c. canalized.
    d. polygenic.

17. A person's genetic heritage is his or her:
    a. genotype.
    b. phenotype.
    c. dominant character.
    d. recessive character.

18. The expression of a person's genetic heritage is his or her:
    a. genotype.
    b. phenotype.
    c. dominant character.
    d. recessive character.

19. The basic premise of the reaction range model is that:
    a. genetic factors determine an infant's range of behavior and environmental factors determine an adult's behavior.
    b. genetic factors determine a possible range of expressions and environmental factors determine the ultimate expression achieved.
    c. most behaviors are determined by genetic factors and the environment constitutes little to human reactions.
    d. most behaviors are determined by the environment and genetic factors contribute little to human reactions.

20. The narrow path marking the development of characteristics that appear immune to vast changes in environmental events is called:
    a. canalization.
    b. meiosis.
    c. phenotype.
    d. heredity.

21. Which of the following is the best example of canalization?
    a. Twins reared apart in very different environments have different temperaments.
    b. Two brown-eyed parents have a blue-eyed child.
    c. An extra X chromosome causes genetic abnormalities.
    d. Infants smile at exactly 40 weeks after conception, regardless of when they are born.

22. Behavioral geneticists believe that behaviors are determined by:
    a. only biological factors.
    b. only environmental factors.
    c. biological factors at birth and environmental factors throughout the rest of life.
    d. a continuous interaction between biological and environmental factors.

23. If heredity is an important determinant of a specific behavior, what prediction can we make about expression of the behavior in identical twins reared apart compared to its expression in fraternal twins reared apart?
   a. Fraternal twins will express the behavior more similarly than identical twins.
   b. There will be little similarity in the expression of the behavior in either set of twins.
   c. Identical twins will express the behavior more similarly than fraternal twins.
   d. The behavior will be expressed similarly by identical twins and fraternal twins.

24. In adoption studies, psychologists compare the behavior of:
   a. identical fraternal twins.
   b. family members and randomly selected others.
   c. fraternal twins with each other.
   d. children living with adoptive parents and children living with biological parents.

25. Jensen argues that heredity is a more important determinant of intelligence than environment because the:
   a. educational level of biological parents correlates more strongly with children's IQs than do IQs of adoptive parents.
   b. IQs of DZ twins are as highly correlated as the IQs of MZ twins.
   c. IQs of MZ twins reared apart are as highly correlated as those of MZ twins reared together.
   d. correlation between DZ twins' IQs is similar to correlations of siblings' IQs.

26. What do Arthur Jensen's views have in common with those of Richard Hernstein and Charles Murray?
   a. Their specific views illustrate the more general issue of heredity's influence on development.
   b. These individuals are on the same side with regard to the debate concerning shared and nonshared environmental influences.
   c. Their specific views illustrate the more general issue of an evolutionary perspective.
   d. These individuals are proponents of genetic counseling.

27. In Jensen's review of studies on intelligence, he discovered that _____ had the highest correlated IQ scores.
   a. identical twins reared together
   b. identical twins reared apart
   c. fraternal twins reared together
   d. fraternal twins reared apart

28. Children who are highly active, easily distracted, and move very fast frequently elicit adult attempts to quiet them down, punishment for lack of concentration, and angry warnings to slow down. This describes an example of a(n) _____→ environment interaction.
   a. passive genotype
   b. active genotype
   c. niche-picking genotype
   d. evocative genotype

29. Allan, Amanda, and Adam Brodsky all grew up in the same house, went to the same school, and observed their parents' dedication to charitable work. These experiences constitute the children's:
   a. shared environmental influences.
   b. nonshared environmental influences.
   c. niche-picking experiences.
   d. heritability.

30. Ramey (1988) studied the effects of early intervention on intelligence by recruiting pregnant women whose IQ averaged 80. Ramey found that _____ can significantly raise the intelligence of young children from impoverished environments.
   a. providing medical care and dietary supplements
   b. high-quality early educational day care
   c. teaching mothers parenting skills
   d. placing the child into an adoptive home with highly intelligent parents

31. All of the following are important with respect to intervention programs having a positive effect on children's well-being *except*:
   a. beginning as early as possible.
   b. providing services to parents as well as to the child.
   c. having minimal parental involvement with the child during the intervention.
   d. having a low child-teacher ratio.

32. Behavioral geneticist Robert Plomin argues that differences between siblings' personalities are primarily a result of:
   a. genetics.
   b. nonshared environmental experiences.
   c. random variance.
   d. shared environmental experiences.

33. Behavioral geneticist Sandra Scarr argues that:
   a. most aspects of family context are shared by all siblings within the family.
   b. the environment parents select for their children is due, in part, to the parents' genotypes.
   c. only cross-cultural studies can be used to support the role of genetics in determining behavior.
   d. females are genetically superior to males in all aspects of development except physical strength.

34. Which of the following statements best describes the role and function of a genetic counselor?
   a. counseling couples who have a baby that is genetically abnormal
   b. administering in vitro fertilization
   c. helping a couple decide how likely they are to have a genetically defective baby
   d. suggesting to a couple that they should terminate a pregnancy when tests find the fetus to have genetic defects

Self-Test B: Matching

Match the persons in the left column with the ideas, statement, or programs they are associated with in the right column.

1. Diana Baumrind   a. Each individual has a range of potential but won't exceed that range
2. Thomas Bouchard   b. Intelligence is primarily inherited
h 3. Charles Darwin   c. High-quality early educational day care can raise intelligence
4. Richard Hernstein   d. Children reared in the same environment often have different personalities
d 5. Robert Plomin   e. Minnesota Study of Twins Reared Apart
b 6. Arthur Jensen   f. Many important aspects of family contexts are shared by all family members
7. Craig Ramey   g. Co-author who said America is evolving an intellectually deprived underclass
8. Sandra Scarr   h. Natural selection; survival of the fittest

Self-Test C: Matching Genetic Disorders

Match the disorders in the left column with the descriptions in the right column.

1. Anencephaly   a. Group of inherited blood disorders causing anemic symptoms
2. Cystic fibrosis   b. Neural tube disorder causing brain & skull malformation
3. Down syndrome   c. Accumulation of lipids in the nervous system; deceleration of mental & physical development
4. Hemophilia   d. Glandular dysfunction; interferes with mucus production
5. Klinefelter syndrome e. Excess muscle in upper intestine; can cause severe vomiting & death
6. Phenylketonuria (PKU) f. Extra or altered 21st chromosome; causes mild to severe retardation
7. Pyloric stenosis   g. Lack of clotting factors; causes excessive internal & external bleeding
8. Sickle-cell anemia   h. A missing or altered X chromosome may cause mental retardation
9. Spina bifida   i. Metabolic disorder; untreated causes mental retardation
10. Tay-Sachs disease   j. Blood disorder; limits body's oxygen supply
11. Thalassemia   k. Extra X chromosome; causes physical abnormalities
12. Turner syndrome   l. Neural tube disorder that causes brain & spine abnormalities

Essay Questions:

1. Imagine that you are a genetic counselor and a couple has come to you because they are concerned about whether they should have children. The wife is 40 years old and comes from an Eastern European Jewish background; her husband is a 42-year-old African American. What potential problems might this couple's children have? How would you counsel them?

2. Your roommate is studying sociobiology and has determined that you will never become a major success in life because your hereditary background will limit you to mediocrity. Consider what you know about sociobiology; then examine the various theories that address heredity and environment in an effort either to support or refute your roommate's assertions.

Key to Self-Test A:

1.	c	p.	66	18.	b	p.	77
2.	a	p.	66	19.	b	p.	78
3.	d	p.	66	20.	a	p.	78
4.	d	p.	66	21.	d	p.	78
5.	d	p.	67	22.	d	p.	79
6.	a	p.	67	23.	c	p.	79
7.	c	p.	68	24.	d	p.	79
8.	b	p.	68	25.	c	p.	80
9.	a	p.	69	26.	a	p.	80
10.	b	p.	70	27.	a	p.	80
11.	d	p.	70-71	28.	d	p.	81
12.	a	p.	71-72	29.	a	p.	82
13.	b	p.	72	30.	b	p.	82
14.	d	p.	74	31.	c	p.	82
15.	a	p.	74	32.	b	p.	82
16.	d	p.	76	33.	b	p.	82-83
17.	a	p.	76	34.	c	p.	85

Key to Self-Test B:

1.	f	5.	d
2.	e	6.	b
3.	h	7.	c
4.	g	8.	a

Key to Self-Test C:

1.	b	7.	e
2.	d	8.	j
3.	f	9.	l
4.	g	10.	c
5.	k	11.	a
6.	i	12.	h

Key to Essay Questions:

1. First of all you would need to look at the potential risk factors for Tay-Sachs (mother's background), Down syndrome (mother's age), and sickle-cell anemia (father's background). Discuss how you might do this (look at family history). In terms of counseling on how they should proceed, you would help them consider their own wishes and options (what kinds of tests would you suggest? what other options/procedures might be available?). What personal issues (e.g., the couple's ethical and religious beliefs) might you consider?

2. Here you would need to discuss what sociobiology is and what the criticisms are of this position. Present the notion of range of potential but look also at the evidence stating that environmental factors are dominant in development. Discuss the various forms of heredity-environment interactions (e.g., passive genotype→environment interactions), as well as the findings from twin studies and adoption studies. Based on your evaluation of this research, state which position you find most compelling.

Research Project 1: Heritability of Height*

To help you understand the concept of heritability, collect data from two families (one may be your own). Record the height of all family members over the age of 18, and, separating the males from the females, calculate the mean height and range of heights for both the males and the females. Use the tables provided below for recording the heights, then answer the following questions.

Questions:

1. On average, which family in your sample is taller for both males and females?
2. Of the taller family, how many females are taller than the females in the shorter family? How many of the males are taller than the males in the shorter family?
3. Based on your data, does heritability appear to be a factor in height?
4. What is the advantage of studying a variable like height rather than a variable such as intelligence or personality?

Data

	Family 1	Family 2
Average Female Height		
Average Male Height		
Tallest Female Height		
Tallest Male Height		
Shortest Female Height		
Shortest Male Height		

Family 1			Family 2		
Person	**Sex**	**Height**	**Person**	**Sex**	**Height**
Self					
Mother			Mother		
Father			Father		
Grandmother 1			Grandmother 1		
Grandmother 2			Grandmother 2		
Grandfather 1			Grandfather 1		
Grandfather 2			Grandfather 2		
Sibling			Sibling		
Sibling			Sibling		
Sibling			Sibling		
Aunt			Aunt		
Aunt			Aunt		
Aunt			Aunt		
Uncle			Uncle		
Uncle			Uncle		
Uncle			Uncle		
Cousin			Cousin		
Cousin			Cousin		
Cousin			Cousin		
Other			Other		

Note that if there are fewer of one category of siblings, aunts, uncles, and cousins, but more of another, feel free to change category names (e.g., from "siblings" to "cousins").

*Adapted from Keniston, A. H., & Peden, B. F. (1995), *Student Study Guide to accompany Children,* 4th ed. (Santrock, J. W.)

Chapter 4   Prenatal Development and Birth

Learning Objectives

1. Describe the germinal, embryonic, and fetal periods of prenatal development.

2. Define placenta and umbilical cord, and explain how they prevent the transmission of harmful substances from mother to infant.

3. Define organogenesis and explain its importance.

4. Define and distinguish between miscarriage and abortion and list some causes of miscarriage.

5. Explain how maternal characteristics affect prenatal development.

6. Discuss maternal diseases and conditions that influence prenatal development such as rubella, syphilis, herpes, and HIV/AIDS.

7. Describe the three stages of birth.

8. Summarize what researchers know/do not know about the effects of drugs administered to a woman during childbirth.

9. Contrast the different childbirth strategies, noting the pros and cons of each.

10. Define and distinguish between preterm infants and low-birthweight infants.

11. Describe some of the physical, emotional, and psychological adjustments women have to make after pregnancy.

Describe the germinal period and the two components of cell division during the germinal period.

Explain what process occurs during spontaneous abortion.

Describe the embryonic period of prenatal development and the three components of the embryo.

What maternal characteristics are of particular importance during the prenatal period?

What are the placenta and the umbilical cord?

What is "lanugo"? When does it first appear and when does it typically disappear?

Define the amnion and its importance during prenatal development.

Explain the concept of "teratology." What is a teratogen?

Explain organogenesis.

What are the potential effects for the child when the mother is exposed to the following diseases: rubella, syphilis, genital herpes & HIV/AIDS?

Explain what changes occur during the fetal period.

Describe the disorder that a child may acquire if the mother consumes alcohol during pregnancy.

Miscarriage (spontaneous abortion) occurs when pregnancy ends before the developing organism is mature enough to survive outside the womb; embryo separates from uterine wall & is expelled by the uterus,
About 15-20% of all pregnancies end in spontaneous abortion, most in the first 2-3 months.

Germinal period: period of prenatal development the first 2 weeks after conception: creation of zygote, continued cell division, & attachment of zygote to uterine wall
Blastocyst: the inner layer of cells
Trophoblast: outer layer of cells; provides nutrition & support for the embryo
Implantation: attachment of zygote to uterine wall (about 10 days after conception)

Mother's age: infants born to adolescents are often premature & mortality rate is double that of mothers in their 20s; after age 30 increased risk of Down syndrome & lowered fertility
Nutrition: mother's nutrition involved in ability to reproduce & malformation, mortality, and performance of child
Emotional states/stress: affect child's activity levels

Embryonic period: 2 to 8 weeks after conception; rate of cell differentiation intensifies, support systems for cells form, & organs appear
Endoderm: inner layer of cells develops into digestive & respiratory systems
Ectoderm: outermost layer, becomes nervous system, sensory receptors, & skin parts
Mesoderm: middle layer becomes circulatory system, bones, muscle, excretory; & reproductive systems

Lanugo: downy hair that covers infant during 2nd & most of 3rd trimesters; typically is mostly gone by end of third trimester (36-38 weeks)

Placenta: life-support system consisting of a disk-shaped group of tissues in which small blood vessels from mother & offspring intertwine (but do not join)
Umbilical cord: life-support system with 2 arteries & 1 vein connecting embryo to placenta

Teratology: the field of study that investigates the causes of birth defects
Teratogen: any agent that causes a birth defect (these can include environmental hazards, drugs, exposure to diseases, etc.); structural defect greatest early in embryonic period while organs are being formed; during fetal period, stunt growth or create problems with organ functioning

Amnion: life-support system: a bag or envelope containing a clear fluid in which the developing embryo floats; amniotic fluid provides temperature & humidity control, & shockproof environment for the fetus

Rubella: mental retardation, blindness, deafness, & heart problems
Syphilis: damage organs after they're formed; eye lesions (can cause blindness), skin lesions; at birth: CNS & gastrointestinal tract problems
Genital herpes: may cause death, brain damage
HIV/AIDS: transmission to child; death in first four years

Organogenesis: the process of organ formation that takes place during the first 2 months of prenatal development

Fetal alcohol syndrome (FAS): a cluster of abnormalities appearing in the offspring of mothers who drink alcohol during pregnancy; may result in facial deformities, defective limbs, face, & heart; below-average intelligence/mental retardation; reduced attention & alertness; may be avoided by avoiding alcohol during pregnancy

During the **fetal period** (2 to 9 months after conception); fetus becomes active, moves its arms & legs, opens & closes mouth, moves head, skin structures form, coordinates movements, respiration & organ systems become regulated; grows from less than 1" to about 20" & from less than 3 oz to about 7 lbs

What are the potential effects on the unborn child when the pregnant mother smokes cigarettes, uses marijuana, is addicted to heroin, or uses cocaine?

What is oxytocin?
Explain the controversy about its use.

What environmental toxins have been shown to endanger the fetus and what problems might they cause?

Describe the different childbirth strategies discussed in the text.

What is toxoplasmosis?
What effect does that have on the unborn child?
How can it be avoided?

Compare the preterm infant with the low-birthweight infant.

What are the three stages of childbirth?

Describe the two scales used to measure neonatal health.

Explain the three delivery complications described in the text.

Describe the postpartum period and the process of involution.
State the signs that may indicate a need for professional counseling about postpartum adaptation.

What is a cesarean section and when is it typically performed?

What is bonding?

Oxytocin: a hormone that stimulates & regulates rhythmicity of uterine contractions; widely used as a drug to speed delivery. Controversy: can save mother's life & keep infant from damage, but baby more likely to be jaundiced, induced labor requires more painkilling drugs, greater medical care required postnatally results in separation of mother & infant

Cigarettes: greater risk of fetal & neonatal death; preterm births, low birthweight, respiratory problems, SIDS

Marijuana: more tremors & startles; poorer verbal & memory development

Heroin: addiction; withdrawal symptoms (e.g., tremors, irritability); behavioral problems; attention deficits

Cocaine: lower birthweight/length; more congenital abnormalities (may be from associated factors)

Standard: in hospital mother has enema, pubic hair is shaved; delivery room is like an operating room

Leboyer: baby put on mother's stomach, bathed in warm water, umbilical cord intact several minutes

Prepared: mother knows what will happen, comfort measures for childbirth, little or no medication, participates in decision making if complications arise

Lamaze: similar to prepared childbirth but breathing techniques more central & active; father often involved

Environmental hazards: radiation (gene mutation; chromosomal abnormalities); pollutants & toxic wastes (e.g., carbon monoxide & lead) (affect mental development); PCBs (smaller, preterm infants; problems with visual discrimination & short term memory); VDTs (unknown effects)

Preterm (premature) infant: one who is born prior to 38 weeks after conception

Low-birthweight infant: born after regular gestation period (38-42 weeks) but weighs less than 5-1/2 lbs

Both are considered at risk.

Toxoplasmosis: mild infection causing coldlike symptoms or no apparent illness in adults may cause eye defects, brain defects, & premature birth for infants; often transmitted by cats-- expectant mothers may pick up organisms by handling cats, litter boxes, or raw meat; have someone else clean the litter box, wash hands after handling cats, litter boxes, raw meat

Apgar scale: widely used to assess newborn's health 1 & 5 minutes after birth; evaluates heart rate, respiratory effort, muscle tone, body color, & reflex irritability

Brazelton Neonatal Behavioral Assessment Scale: hours after birth assesses neurological development, reflexes, & reactions to people

1ˢᵗ stage: (may last 12-24 hrs) uterine contractions 15-20 minutes apart; by end, contractions 2-5 minutes & cervix dilated to 4"

2ⁿᵈ stage: baby's head moves through cervix & birth canal (usually 1-1/2 hrs)

Afterbirth: the placenta, umbilical cord, & other membranes are detached & expelled (lasts a few minutes)

Postpartum period: after childbirth or delivery woman adjusts physically & psychologically to childbearing; lasts about 6 weeks or until body adjusts & returns to near prepregnant state

Involution: process by which uterus returns to prepregnant size

5 signs: excessive worrying, depression, extreme changes in appetite, crying spells, sleep inability

Precipitate delivery: takes place too rapidly; can disturb infant's normal flow of blood & pressure on head can cause hemorrhaging

Anoxia: insufficient supply of oxygen can cause brain damage (if delivery takes too long)

Breech position: baby's uterus position causes buttocks to emerge first, may cause respiratory problems; may need C-section delivery

Bonding: the occurrence of close contact, especially physical, between parents & newborn in the period shortly after birth; important emotional attachment providing foundation for optimal development in years to come

Cesarean section (C-section): surgical removal of the baby from the uterus; usually performed if baby's in breech position, is lying crosswise in uterus, baby's head is too large to pass through mother's pelvis, baby develops complications, or mother is bleeding vaginally

Self-Test A: Multiple Choice

1. Which of the following is true concerning conjoined twins?
   a. They are always identical.
   b. About 60% are still-born.
   c. They are becoming more common.
   d. They share the same thought patterns.

2. Human fertilization typically takes place in the:
   a. ovary.
   b. fallopian tube.
   c. uterus.
   d. vaginal canal.

3. A fertilized ovum is called:
   a. a zygote.
   b. a blastocyst.
   c. an egg.
   d. an embryo.

4. The period of prenatal development that occurs in the first two weeks after conception is called the _____ period.
   a. fetal
   b. germinal
   c. embryonic
   d. blastocystic

5. A skin defect might be traced back to an initial problem with the embryo's _____ cells.
   a. mesoderm
   b. ectoderm
   c. microderm
   d. endoderm

6. How does the placenta/umbilical cord life-support system prevent harmful bacteria from invading a fetus?
   a. Bacteria are too large to pass through the placenta walls.
   b. The placenta generates antibodies that attack and destroy bacteria.
   c. Bacteria become trapped in the maze of blood vessels of the umbilical cord.
   d. No one understands how the placenta keeps bacteria out.

7. During the second trimester, the amniotic sac is filled mainly with:
   a. blood.
   b. mucus.
   c. urine.
   d. air.

8. Organogenesis takes place during which stage of development?
   a. germinal
   b. zygotic
   c. embryonic
   d. fetal

9. The fetal period is best described as a time when:
   a. major organ systems emerge from the less differentiated endoderm and mesoderm.
   b. support systems that sustain the fetus become fully formed and functioning.
   c. fine details are added to systems that emerged during the embryonic period.
   d. teratogens are most likely to impair development.

10. A 1989 study on the psychological effects of abortion found that:
    a. unwanted pregnancies are stressful for most women.
    b. the decision to abort typically has long-term negative effects on women undergoing the abortion.
    c. family/friend support does little to ease the stress levels of women undergoing an abortion.
    d. most women are anti-abortion.

11. Which of the following statements about the relationship between age and pregnancy outcome is most accurate?
    a. Adolescent mothers are most likely to have retarded children.
    b. Artifically inseminated women in their thirties and forties are more likely to become pregnant than those in their twenties.
    c. Mothers over age thirty are most likely to have retarded babies.
    d. Adolescent mothers suffer the lowest infant mortality rates of any age group.

12. Researchers now believe that maternal stress may lead to birth defects by:
    a. reducing the amount of oxygen received by the embryo and fetus.
    b. increasing the mother's susceptibility to viruses.
    c. reducing the likelihood of a good placenta-to-uterus connection.
    d. increasing the likelihood of an unusual chromosome split during meiosis.

13. Which phrase best defines a teratogen?
    a. a life-support system that protects the fetus
    b. an agent that stimulates the formation of organs
    c. an abnormality in infants of alcoholic mothers
    d. an environmental factor that produces birth defects

14. While looking over a newborn, a physician notes that the neonate's outer ears are severely deformed. Based on her knowledge of prenatal development, the physician would suspect the damage occurred during the _____ stage of development.
    a. germinal
    b. zygotic
    c. embryonic
    d. fetal

15. Which of the following statements about fetal alcohol syndrome is most accurate?
    a. The infant is often physically deformed and below average in intelligence.
    b. It commonly results in miscarriages.
    c. It causes ectopic pregnancies.
    d. Babies suffering from this syndrome are often born before term and with low birthweights.

16. A common characteristic of babies born to women who smoke during their pregnancies is:
    a. a missing arm or leg.
    b. facial deformities and below-average intelligence.
    c. restlessness and irritability.
    d. lower birthweights.

17. All of the following are environmental hazards to prenatal development *except*:
    a. cats.
    b. dogs.
    c. carbon monoxide.
    d. video display terminals.

18. All of the following are reasons stated for the high incidence of low-birthweight occurrence in the United States *except*:
    a. pregnant women in the United States do not receive the uniform prenatal care that women in other industrialized countries receive.
    b. the United States lacks a national health-care policy to assure high-quality assistance for pregnant women.
    c. more than 25% of all American women of prime childbearing age do not have insurance to cover hospital costs.
    d. nearly 20% of pregnant women do not receive adequate prenatal care.

19. Mrs. Peters is bearing down hard with each contraction. She is in the ____ stage of labor.
    a. first
    b. second
    c. third
    d. final

20. A physician who has just witnessed a precipitate delivery would likely say:
    a. "It's okay for a child to come out feet first."
    b. "Wow! That delivery certainly went fast."
    c. "That abdominal scar will heal within a week."
    d. "One's a girl, the other's a boy."

21. Which of the following can lead to anoxia during the birth process?
    a. having the umbilical cord tighten around the neck of the fetus
    b. use of forceps to help ease the infant from the birth canal
    c. an episiotomy (surgically widening the vaginal opening)
    d. Braxton-Hicks contractions

22. A physician might elect to give a pregnant mother oxytocin if:
    a. her contractions have stopped.
    b. she is bleeding vaginally.
    c. she has stopped ovulating.
    d. her placenta has partially detached.

23. During the 1980s, the rate of cesarean sections performed in the United States:
    a. increased dramatically.
    b. increased slightly.
    c. decreased slightly.
    d. decreased dramatically.

24. Which statement about the influence on newborns of drugs used during birth is the most accurate?
    a. Experiments on the effects of drugs on childbirth raise few ethical questions.
    b. Methodological problems complicate the results of studies of drug use during labor.
    c. Drugs affect all infants in almost the same way.
    d. Most mothers choose standard childbirth, so researchers are able to learn about how drugs affect labor.

25. A mother delivers a baby that is placed on her stomach immediately after birth, then placed in a bath of warm water to relax. The mother is using which method of childbirth?
    a. LaLeche
    b. Lamaze
    c. Leboyer
    d. standard

26. The main premise of natural or prepared childbirth is summarized by the phrase:
    a. "knowledge is power."
    b. "always say 'no' to drugs."
    c. "it takes two to tango."
    d. "easy does it."

27. Most modern birthing practices encourage relaxation by the mother because it:
    a. makes birth less traumatic for the infant.
    b. eliminates the mother's pain.
    c. enables the mother to participate fully in the birth.
    d. helps the attending physician to control the birth process.

28. Today more fathers participate in childbirth because:
    a. they need to do this to bond with their infants.
    b. doing so can be an important experience to share with their wives.
    c. they are the best possible support for their wives.
    d. physicians require fathers to be present.

29. A "preterm" baby cannot have gestated for more than _____ weeks.
    a. 38
    b. 34
    c. 30
    d. 26

30. Which of the following statements about a shortened gestation period is most accurate?
    a. It is common for low-birthweight infants.
    b. It often leads to organ malformation.
    c. It is almost always devastating.
    d. It alone does not necessarily harm an infant.

31. In contrast to the Brazelton scale, the Apgar primarily assesses a newborn's:
    a. psychological status.
    b. reflexes.
    c. physiological health.
    d. responsivity to people.

32. Two-day-old Terry's very low Brazelton Neonatal Behavioral Assessment Scale score is often a good indicator that:
    a. he has brain damage.
    b. his mother took heroin while she was pregnant.
    c. he will develop a "difficult" temperament.
    d. he is unlikely to bond with his primary caregiver.

33. Which of the following terms refers to a physical change that occurs to women after childbirth?
    a. decompensation
    b. decompression
    c. involution
    d. menarche

34. Which of the following statements about close contact between mothers and newborns enjoys supporting evidence?
    a. The newborn must have close contact with the mother in the first few days of life to develop optimally.
    b. Close contact between infant and mother can only occur after standard childbirth.
    c. Close contact with mothers is helpful to preterm infants.
    d. Close contact with the mother is more important than close contact with the father.

35. Recent evidence suggests that _____ can lead to significant weight gain in preterm infants.
    a. a strong parental bond
    b. exercise and massage
    c. fat-free infant formulas
    d. exposure to parental voices

36. Whether a mother chooses to stay home with her newborn or return to work:
    a. only she will know if she made the right choice.
    b. she is likely to make sacrifices and have misgivings.
    c. is primarily dependent on the health of the baby.
    d. is no longer a question that presents major concerns.

Self-Test B: Matching

Match the individuals in the left column with the appropriate descriptors in the right column.

1. Virginia Apgar
2. Fernand Lamaze
3. Arlene Eisenberg, Heidi Murkoff, & Sandee Hathaway
4. Frederick Leboyer
5. Tiffany Field
6. T. Berry Brazelton
7. Abigail Hensen

a. one member of a pair of conjoint twins
b. guidelines to help mothers decide whether to work outside home
c. advocated a procedure referred to as "birth without violence"
d. developed a form of natural childbirth widely used today
e. neonatal assessment of health 1 to 5 minutes after birth
f. the role of touch & massage in development
g. assessment of neurological development, reflexes, & reactions to people

Self-Test C: Matching Teratogens and Consequences

Match the teratogens in the left column with some of their potential consequences in the right column.

1. rubella
2. syphilis
3. alcohol
4. nicotine
5. tranquilizers
6. heroin
7. marijuana
8. cocaine
9. radiation
10. toxoplasmosis

a. poor attention; facial & limb deformities; below-average intelligence
b. low birthweight with increased health problems
c. cleft palate or other congenital malformations
d. increased tremors & startles; poorer verbal & memory development
e. addiction; tremors, restlessness; irritability
f. gene mutation; chromosomal abnormalities
g. neonatal deaths; mental retardation, blindness, deafness, heart problems
h. eye defects, brain defects, premature birth
i. dependency, withdrawal; hypertension, heart problems, learning difficulties
j. eye lesions resulting in blindness, skin lesions, CNS & gastrointestinal problems

Essay Questions:

1. You are asked to talk to a high school class about potential hazards to prenatal development. The principal of the high school has suggested that you discuss not only alcohol and other drugs, but environmental hazards and maternal diseases as well. She has asked that you be honest about the different agents that can cause problems, the problems they may cause, and how these problems can be avoided. What would you tell these students about teratogens and prenatal care?

2. One of your friends has recently gotten married and has now confided in you that she is pregnant. She knows you're taking this class in life-span development and asks for your input concerning what she can expect when giving birth, and wants your suggestions concerning her childbirth options. What would you tell her about the three stages of birth, complications she might expect, options about use of drugs, and the childbirth strategies that are available to her?

Key to Self-Test A:

1.	a	p.	89	19.	b	p.	104
2.	b	p.	89	20.	b	p.	105
3.	a	p.	89	21.	a	p.	105
4.	b	p.	90	22.	a	p.	105
5.	b	p.	90	23.	a	p.	105
6.	a	p.	91	24.	b	p.	106
7.	c	p.	91	25.	c	p.	106
8.	c	p.	91	26.	a	p.	106
9.	c	p.	92	27.	c	p.	106-108
10.	a	p.	93	28.	b	p.	108
11.	c	p.	93	29.	a	p.	108
12.	a	p.	96	30.	d	p.	108
13.	d	p.	96	31.	c	p.	109
14.	c	p.	97	32.	a	p.	110
15.	a	p.	98	33.	c	p.	110
16.	d	p.	98-99	34.	c	p.	112
17.	b	p.	100-101	35.	b	p.	112, 115
18.	d	p.	101	36.	b	p.	113

Key to Self-Test B:

1.	e		5.	f
2.	d		6.	g
3.	b		7.	a
4.	c			

Key to Self-Test C:

1.	g		6.	e
2.	j		7.	d
3.	a		8.	i
4.	b		9.	f
5.	c		10.	h

Key to Essay Questions:

1. An appropriate answer should include alcohol and other drugs, such as marijuana and cocaine, and their potential effects on the developing embryo/fetus, noting when during development the particular organs are most vulnerable (note that no amount of alcohol is considered safe during pregnancy). You should also discuss what is known about the effects of certain diseases, such as rubella, syphilis, HIV/AIDS, etc., and about environmental hazards such as radiation, lead, etc. Explain how each of these problems can be avoided (e.g., do not consume alcohol or other drugs during pregnancy); and then describe the type of prenatal care that a pregnant woman should get to ensure the health of her child.

2. Describe the three stages of birth (e.g., first stage, the longest, lasts an average of 12 to 24 hours, with contractions first being 15 to 20 minutes apart); discuss possible complications (e.g., precipitate delivery and breech position); explain why she may or may not want to use drugs during childbirth, which drugs might be used, and potential consequences of using drugs for mother and child; and finally, describe the different childbirth strategies, such as standard childbirth, the Leboyer method, etc., and why she might prefer one over another. Be sure to discuss also the benefits of having her husband present during the birth process.

Research Project 1: Child Delivery Practices*

This project looks at generational differences in delivery practices. Work with three other students in your class so you can pool your data after you have collected them. Present the following questions to your mother, your grandmother (if she's not alive, ask another woman you would be comfortable talking to who would be your grandmother's age), and a woman who has a child under two years of age and circle the response:

	Grandmother	Mother	Other
Was the delivery cesarean or vaginal?	C/V	C/V	C/V
Were medications used?	Y/N	Y/N	Y/N
Was the father present in the delivery room?	Y/N	Y/N	Y/N
Did the pregnant woman attend childbirth classes?	Y/N	Y/N	Y/N

After comparing responses with your group members, answer the following questions:
1. What might you conclude about the use of medication during delivery over the past three generations?
2. Has the percentage of cesarean deliveries relative to vaginal deliveries changed during that time period?
3. What might you conclude about the presence of fathers during delivery over this time period?
4. What change might be noted, if any, in terms of the percentage of women attending childbirth classes?
5. Are your data consistent with the research described in the text? Explain.

*Adapted from Simons, J. A. (1994). *Student Study Guide for Child Development*, 6th ed. (Santrock, J. W.)

Research Project 2: Women's Health Practices

The text discusses certain behaviors that are potentially harmful to the unborn child, such as smoking or use of alcohol and other drugs; it also discusses healthful practices, such as good nutrition, safe exercise, prenatal care, etc. Talk to women you know who are of childbearing age to see how much they know about what is both harmful and healthful for their unborn child; assess the behaviors in which they engage; and for those who smoke, drink, or use other drugs, have them tell you why they do so, whether they will when they are pregnant, and what they expect the consequences might be for their child. If they are unaware of the potential harmful effects of teratogens, explain these to them, then ask if they would engage in these practices while pregnant. Compare the responses you get to see if you can draw any conclusions. What type of campaign do you think might be useful to have women discontinue unhealthy behaviors and engage in healthful ones instead?

Chapter 5   Physical Development in Infancy

Learning Objectives

1. Distinguish between cephalocaudal and proximodistal growth patterns.

2. Define REM sleep and explain the purpose of REM sleep.

3. Describe sudden infant death syndrome (SIDS), and list factors related to an infant's risk of SIDS.

4. Discuss the pros and the cons of breast- versus bottle-feeding.

5. Describe both the macro and micro levels of brain organization/structure.

6. Explain the importance of infant reflexes and distinguish between the sucking and rooting reflexes, and between the Moro and grasping reflexes.

7. Explain how the development of gross motor skills and fine motor skills follow the principles of cephalocaudal and proximodistal sequences.

8. Define sensation and perception, then discuss the two main theories of perceptual development.

9. Describe infants' visual abilities, including visual acuity, color vision, and visual preferences.

10. Describe the development of size constancy and depth perception.

11. Explain how we know that infants can hear before birth.

12. Identify odors and tastes that newborns can discriminate.

13. Define intermodal perception.

Contrast the cephalocaudal and proximodistal patterns of development.

What is the importance of neurons?

What are developmentalists referring to when they use the term "states" to describe infants?
What is REM?

Differentiate between an axon and a dendrite.

What is SIDS?
What do we know about its possible causes?

What is the myelin sheath and what are its primary purposes?

What is marasmus and what is its primary cause?

What are reflexes?

Describe the location and functions (presented in the text) of the hindbrain, midbrain, and forebrain.

What are the sucking & rooting reflexes?
What purpose do they serve?

Explain the location and primary functions of the occipital lobe, temporal lobe, frontal lobe, and parietal lobe.

What is the Moro reflex?
What is its purpose?

Neurons are nerve cells that handle information processing at the cellular level.

Cephalocaudal pattern: the sequence in which the greatest growth occurs at the top (head); physical growth & feature differentiation goes from top to bottom
Proximodistal pattern: the sequence in which growth starts at the center of the body & moves toward the extremities

Axon: the part of the neuron that carries information away from the cell body to other cells
Dendrite: the receiving part of the neuron; it collects information & routes it to the cell body

"States": the infant's level of awareness; Thomas et al. (1981) describe eight states: no REM sleep; active sleep without REM; REM sleep; indeterminate sleep; drowsy; inactive alert; active awake; and crying
REM (rapid eye movement) **sleep**: recurring sleep during which vivid dreams commonly occur

Myelin sheath: a layer of fat cells encasing most axons; insulates nerve cells and helps the nerve impulse travel faster

SIDS: sudden infant death syndrome, a condition that occurs when an infant stops breathing, usually during the night, & suddenly dies without apparent cause
Risk factors: prematurity, low birthweight, low Apgar, respiratory problems, second-hand smoke, lying on stomach, elevated fetal hemoglobin

Reflexes are built-in reactions to stimuli (initially they provide infants with adaptive responses to the environment before they have had the opportunity to learn).

Marasmus: a wasting away of body tissues in the infant's first year caused by severe protein-calorie deficiency
Main cause: early weaning from breast milk to inadequate nutrients (e.g., unsuitable & unsanitary cow's milk formula

Sucking: newborns automatically suck objects placed in their mouths (helps get nourishment before they have associated a nipple with food)
Rooting: when infant's cheek is stroked or side of mouth is touched, infant turns its head toward the side that was touched (helps infant find something to suck)

Hindbrain: (at rear of skull) contains cerebellum, important in motor development & control
Midbrain: (between hindbrain & forebrain) relays information between brain & eyes/ears via ascending & descending fibers
Forebrain: (at front of brain) of its many structures, the cerebrum is important for higher cognitive functions

Moro reflex: a neonatal startle response that occurs in response to a sudden, intense noise or movement; when startled, the newborn arches its back, throws its head back, flings out its arms & legs, then rapidly closes arms & legs to the center of the body
(vestige from primate ancestry)

Occipital: (at rear of brain) involved in vision
Temporal: (lateral side of brain) involved in hearing
Frontal: (at front of brain) involved in control of voluntary muscles & intelligence
Parietal: (above temporal & occipital) involved in processing body sensations

What is the grasping reflex?

What is the ecological view of development?

Explain nonnutritive sucking.

Define the concept referred to as "affordances."

Differentiate between gross motor skills and fine motor skills.

How does size constancy relate to the infant's world?

Explain developmental biodynamics.

What is involved in intermodal perception?

Contrast sensation and perception.

What is the constructivist view of development?

Ecological view: perception has a functional purpose of bringing the organism into contact with the environment & increasing adaptation (even complex things can be perceived directly without constructive activity)

Grasping reflex: when something touches the infant's palms, the infant responds by grasping tightly

Affordance: (a concept of ecological view) opportunities for interaction that an object offers (by sensing information from the environment we directly & accurately perceive affordances); they are needed to perform functional activities (sitting in a chair, walking on concrete, etc.)

Nonnutritive sucking: sucking behavior that is unrelated to the infant's feeding; the primary response measure used to assess infant attention & learning

Size constancy: recognizing an object is the same size even though the retinal image of the object changes (absent prior to 3 months); lacking perceptual constancy, each time we perceive an object at different distance, orientation, etc., it would be perceived as a different object

Gross motor skills: involve large muscle activities, such as moving one's arms & walking
Fine motor skills: involve finely tuned movements, such as finger dexterity
Gross motor skills develop before fine motor skills.

Intermodal perception: the ability to relate & integrate information about two or more sensory modalities, such as vision & hearing

Developmental biodynamics: a developmental perspective that seeks to explain how motor behaviors are assembled for perceiving & acting (outgrowth of developments in the neurosciences, biomechanics, & behavioral sciences)

Sensation occurs when information interacts with sensory receptors (eyes, ears, tongue, nostrils, & skin).
Perception is the interpretation of what is sensed.

Constructivist view: perception is a cognitive construction based on sensory input plus information retrieved from memory; perception is a kind of representation of the world that builds up as the infant constructs an image of experiences
(advocated by Piaget & information-processing psychologists)

Self-Test A: Multiple Choice

1. Which best demonstrates the basic principle of cephalocaudal development?
   a. an infant first producing an endogenous smile, then an exogenous smile, then a laugh
   b. an infant first being able to raise the head, then sit up, then stand up
   c. an infant obtaining visual skills, then olfactory skills, then auditory skills
   d. an infant cooing, then babbling, then the first word, then language

2. The proximodistal progression pattern is seen in children's:
   a. drawings, which are first done using the entire arm, and eventually using only the wrist and fingers.
   b. toileting behavior, which proceeds from urine control to bowel control.
   c. head size, which originally comprises about one-fourth of the body, and eventually only one-eighth of the body.
   d. memory, which proceeds from sensory store to short-term store to long-term store.

3. If an alien randomly drops in on ten newborns, it might conclude humans spend their entire first months of life:
   e. sleeping.
   f. crying.
   g. eating.
   h. playing.

4. Which statement most accurately describes height and weight changes during infancy?
   a. Both increase more rapidly during the second year than during the first year.
   b. Girls increase in height and weight faster than boys do during infancy.
   c. The sexes grow at the same rate during infancy.
   d. Both height and weight increase more rapidly during the first year than during the second year.

5. Which statement most accurately portrays the sleep-wake cycle of infants?
   a. Infants sleep less as they grow older.
   b. Newborn sleep is reflexive, whereas infant sleep is intentional.
   c. Infants eventually sleep more during the day than they do at night.
   d. Infants spend less time sleeping than do adults.

6. Juan was a low-birthweight infant, while Serge was a premature infant. Which statement applies to them?
   a. Neither is vulnerable to SIDS.
   b. Juan is less vulnerable to SIDS than Serge.
   c. Juan is more vulnerable to SIDS than Serge.
   d. Both are vulnerable to SIDS.

7. Infants require about _____ calories a day for each pound they weigh.
   a. 25
   b. 50
   c. 75
   d. 100

8. Breast-feeding is superior to bottle-feeding because:
   a. breast-feeding is more convenient and more adaptable to the time requirements of demand feeding.
   b. breast milk is a superior source of the nutrients that babies need.
   c. bottle-fed infants suffer psychological damage because they become only weakly attached to their mothers.
   d. breast-feeding is not superior to bottle-feeding; this is a myth.

9. A child who eats a low-fat, low-calorie diet experiences _____, while a child who eats a restricted-protein diet experiences _____.
   a. breast-feeding; bottle-feeding
   b. delirium; toxic shock
   c. malnourishment; marasmus
   d. marasmus; SIDS

10. Which of the following conditions **is not** necessary for a young child to be toilet trained?
    a. adequate motivation
    b. cognitive maturity
    c. passage from the anal to the phallic stage
    d. muscular control

11. Which of the following **is not** one of the characteristics of the infant brain?
    a. increasing experience increases the number of neurons
    b. increasing experience increases the number of connections between neurons
    c. the dendrites branch out with increasing age
    d. neurotransmitters change with increasing age

12. Which statement best characterizes infant reflexes?
    a. Reflexes are vestigial remnants of early evolutionary processes.
    b. Reflexes are genetically coded survival mechanisms for all infants.
    c. Modern infants rely more on learning than on reflexes.
    d. All reflexes disappear by the end of infancy.

13. Which of the following **is not** a characteristic of a neonatal reflex?
    a. genetically based
    b. a survival mechanism
    c. involves motor functions
    d. alterable by the newborn

14. The sucking style of an infant is dependent on all but which of the following?
    a. the way the milk is coming out of the bottle or breast
    b. the infant's sucking speed and temperament
    c. the way the infant is held
    d. the nourishment being offered

15. Which infant motor event typically occurs first?
    a. stands with support
    b. cruises around furniture
    c. rolls over
    d. sits without support

16. Finger dexterity is to walking as _____ is to _____.
    a. gross motor skills; gross motor skills
    b. fine motor skills; fine motor skills
    c. fine motor skills; gross motor skills
    d. gross motor skills; fine motor skills

17. Which of the following is a sensation?
    a. sound waves hitting the ear
    b. seeing your mother's face
    c. feeling the roughness of your father's beard
    d. hearing the sound of your brother crying

18. Was William James right when he proclaimed that newborns experience a blooming, buzzing confusion?
    a. No, because infants display visual preferences.
    b. Yes, because infants' visual acuity is less than that of adults.
    c. Yes, because infants sense the world but do not perceive it.
    d. No, because infants display sensitivity to pinpricks.

19. Researchers have found that young infants prefer to look at items with a great deal of:
    a. color.
    b. contrast.
    c. brightness.
    d. rapid movement.

20. Fantz (1963) found that two-day-old infants:
    a. were beginning to focus on their mothers' eyes.
    b. were able to distinguish contour.
    c. showed a preference for patterned stimuli over plain stimuli.
    d. began to perceive the oval shape of the head.

21. When infants were placed on one side of the visual cliff, they refused to go to their mothers who were coaxing them from the other side. This result was cited as evidence for:
    a. depth perception.
    b. failure of visual acuity.
    c. inability to hear at a distance.
    d. inability to crawl.

22. What evidence indicates that a fetus can hear?
    a. A fetus moves when a loud noise occurs.
    b. Newborns prefer their mother's voice to strangers' voices.
    c. Hearing is more sensitive and better developed among newborns who have been experimentally stimulated before birth.
    d. Newborns prefer to hear stories that were read to them in their mothers' womb.

23. One current controversy concerning the medical treatment of infants involves:
    a. the use of small amounts of cocaine to stimulate the heart rate of sluggish neonates.
    b. the rule of not allowing mothers to hold their at-risk low-birthweight neonate immediately after birth .
    c. not using any anesthetics when performing surgery on young infants.
    d. the fact that a mother's opinion outweighs a father's when it comes to a decision of whether a child should be given a heart transplant.

24. Which of the following smells do infants like the *least*?
    a. vanilla
    b. fish
    c. their mothers' milk
    d. strawberries

25. When an infant turns its head at the sound of footsteps in the hall, and then smiles when it sees Mom come into the room, the infant is using:
    a. depth perception.
    b. intermodal perception.
    c. auditory perception.
    d. visual perception.

26. According to the ecological perception view:
    a. bimodal perception is possible at birth.
    b. perceptual abilities are uncoordinated at birth.
    c. bimodal perception depends on internal representations of the perceptions from different senses.
    d. experience with all of the senses is needed before bimodal perception can occur.

27. The constructivist view of intermodal perception states that:
    a. perceptual abilities are not coordinated early in infancy.
    b. perceptual abilities are inborn.
    c. neonates show an ability to make connections between the different sensory modalities.
    d. perception guides action.

28. Which of the following statements about infant fitness classes is *false*?
    a. Swimming lessons can result in brain swelling because infants swallow too much water.
    b. Everyday activities are optimal for normal infant physical development.
    c. Infants are not capable of aerobic exercise.
    d. Infants exposed to swimming will be less frightened of water later in life.

Self-Test B: Matching

Match the individuals in the left column with the appropriate descriptors in the right column.

1.	Elizabeth Spelke	a.	used looking chambers to see infants' visual preferences
2.	Eleanor Gibson	b.	grasping is guided by proprioception rather than vision
3.	Jean Piaget	c.	studied how newborns cope with stress
4.	T. Berry Brazelton	d.	proponent of constructivist view of intermodal perception
5.	Robert Frantz	e.	pediatrician; observed development of infant sucking
6.	Megan Gunnar	f.	used the visual cliff to study infant depth perception
7.	Rachel Clifton	g.	infants have a biological core knowledge of the perceptual world

Self-Test C: Matching Infant States

Match the infant states of consciousness in the left column with some of their descriptions in the right column.

1. No REM sleep
2. Active sleep without REM
3. REM sleep
4. Indeterminate sleep
5. Drowsy
6. Inactive alert
7. Active awake
8. Crying

a. eyes wide open; relatively inactive, occasional limb movement
b. eyes closed & still; occasional startle, rhythmic mouthing
c. eyes open or closed; motor activity & agitated vocalizations
d. eyes open; motor activity present
e. eyes closed & still; motor activity present
f. eyes opening & closing but dull; minimal motor activity
g. eyes closed; rapid eye movements detectable
h. transitional state

Self-Test D: Matching Reflexes

Match the reflexes in the left column with their descriptions in the right column.

1. Blinking
2. Babinski
3. Grasping
4. Moro (startle)
5. Rooting
6. Stepping
7. Sucking
8. Swimming
9. Tonic neck

a. automatically sucks when object touches mouth
b. makes coordinated swimming movements when put face down in water
c. forms fists & turns head to right when placed on back
d. feet move as if walking if held above surface, then feet touch surface
e. fans out toes, twists foot in when sole of foot stroked
f. turns head, opens mouth, begins sucking at stroke of cheek
g. closes both eyes to flash of light, puff of air
h. grasps tightly when palms touched
i. arches back, throws head back, flings arms & legs, then closes them to center of body at sudden stimulation

Essay Questions:

1. A good friend of yours just had a baby and, knowing you are taking this course in Life Span Development, confides in you about her concerns. She says her baby sleeps "almost all the time" and doesn't seem to look at her when she feeds, rocks, or talks to the child, and because of this your friend is particularly worried about her baby's hearing and vision. She's also told you that her baby seems to "thrash about" at things and doesn't seem very coordinated. What would you tell her about sleep patterns that a normal baby experiences? How would you explain the development of motor skills as well as sensory and perceptual development, addressing the constructivist and ecological views to your friend? What strategies might you suggest to your friend for helping her infant develop competently?

2. Your high school psychology teacher has learned that you are taking this course in Life Span Development and has asked you to talk to her class about the course of infant development. She has asked that you describe the patterns of cephalocaudal and proximodistal development, gross versus fine motor skills, and the development of sensation and perception. When you talked to her about this presentation, you noted she has assumed you know all about intermodal perception because she wants you to explain that to her class as well. Remembering that this was your favorite teacher in high school, what would you tell these high school students in response to her request?

Key to Self-Test A:

1.	b	p.	121		15.	c	p.	131
2.	a	p.	122		16.	c	p.	131-132
3.	a	p.	122		17.	a	p.	134
4.	d	p.	122		18.	a	p.	136
5.	a	p.	122		19.	b	p.	136
6.	d	p.	122-123		20.	c	p.	136
7.	b	p.	123		21.	a	p.	137
8.	b	p.	123-124		22.	d	p.	138
9.	c	p.	124		23.	c	p.	140
10.	c	p.	124		24.	b	p.	140
11.	a	p.	126-128		25.	b	p.	140
12.	b	p.	128		26.	a	p.	141
13.	d	p.	128		27.	a	p.	141
14.	d	p.	130		28.	d	p.	143

Key to Self-Test B:

1.	g		5.	a
2.	f		6.	c
3.	d		7.	b
4.	e			

Key to Self-Test C:

1.	b		5.	f
2.	e		6.	a
3.	g		7.	d
4.	h		8.	c

Key to Self-Test D:

1.	g		6.	d
2.	e		7.	a
3.	h		8.	b
4.	i		9.	c
5.	f			

Key to Essay Questions:

1. An appropriate answer should include discussion of infant states, noting that the typical neonate will sleep about 17 hours a day, but may range from 10 to 21 hours a day. Then discuss the notions of cephalocaudal and proximodistal development, noting that development proceeds from head down and from inside out, and that infants are first learning to coordinate gross motor skills before they can develop fine motor skills. In terms of your friend's concern about eye contact, tell her about the infant's visual limitations, then explain to her what we know about development of the other sensory modalities; here you should incorporate the constructivist view (perception is a kind of representation of the world that builds up as the infant constructs an image of experiences) and the ecological view (perception has a functional purpose of bringing the organism into contact with the environment & increasing adaptation). Finally, you would want to make some suggestions for how your friend can maximize her baby's development and ensure that the baby is well, so this would include: (a) discussing her concerns

with her pediatrician; (b) being flexible about the baby's own rhythms; (c) providing good nutrition; and (d) being supportive and encouraging while providing a safe yet stimulating environment.

2. As in the previous question, you would discuss the notions of cephalocaudal and proximodistal development, noting that development proceeds from head down and from inside out, and that infants are first learning to coordinate gross motor skills before they can develop fine motor skills (for example, a child will first grasp a crayon with her fist before she is able to control a pencil with her fingers). You would then add the discussion on intermodal perception (the ability to relate & integrate information about two or more sensory modalities, such as vision & hearing), being sure to provide understandable examples.

Research Project 1: Gross Motor Activity*

This project will assist you in understanding the gross motor activities of infants. With one or two of your classmates, get permission to observe children either at your campus day-care center or at another day-care center that has children as young as one year old. Observe two children--one child should be about 12 months old and the other about 24 months old. After watching them for five or ten minutes, select the same five specific behaviors to observe for both children (running, swinging, jumping, drawing, etc.). Describe each of the five behaviors for each child, noting their similarities and differences in performance. Record your observations in the chart below, then answer the questions that follow.

Behavior	Description of Observations

Child 1: Age _____ Sex _____ Child 2: Age _____ Sex _____

1. What similarities did you notice between the two children in the way they performed each behavior?
2. What differences did you notice between the two children in the way they performed each behavior?
3. What patterns of development did you notice when comparing the two children in terms of the material discussed in this chapter?
4. Were your observations consistent with what you might expect from the research described? Explain your response.
5. What might you conclude about development of these skills based on your observations?

*Adapted from Keniston, A. H., & Peden, B. F. (1995), *Student Study Guide for Children* 4th ed. (Santrock, J. W.)

Research Project 2: Mapping the Brain

Review the information in the chapter. Then, using the diagrams below, or others that you prefer, indicate each area of the brain and what functions it controls for the infant. Explain how the brain develops and how that affects the infant's various cognitive and motor abilities.

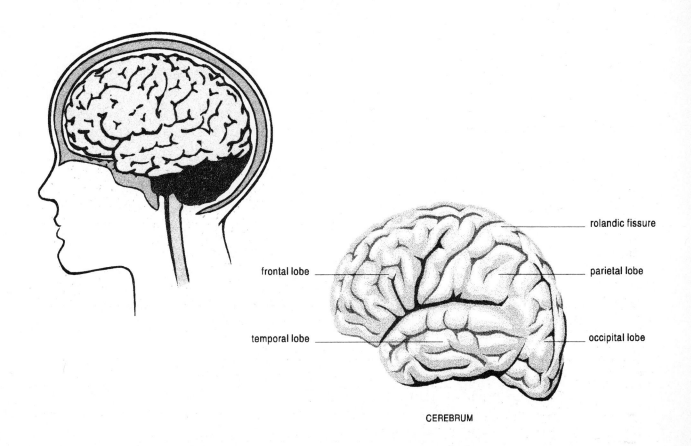

CEREBRUM

Chapter 6   Cognitive Development in Infancy

Learning Objectives

1. Describe Piaget's sensorimotor stage of development, including the six substages.

2. Discuss the criticisms that have been made regarding Piaget's ideas based on research on the perceptual and conceptual development of infants.

3. Explain how the information-processing view differs from the Piagetian view of cognitive development and explain habituation and dishabituation.

4. Describe the memory and imitation abilities of infants.

5. Discuss the relationship between infant cognitive abilities and cognitive functioning in childhood and adolescence.

6. Understand the different components of language.

7. Describe how biological development influences the development of language and cite evidence to support Chomsky's view of language development and the concept of a critical period for learning language.

8. Describe the behavioral view of language development and be able to indicate how environmental factors influence the development of language.

9. Understand the developmental progression of language.

Explain Piaget's concepts of schemes (schema/schemata).

Explain coordination of secondary circular reactions.

List the six substages of the sensorimotor stage.

Describe tertiary circular reactions, novelty, & curiosity.

Describe simple reflexes as they relate to the sensorimotor stage.

Explain the internalization of schemes.

Describe first habits & primary circular reactions.

What is object permanence?

Describe primary circular reactions.

Contrast habituation with dishabituation.

Describe secondary circular reactions.

How does deferred imitation relate to memory?

Coordination of secondary circular reactions: Piaget's 4th sensorimotor substage, develops between 8 & 12 months; significant changes involve the coordination of schemes and intentionality
Infant combines & recombines previously learned schemes in a coordinated way.

Scheme (schema): refers to the basic unit (or units) for an organized pattern of sensorimotor functioning
(also relates to the basic units individuals have for organized patterns of cognitive functioning generally)

Tertiary circular reactions, novelty, & curiosity: Piaget's 5th sensorimotor substage, develops between 12 & 18 months; infants become intrigued by the variety of properties that objects possess & by the many things they can make happen to objects
Infant purposely explores new possibilities with objects.

The ***six sensorimotor substages*** are: (1) simple reflexes; (2) first habits & primary circular reactions; (3) secondary circular reactions; (4) coordination of secondary circular reactions; (5) tertiary circular reactions; & (6) internalization of schemes

Internalization of schemes: Piaget's 6th sensorimotor substage, develops between 18 & 24 months; the infant's mental functioning shifts from a purely sensorimotor plane to a symbolic plane; infant also develops the ability to use primitive symbols (i.e., an internalized sensory image or word that represents an event)

Simple reflexes: Piaget's 1st sensorimotor substage; corresponds to the 1st month after birth. The basic means of coordinating sensation & action is through reflexive behaviors, including rooting & sucking.
The infant develops ability to produce reflex-like behaviors in the absence of obvious reflex stimuli.

Object permanence: the Piagetian term for the infant's ability to understand that objects & events continue to exist even when they cannot directly be seen, heard, or touched

First habits & primary circular reactions: Piaget's 2nd sensorimotor substage, develops between 1-4 months; coordination of sensation & types of schemes or structures--i.e., habits (a scheme based on simple reflexes separated from eliciting stimulus) & primary circular reactions

Habituation: repeated presentation of the same stimulus causes reduced attention to the stimulus
Dishabituation: infant's renewed interest in a stimulus
Habituation is used to assess infant's maturity well-being.

Primary circular reactions: schemes based on the infant's attempt to reproduce an interesting or pleasurable event that initially occurred by chance

Memory: a central feature of cognitive development, pertains to all situations in which an individual retains information over time
Deferred imitation: imitation that occurs after a time delay of hours or days (thus indicating that the infant has memory for a previous event)

Secondary circular reactions: Piaget's 3rd sensorimotor substage, develops between 4 & 8 months; infant becomes more object-oriented or focused on the world, moving beyond preoccupation with the self in sensorimotor interactions

Explain the developmental quotient (DQ).

What is motherese?

Describe the Bayley Scales of Infant Development & how they are used.

Explain the language acquisition strategies of recasting, echoing, expanding, & labeling.

Define the term "language." Explain the concept of infinite generativity as it relates to language.

What is receptive vocabulary and when does it begin?

Explain the concepts of phonology, syntax, semantics, & pragmatics.

Explain the holophrase hypothesis.

What is the language acquisition device (LAD)? Who has suggested its existence?

Describe telegraphic speech.

How do critical periods relate to language acquisition?

What are MLUs? What is their purpose? Who proposed this concept?

Motherese: the kind of speech often used by mothers & other adults to talk to babies (in a higher pitch than normal & with simple words & sentences)

Developmental quotient (DQ): an overall developmental score that combines subscores in motor, language, adaptive, & personal-social domains in Arnold Gesell's assessment of infants (a clinical assessment)

Recasting: rephrasing a statement the child has made, perhaps turning it into a question
Echoing: repeating what a child says, especially if it is an incomplete phrase or sentence
Expanding: restating what a child says in linguistically sophisticated form
Labeling: identifying the names of objects

The Bayley Scales of Infant Development: (developed by Nancy Bayley, 1969) widely used to assess infant development; three components: mental scale, motor scale, infant behavior profile (used to predict later development)

Receptive vocabulary refers to the words an individual understands (as opposed to those that the individual can actually produce).
It begins at approximately 6 to 9 months of age.

Language: a system of symbols used to communicate with others; human language is characterized by infinite generativity & rule systems
Infinite generativity: an individual's ability to generate an infinite number of meaningful sentences using a finite set of words & rules

The holophrase hypothesis: a single word can be used to imply a complete sentence; infants' first words are characteristically holophrastic (e.g., "ball" may mean "that's the ball," "let's play ball," "I want the ball," etc.)

Phonology: study of language's sound system
Syntax: the ways words are combined to form acceptable phrases & sentences
Semantics: meanings of words & sentences
Pragmatics: use of appropriate conversation & knowledge underlying the use of language in context

Telegraphic speech: the use of short & precise words to communicate; it characterizes young children's two- or three-word combinations (unnecessary words such as articles, auxiliary verbs, & other connectives are omitted)

Language acquisition device (LAD): a biological endowment that enables a child to detect certain language categories, such as phonology, syntax, & semantics
Noam Chomsky's theoretical construct flowing from evidence of the biological basis of language

Mean length of utterance (MLU): Roger Brown's (1973) notion that an index of language development based on the number of morphemes per sentence a child produces in a sample of about 50 to 100 sentences is a good index of language maturity

Critical period: a period in which there is learning readiness; beyond this period learning is difficult or impossible
Observing children like Genie, the "Wild Boy of Aveyron," & Kamala suggests language falls within this notion.

Self-Test A: Multiple Choice

1. Jean Piaget gathered the information for his theories about cognitive development by:
   a. reviewing the literature on cognitive development.
   b. surveying thousands of parents.
   c. observing his own children.
   d. testing hundreds of children in his laboratory.

2. Piaget's theory is a qualitative theory of cognitive development, which means that it:
   a. uses standardized tests to measure and describe thought.
   b. explains what kinds of knowledge are typical of children at different ages.
   c. identifies different kinds of thinking children perform at different ages.
   d. provides ways to determine how well children think at different stages.

3. In a Piagetian model, the basic mental units for organizing information are referred to as:
   a. memories.
   b. images.
   c. cognitions.
   d. schemas.

4. According to Piaget, during the first sensorimotor substage, infants' behaviors are:
   a. reflexive.
   b. maladaptive.
   c. unchanging.
   d. reinforced.

5. Laurent has problems retrieving a ball that rolled out of reach, so he uses a Tinkertoy stick to hit it. He is in the:
   a. primary circular reactions substage.
   b. secondary circular reactions substage.
   c. coordination of secondary circular reactions substage.
   d. tertiary circular reactions substage.

6. Which is the best example of Piaget's concept of a habit?
   a. learning to suck on a nipple and later being able to do it while sleeping
   b. accidentally shaking a rattle, which produces a sound, and then purposefully shaking the rattle to produce the sound
   c. initially blinking reflexively in response to a bright light and then blinking when no stimulus is present
   d. learning to laugh at people who slip on ice and fall down

7. If a child is able to track an object that disappears and reappears in several locations in rapid succession, but does not do well with visible displacements, she is in substage ____ of the sensorimotor stage.
   a. three
   b. four
   c. five
   d. six

8. Infants whose parents use sign language have been observed to start using conventional signs at about ____ months of age.
   a. three
   b. six
   c. ten
   d. thirteen

9. A critical difference between information-processing theorists and Piagetian theorists is that information-processing theorists:
   a. are concerned with the way in which infants think, while Piagetians are concerned with the way infants act.
   b. believe that infants do not develop the ability of conceptualizing objects as solid until they are about two years old.
   c. reject the notion of stages of development.
   d. believe that children develop at a much slower rate than Piagetians.

10. If a child is listening to a tape of a story being read by a male voice and the voice of the storyteller changes to a female voice, most likely the child's sucking rate will:
   a. not change.
   b. stop.
   c. increase.
   d. decrease.

11. _____ occurs when repeated exposure to the same stimulus results in a reduced reaction to that object.
   a. Habituation
   b. Object permanence
   c. Transference
   d. Dishabituation

12. Which is an example of dishabituation?
   a. the excitement students exhibit when a boring professor shows a film instead of lecturing
   b. first being bothered by wearing a new wristwatch, but then getting so used to it that you forget you're wearing it
   c. realizing that when a jet flies off into the distance it still exists
   d. a drinker who believes she is not responsible for her actions

13. Evidence that infants can imitate adult facial expressions shortly after birth indicates:
   a. imitative abilities are learned quickly.
   b. imitation has a biological base.
   c. infants have a full range of emotional expression at birth.
   d. imitation is a form of emotional expression.

14. Contrary to Piaget's view, infants have demonstrated the ability to engage in deferred imitation by age _____ months.
   a. three
   b. six
   c. nine
   d. eighteen

15. The developmental quotient is a global developmental score that combines subscores in the following areas *except*:
   a. motor ability.
   b. language ability.
   c. physical ability.
   d. personal-social abilities.

16. Siegler (1998) demonstrated that infants have some rudimentary understanding of numbers, and can often discriminate one object from two, and two objects from three:
   a. at birth.
   b. by one month of age.
   c. by two months of age.
   d. by six months of age.

17. The _____ has been predictive of academic achievement at six or eight years of age.
   a. Piagetian Sensorimotor Scales
   b. Bayley Scales of Infant Development
   c. Gesell Developmental Schedules
   d. Brazelton Neonatal Behavioral Assessment Scales

18. Infant intelligence scales are appropriate for all of the following *except:*
   a. assessing the effects of malnutrition
   b. predicting childhood intelligence
   c. determining developmental effects of environmental stimulation
   d. measuring detrimental effects of a mother's prenatal drug-taking habits

19. Language is most accurately defined as a system of _____ that allow for communication with others.
   a. images
   b. vocalizations
   c. symbols
   d. words

20. All of the following are part of the system of rules needed in a language *except*:
   a. generativity.
   b. phonemes.
   c. morphemes.
   d. semantics.

21. Phonological rules ensure that:
   a. word meaning will be communicated.
   b. speakers will take turns when talking.
   c. only certain sound sequences will occur in speech.
   d. surface structure will reflect deep structure.

22. Which of the following components of language is closely related to grammar?
   a. semantics
   b. pragmatics
   c. syntax
   d. morphology

23. The best estimate is that human language evolved about _____ years ago.
   a. 20,000 to 70,000
   b. 70,000 to 100,000
   c. 100,000 to 500,000
   d. 500,000 to 1,000,000

24. The evidence favors the conclusion that animals other than humans:
   a. cannot communicate with one another.
   b. may communicate with one another but cannot learn syntax.
   c. may communicate with one another and may learn syntax.
   d. may learn language with all of the characteristics of human language.

25. If a child were reared in isolation from people for the first ten or eleven years of life, he would likely:
   a. never learn to communicate effectively with humans.
   b. learn to communicate if given speech and language therapy.
   c. learn to communicate if placed in a warm, comfortable environment.
   d. learn to communicate in his own personal language system understood by a few people.

26. Dr. Jones claims Marie can make a negative statement because that use was reinforced. Dr. Jones most likely takes which view?
   a. biological
   b. behavioral
   c. cognitive
   d. interactionist

27. When Jennifer said, "The deer was running," Mother asked, "Where was the deer running?" Mother's strategy is:
   a. echoing.
   b. expanding.
   c. recasting.
   d. labeling.

28. A 1989 study by Shirley Brice Heath found that urban housing projects:
   a. impede the ability of young children to develop cognitive and social skills.
   b. provide an opportunity for positive social interactions among children, but may restrict intellectual development.
   c. enhance the cognitive development, but not the social development, of children.
   d. provide excellent social opportunities for parents, but restrict the child's development.

29. A child's first word is uttered at around ___ months.
   a. 3
   b. 9
   c. 12
   d. 18

30. Andrew sees a cat walk on the lawn then turns to his mother and says, "Kitty." The notion that Andrew is using that one word to imply a whole sentence, such as "That's a kitty," would be suggestive of the _____ hypothesis.
   a. generalization
   b. generativity
   c. cognitive
   d. holophrase

31. The mean length of utterance (MLU) is a good index of:
   a. holophrastic speech.
   b. overextension.
   c. language maturity.
   d. language generation.

32. Naomi Baron recommends all of the following ways to facilitate language development in infants *except*:
   a. being an active conversational partner.
   b. avoiding sexist language.
   c. talking as if the infant understands you.
   d. using a language style comfortable to you.

Self-Test B: Matching Researchers

Match the individuals in the left column with the appropriate descriptors in the right column.

1. Arnold Gesell
2. Carolyn Rovee-Collier
3. Nancy Bayley
4. Andrew Metzhoff
5. Naomi Brown
6. Roger Brown
7. Shirley Brice Heath
8. Jean Piaget

a. devised the most commonly used infant intelligence test
b. contributed to his cognitive theoryby observing his own children
c. developed MLU to measure language maturity
d. suggested ways parents can assist language development
e. studied imitation and deferred imitation by infants
f. studied language traditions of poor urban African Americans
g. developed a clinical measure to assess potential abnormality
h. demonstrated detailed memory in 2- to 3-month old infants

Self-Test C: Matching Terms

Match the terms in the left column with the appropriate descriptions in the right column.

1. scheme
2. phonology
3. telegraphic speech
4. recasting
5. motherese
6. object permanence
7. deferred imitation
8. habituation

a. high-pitched, simple speech used by adults to talk to babies
b. reduced attention to a stimulus caused by repeated presentation
c. imitation that occurs after a time delay of hours or days
d. study of language's sound system
e. the basic unit for an organized pattern of sensorimotor functioning
f. the use of short & precise words to communicate
g. rephrasing a statement the child has made
h. infant's ability to understand that objects exist even when they cannot directly be seen

Essay Questions:

1. Your next door neighbor is planning to open a day-care center that caters to infants and toddlers. She has had a lot of experience with toddlers, but less experience with infants, and so she has asked you to share what you have been learning in your Life Span Development class. She is familiar with Piaget, but has heard some criticisms of his ideas and asks you what you know about this. She also wants your suggestions on how to provide the best possible environment for the children. What would you tell her?

2. Your 15-month-old nephew has started using two-word sentences. Explain the process of language development, including the stages of language development and explanations of the biological and behavioral theories involved. On the basis of what you know, do you think your nephew's language development is advanced, delayed, or typical? Give your reasons.

Key to Self-Test A:

1.	c	p.	147	17.	b	p.	156
2.	c	p.	148	18.	b	p.	156-157
3.	d	p.	148	19.	c	p.	158
4.	a	p.	148	20.	a	p.	158
5.	c	p.	148-149	21.	c	p.	158
6.	c	p.	148	22.	c	p.	159
7.	c	p.	149	23.	a	p.	159
8.	b	p.	151	24.	c	p.	159
9.	c	p.	151	25.	a	p.	160
10.	b	p.	152	26.	b	p.	161
11.	a	p.	152	27.	c	p.	162
12.	a	p.	152	28.	a	p.	162
13.	b	p.	153	29.	c	p.	163
14.	c	p.	154	30.	d	p.	163
15.	c	p.	154	31.	c	p.	164
16.	c	p.	155	32.	b	p.	166

Key to Self-Test B:

1.	g	5.	d
2.	h	6.	c
3.	a	7.	f
4.	e	8.	b

Key to Self-Test C:

1.	e	5.	a
2.	d	6.	h
3.	f	7.	c
4.	g	8.	b

Key to Essay Questions:

1. First you would talk about Piaget's notions of schemes, then describe each of the six substages in the sensorimotor stage, so your neighbor would be familiar with what to expect. Be sure to include object permanence, as well as imitation and deferred imitation, being clear when each develops. Then you would go through the various criticisms of Piaget's theory (such as the research finding that infants go through the stages earlier than Piaget suggested). You should also present the information-processing approach and how that differs from Piaget's. Finally, you would want to offer some advice such as providing a stimulating, but not overstimulating, environment, and being sure to communicate actively with the infant.

2.   This question requires you to explain each stage of language development discussed in this chapter, beginning with receptive language (understanding words about 6 to 9 months of age), the one-word stage (which begins at approximately 12 months), etc. Present the biological influences, such as biological prewiring as suggested by Noam Chomsky (i.e., the language acquisition device) and the evidence for a critical period for learning language; and also discuss the evidence for environmental influences (e.g., the use of "motherese," and the strategies such as recasting that adults use with children). Also present the notion of mean length of utterance with respect to determining a child's language maturity. Finally, it would appear that your nephew is clearly advanced in his language development, since the two-word stage does not typically begin until 18 to 24 months.

Research Project 1: Imitation

Something that I particularly like to do (as a developmental psychologist) is to observe babies when I'm standing in line in the grocery store. The next time you find yourself standing behind an infant, first observe the child to see what you notice that would (or would not) be consistent with what you've read in this chapter. Then, smile at the baby and see what kind of response you get--does the baby smile back, turn away, ignore you, cry? What I've found will help a baby stop crying is to make an "O" with your mouth as if you are sympathizing with the child and acknowledging the child's distress. Whenever I do this I find that the child stops crying, and looks at me in wide-eyed interest. Try opening and shutting your mouth to see if the child will imitate you. You might also trying wiggling your nose or your ears. While people might think you are really weird if you do this in some other context, they seem to understand and either ignore you or become amused when an infant is involved. Typically the parent(s) will acknowledge your presence, and if they do, you might say you are taking this class and ask the baby's age. Based on your observations, answer the questions that follow.

1.   What have you noticed about the child's perceptual abilities? Are they what you would expect for a child of this age?
2.   Did anything the child do surprise you?
3.   What did you learn from observing this interaction?

Research Project 2: Object Permanence*

To do this research project, you will need approval from your school's Institutional Review Board **plus** a signed consent form from each child's parent. Before starting, you will want to develop rapport with each child and ask each child if he or she would like to play a game with you and help you. Do not push any child into participating if that child seems unwilling to participate (an infant has just as much right not to participate as an adult).

Working in groups of two to four classmates, select two children to work with, one from any of the following age groups: 4 to 8 months; 8 to 12 months; 12 to 18 months; or 18 to 24 months. Do the following three tasks with each child and record your responses. Only one person should do the tasks while the others record.

Task Description	Infant Responses	
	Infant 1 Sex_____ Age _____	Infant 2 Sex_____ Age _____
1. Show each infant an interesting object (e.g., ball), then cover it with a cloth. Note the response. Partially remove the cloth so part of the object is visible. Note the response.		
2. Show the child the object again, then move it so it disappears behind a screen. Note the response. Do the task again, but now show the child that you are putting the object behind one screen, and then behind another one that is nearby. Note the response.		
3. Show the child the object, then cover it with a small box. Move the box behind the screen. Let the object remain behind the screen, but bring the box back into view. Note the response.		

1. How do the younger and older children respond in the first task? Do they both understand that the object is under the cloth? When the object is partially exposed does either child seem surprised? Do the children try to reach the object?
2. In the second task, does either child realize the object is behind the screen? Can they follow the action when you move the object from behind screen 1 to behind screen 2? Where do they look for the object?
3. How does each child react when the object is placed in the box? What are their reactions when they see the object is no longer in the box? Do they try to find it? If so, where do they look?
4. Based on your observations, what would you conclude about development of object permanence? Do your observations agree with Piaget's?

*Adapted from Keniston, A. H., & Peden, B. F. (1995). *Student Study Guide for Children* 4th ed. (Santrock, J. W.)

Chapter 7   Socioemotional Development in Infancy

Learning Objectives

1. Understand reciprocal socialization and scaffolding.

2. Define attachment and describe the importance of Harlow and Zimmerman's study on attachment theory.

3. Identify the types of attachment and know what behaviors manifest themselves for each type.

4. Discuss criticisms of attachment theory and the Strange Situation laboratory procedure.

5. Describe the role the father plays in the development of the infant.

6. Indicate what the effects of day care are on the developmental processes in infancy.

7. Understand the concept of temperament, including the three types of temperament and the implications of temperamental variations for parenting.

8. Describe how emotions are assessed in infants and the developmental progression of facial expressions.

9. Discuss early personality development, including trust and the developing sense of self and independence.

10. Describe the nature and frequency of child abuse.

How does reciprocal socialization work?

What is temperament?

Explain the concept of scaffolding.

Explain the three types of temperament commonly seen in children.

How does attachment differ from bonding?

Explain the concept of emotionality and how it relates to temperament.

What is meant by the term "secure attachment"? What types of behaviors would suggest a child is securely attached?

Explain sociability and describe how it relates to temperament.

Compare Type A babies, Type B babies, and Type C babies.

Explain the notion of activity level and how it relates to temperament.

Describe the "Strange Situation" and what it tests. Which researcher designed the Strange Situation?

What is emotion?

Temperament: an individual's behavioral style and characteristic way of responding (a person's temperament is considered to be innate, although it can be altered by the child's environment)

Reciprocal socialization: the view that socialization is bidirectional--children socialize parents just as parents socialize children; the successive actions of the partners are coordinated through mutual synchrony or matching a partner's actions

Easy child: positive mood, regular routines in infancy, adapts easily to new experiences (40%)
Difficult child: reacts negatively, cries often, irregular daily routines, slow to accept new experiences (10%)
Slow-to-warm-up child: low activity level, somewhat negative, low adaptability, low intensity of mood (15%)

Scaffolding: an important caregiver role in early parent-child interaction: through their attention & choice of behaviors, caregivers provide a framework around which they & their infants interact; one function is to introduce infants to social rules, especially role-taking

Emotionality: the tendency to be distressed
Emotionality reflects the arousal of a person's sympathetic nervous system; in infancy, distress develops into fear & anger; children are labeled "easy" or "difficult" on the basis of their emotionality (Buss & Plomin)

Attachment: a close emotional bond between the infant and the caregiver
Bonding is more general--a close emotional tie between two people

Sociability: the tendency to prefer the company of others to being alone; matches a tendency to respond warmly to others;
one of the categories used to label children as "easy," "difficult," or "slow-to-warm-up" (e.g., easy children would have high sociability; slow-to-warm-up children would have low sociability)

Secure attachment: Infants use their caregiver as a secure base from which to explore the environment; secure attachment in 1st year provides important foundation for later psychological development (Ainsworth); infant moves freely away from mother but keeps visually connected; responds positively to being picked up by others; freely moves to play

Activity level: involves tempo & vigor of movement (e.g., as displayed in walking, game preferences, other physical movements); another category used to label children as "easy," "difficult," or "slow-to-warm-up" (e.g., difficult children would have high activity level; slow-to-warm-up chidlren would have low activity level)

Type A (Anxious-Avoidant): exhibit insecurity by avoiding the caregiver
Type B (Secure): use caregiver as a secure base from which to explore environment
Type C (Anxious-Resistant): exhibit insecurity by resisting the caregiver

Emotion: feeling or affect that involves a mixture of physiological arousal (e.g., a fast heartbeat) and overt behavior (e.g., a smile or grimace)

Strange Situation: an observational measure of infant attachment that requires the infant to move through a series of introductions, separations, & reunions with the caregiver & an adult stranger in a prescribed order; designed by Ainsworth

What are positive and negative affectivity (PA & NA)? How are they related to the research on emotion?

What is the social smile and when does it begin to emerge?

Describe the Maximally Discriminative Facial Movement Coding System (MAX).

What is the first of Erikson's eight stages of development? What is the age range for this stage? What is the infant's primary task during this stage?

Describe the baby's basic cry.

Explain the use of the mirror technique in determining whether a child has developed a sense of self.

Describe the baby's anger cry.

What is the second of Erikson's eight stages of development? What is the age range for this stage? What is the child's primary task during this stage?

Describe the baby's pain cry.

How does the term "child abuse" differ from the term "child maltreatment"?

What is a reflexive smile?

What is infantile autism? Describe the symptoms and possible causes.

Social smile: occurs in response to an external stimulus--in early development typically in response to a face;
begins to occur about 2 to 3 months, although some researchers believe infants grin in response to voices as early as 3 weeks

Positive Affectivity (PA): range of positive emotions from high energy, enthusiasm, & excitement to calm, quiet, & withdrawn; involved in joy, happiness, & laughter
Negative Affectivity (NA): negatively toned emotions, e.g., anxiety, anger, guilt, sadness
PA & NA are separate dimensions used by psychologists to classify emotions

Trust versus mistrust: during first year of life is Erikson's first stage;
infants learn trust when cared for in a consistent, warm manner; develop mistrust if not well fed or kept consistently warm;
infants with a sense of trust are more likely to be securely attached, but there must be a balance between trust & mistrust

Maximally Discriminative Facial Movement Coding System (MAX): Izard's system of coding infants' facial expressions related to emotion; MAX coders watch slow-motion & stop-action videotapes of infants' facial reactions to stimuli (e.g., giving an infant ice, putting tape on back of child's hands, giving & taking away a toy)

The mirror technique: used to determine if infants can recognize themselves; mother puts dot of rouge on infant's nose; researcher observes how often infant touches his nose, then places infant in front of mirror to see if nose touching increases; by 18 months usually recognize own image & coordinate mirror image with own actions

Basic cry: a rhythmic pattern that usually consists of a cry, followed by a briefer silence, then a shorter inspiratory whistle somewhat higher in pitch than the main cry, then another brief rest before the next cry
(Note that crying is a newborn's most important means of communicating with their world)

Autonomy versus shame/doubt: Erikson's 2nd stage (1-3 yrs); development of independence; builds on infant's developing mental & motor abilities including control of muscles (e.g., for toilet training); development of autonomy during toddler years gives adolescents courage to be independent & able to guide their future

Anger cry: a variation of the basic cry but more excess air is forced through the vocal cords; mothers tend to infer exasperation or rage from this cry

Child abuse: term used by public & professionals, refers to abuse & neglect; **Child maltreatment**: developmentalists use term to reduce emotional impact of "abuse"; addresses multifaceted nature to include physical & sexual abuse, fostering delinquency, lack of supervision, medical, educational, nutritional neglect, & drug/alcohol abuse

Pain cry: stimulated by high-intensity stimuli; sudden appearance of loud crying without preliminary moaning; characterized by a long initial cry followed by an extended period of breath holding

Infantile autism: severe developmental disorder includes deficiencies in social relationships, abnormalities in communication; restricted, repetitive, stereotyped behavior patterns (onset in infancy); echolalia (echo what they hear); Associated with organic brain dysfunction, may have hereditary basis

Reflexive smile: appears during the first month after birth, usually during irregular patterns of sleep, not when the infant is in an alert state (not occurring in response to external stimuli)

Self-Test A: Multiple Choice

1. Studies of reciprocal socialization during infancy reveal that _____ plays an important role in socialization.
   a. breast feeding
   b. mutual gaze
   c. trust
   d. attachment

2. Reciprocal socialization is best defined in which of the following ways?
   a. Children are products of their parents' socialization techniques.
   b. Parents are products of their children's socialization techniques.
   c. Socialization is bi-directional.
   d. The interactions that children have with people other than their parents determine how they will be socialized.

3. One of the functions of scaffolding is to:
   a. introduce infants to interactive games.
   b. provide a parent support network.
   c. teach infants social rules.
   d. ensure that parents know how to care for their infants.

4. Which of the following research techniques is used to investigate attachment?
   a. watching children as they are separated from and then reunited with their parents
   b. asking parents to describe how emotionally involved they are with their children
   c. watching children play with dolls representing adults and children to see what kinds of interactions they create
   d. asking baby-sitters about how infants behave when their parents are gone

5. The stage that Erik Erikson believes is most relevant to the formation of attachment is the _____ stage.
   a. trust versus mistrust
   b. autonomy versus shame and doubt
   c. phallic
   d. anal

6. Life-span developmentalists agree that secure attachment:
   a. is essential to adult social competence.
   b. is not essential, but is a factor in adult social competence.
   c. is not an important factor in adult social competence.
   d. cannot easily be connected to adult social competence.

7. You are asked to baby-sit your niece for the evening. When the parents put the child down so they can finish getting dressed, she heads toward her toys while she watches the parents find their coats. The child is demonstrating which kind of attachment?
   a. secure
   b. anxious-avoidant
   c. anxious-resistant
   d. insecure

8. Jeremy resists being held closely by his mother, yet hangs on to her when she tries to put him down. He is a type ____ baby.
   a. A
   b. B
   c. C
   d. D

9. Jerome Kagan has emphasized the importance of _____ as a determinant of social competence.
   a. bonding
   b. temperament
   c. peer responsiveness
   d. learning

10. Which statement *is not* a criticism of the theories concerning attachment?
    a. Genetics and temperament have not been accounted for and may play more of a role in development than the nature of the attachment.
    b. The role of multiple social agents and changing social contexts is not included in the study of attachment.
    c. Cultural differences are not considered when explaining how attachment occurs.
    d. The relationship between the parent and the infant is not emphasized enough.

11. Given the opportunity, fathers usually will:
    a. not elect caretaking roles with children.
    b. elect nurturing caretaker roles with infants.
    c. elect inactive child-caretaking roles.
    d. elect involved caretaker roles over occupational roles.

12. The results of a Swedish study indicate that if a mother works and a father stays at home with the baby, the father:
    a. reverses roles and behaves like the typical mother in many respects.
    b. interacts with the baby in his usual fatherly manner.
    c. is more likely to discipline and comfort the infant than the mother is.
    d. plays with the infant in a less physical and arousing manner than does the mother.

13. It can be concluded that day care for American children is:
    a. adequate, but needs to be expanded.
    b. inadequate and has negative outcomes for children.
    c. neither adequate nor inadequate; the results of studies are mixed.
    d. exemplary, a good model for the world community.

14. Research concerning the long-term effects of day care suggests which of the following?
    a. Day care has long-term, detrimental effects.
    b. Day care has no long-term effects.
    c. Day care can facilitate development.
    d. The effects of day care are dependent on the length and type of care given.

15. Temperament is best defined as:
    a. the way an individual reacts to a special person in the environment.
    b. an individual's general behavioral style.
    c. the emotions experienced by infants and children.
    d. the reaction displayed by a parent when a child engages in an unwanted activity.

16. Chess and Thomas believe the _____ child is the most typical temperament for a child.
    a. difficult
    b. easy
    c. slow-to-warm-up
    d. feisty

17. The tendency to prefer the company of others is referred to as:
    a. activity level.
    b. emotionality.
    c. sociability.
    d. temperament.

18. An infant who responds with anger at unpleasant events displays:
    a. rage.
    b. emotionality.
    c. withdrawal.
    d. sociability.

19. _____ influences temperament, but the degree of influence depends on _____ experiences.
    a. Heredity; environmental
    b. Environment; heredity
    c. Affectivity; situational
    d. Environment; long-term

20. Arnold Buss and Robert Plomin use all of the following categories to classify temperament *except*:
    a. activity level.
    b. emotionality.
    c. regularity.
    d. sociability.

21. A child whose temperament does not fluctuate much during development probably has a temperament that _____ the parents.
    a. engages
    b. matches
    c. counters
    d. influences

22. Emotion is a mixture of:
    a. physiological arousal and cognitions.
    b. cognitions and behaviors.
    c. physiological arousal and behaviors.
    d. unconscious and universal processes.

23. Which of the following emotions develops before the others?
    a. guilt
    b. contempt
    c. surprise
    d. shame

24. _____ represent the first language used by infants and parents.
    a. Emotions
    b. Facial expressions
    c. Words
    d. Gazes

25. The _____ cry is a rhythmic pattern that usually consists of a cry, followed by a briefer silence, then a shorter inspiratory whistle somewhat high in pitch.
    a. basic
    b. anger
    c. pain
    d. colicky

26. The _____ smile does not appear in response to external stimulation.
    a. social
    b. reflexive
    c. internal
    d. reciprocal

27. Mary Ainsworth believes that attachment security depends on:
    a. how sensitive and responsive the caregiver is to infant signals.
    b. the mother's love and concern for the welfare of her child.
    c. the consistency of parental responses during the child-care routine.
    d. reinforcement of attachment behaviors by the caregiver.

28. According to Erik Erikson, children will develop an excessive sense of shame and a sense of doubt about their abilities under all but which of the following circumstances?
    a. when impatient parents do things children can do for themselves
    b. when children are consistently overprotected
    c. when accidents the children have had or caused are criticized
    d. when children are allowed to express their emotions unchecked

29. The human infant learns to recognize his or her image in a mirror at approximately ___ months.
    a. two
    b. six
    c. nine
    d. eighteen

30. Reductions in incidents of child abuse have been shown to be related to all of the following *except*:
    a. the presence of community support systems.
    b. the availability of support from relatives and friends.
    c. harsh laws punishing abusers.
    d. family income.

31. A child using echolalia will say what in response to the question, "Is that your ball?"
    a. "My ball."
    b. "Is that your ball?"
    c. "No, it's my ball."
    d. "Yes, it's your ball."

32. Which of the following countries has no national policy permitting paternity leave?
    a. Norway
    b. the United States
    c. Portugal
    d. Spain

33. If you were listening to LaVisa Wilson lecture on competent caregivers, you would hear her describe all of the following characteristics *except*:
    a. patience.
    b. physical health.
    c. economic stability.
    d. flexibility.

Self-Test B: Matching

Match the individuals in the left column with the appropriate descriptors in the right column.

1.	Carroll Izard	a.	Studied nontraditional gender roles in Swedish families
2.	Edward Zigler	b.	Proposed a solution to day-care needs for many U.S. families
3.	Mary Ainsworth	c.	The researcher whose work illustrates the new functionalism in emotion
4.	John Bowlby	d.	Described easy, difficult, & slow-to-warm-up temperaments in infants
5.	Margaret Mahler	e.	Tested Freud's theory of attachment via oral gratification using monkeys
6.	Michael Lamb	f.	Created Maximally Discriminative Facial Movement Coding System (MAX)
7.	Harry Harlow	g.	Devised the "Strange Situation" to measure attachment in children
8.	Alan Sroufe	h.	Developmentalist who said children go through separation & individuation
9.	Alexander Chess & Stella Thomas	i.	Ethological researcher who stated that attachment has a biological basis

Self-Test C: Matching Infant Styles

Match the infant styles of attachment or temperament in the left column with the characteristics in the right column.

1.	Type A babies	a.	Exhibit insecurity by resisting the mother
2.	Type B babies	b.	Low activity level, adaptability, & intensity of mood; somewhat negative
3.	Type C babies	c.	Use the caregiver as a secure base from which to explore the environment
4.	Easy	d.	Exhibit insecurity by avoiding the mother
5.	Difficult	e.	Positive mood, regular routines, adapts easily to new experiences
6.	Slow-to-warm-up	f.	Reacts negatively, cries frequently, irregular daily routines, slow to adapt

Essay Questions:

1. Your sister and brother-in-law both work for the same internationally based company that has branches in fifty countries and every continent around the world. Your sister has confided in you that she would like to have children but, while she feels guilty about it, she would really rather work than stay at home with them while they are growing up. She said her husband also wants children, and he has said he'd be willing to stay home with them for a while so your sister could continue working, but he's concerned about the loss of income if he doesn't work for several months. They both would like to spend some time at home with their children, but would want to put them into day care even though they feel guilty about doing that. Assuming that you think they would actually be good parents, what information would you give them about where in the world they might live to maximize their ability for both to have time with their newborn children; and what would you advise them about placing their children in day care?

2. The local PTA has asked you to come talk to their parents and teachers about working with young children. They have specifically asked you to address the idea of attachment--what it is, the research supporting a notion of attachment, the different forms of attachment, and how to help a child become securely attached--and the different types of temperament, including how to deal effectively with children according to their temperamental styles. What will you tell these parents and teachers?

Key to Self-Test A:

1.	b	p.	171		18.	b	p.	180
2.	c	p.	171		19.	a	p.	180
3.	c	p.	171		20.	c	p.	180
4.	a	p.	172		21.	b	p.	181
5.	a	p.	173		22.	c	p.	182-183
6.	d	p.	174		23.	c	p.	184
7.	a	p.	174		24.	a	p.	184
8.	c	p.	174		25.	a	p.	185
9.	b	p.	174		26.	b	p.	185-186
10.	d	p.	174-175		27.	a	p.	186
11.	a	p.	175		28.	d	p.	186
12.	b	p.	175-176		29.	d	p.	187
13.	c	p.	178		30.	c	p.	189
14.	d	p.	178		31.	b	p.	189
15.	b	p.	179		32.	b	p.	177
16.	b	p.	180		33.	c	p.	191
17.	c	p.	180					

Key to Self-Test B:

1.	f		6.	a
2.	b		7.	e
3.	g		8.	c
4.	i		9.	d
5.	h			

Key to Self-Test C:

1.	d		4.	e
2.	c		5.	f
3.	a		6.	b

Key to Essay Questions:

1. You would need to explore the maternity and paternity leave policies of different countries around the world, including the United States, which presently does not have a paternity leave policy, and also discuss the various child-care policies around the world (Sweden, of course, comes to mind as an excellent example of a country that provides paid leave to both parents during the first year of a child's life). You would also need to discuss the benefits and problems that would arise from having only one or both parents involved in early child-rearing, and placement of infants and young children into day care facilities. The issue of day care for both infants and young children needs to be discussed, including the different types of day care that exist in the United States and abroad, the effects of day care on children based on the research to date, and how widely the quality of day care varies. Note that while Belsky concluded that extensive day care during the first year of life is detrimental, other researchers have contradicted this finding, so you should discuss that as well as the tips given in the chapter for determining what defines quality day care. As for the issue of feeling guilty, sometimes it is not an option (either financially or emotionally) for the mother to stay home with the children, so you would want to address this issue as well.

2. Here you would define attachment, then look at the various research studies that have explored attachment, including, among others, the research of Harry and Margaret Harlow and Robert Zimmerman with the rhesus monkeys, and Ainsworth's Strange Situation research. Talk about the different types of attachment that Ainsworth described, and discuss ways to promote secure attachment so that children will feel safe to explore new environments and take on new challenges (be sure to include Erikson's stage of trust versus mistrust in your discussion). Then look at the work by Chess and Thomas on temperament, discussing the three types they describe (note that only 65% of children are clearly able to be designated into one of the three types), as well as the descriptors that Buss and Plomin use (e.g., emotionality). Finally, using the guidelines in the chapter, provide some strategies for the parents and teachers to use to work most effectively with children's different temperaments.

Research Project 1: Prevention of Child Maltreatment

Child abuse, neglect, and maltreatment are not new phenomena. Nonetheless, they create major problems for the children who are abused and for society as a whole. Using the chart below, describe the different types of abuse/neglect/maltreatment (e.g., physical abuse, sexual abuse, etc.), the possible effects that are likely to result from each (note there may be a great deal of overlap), and the types of intervention that might help alleviate these problems (feel free to add more spaces). Then design a program for junior high school students, senior high school students, and parents to educate them about the problems of child abuse; develop a model of intervention to benefit the maltreated children and their families; and develop a list of resources available to children and families to help them deal with and reduce the incidence of abuse, neglect, and/or maltreatment.

Type of Behavior	Possible Effects	Possible Interventions

Research Project 2: Parental Leave and Child Care

In a group with other students in your class, prepare a chart that compares parental leave policies around the world, different types of child-care facilities, and what the research indicates are the effects that parental leave and various forms of child care have on the developing child. After comparing and contrasting each of these variables, write a paper that presents a policy statement concerning what you believe would be the best possible situation in the United States to ensure optimal development of our next generation. You may wish to go a step further and write a letter based on your findings to your elected officials in Washington and in your own home state. You would then want to report back to the class whether you received any response to your letter, what that response was, and how it relates to the information in this chapter.

Chapter 8 Physical and Cognitive Development in Early Childhood

Learning Objectives

1. Understand the changes in height and weight during the preschool years, and note factors associated with individual differences in height and weight.

2. Define myelination, and discuss its contribution to brain development.

3. Explain how gross motor skills and fine motor skills change during the preschool years.

4. Define basal metabolism rate (BMR), and explain why early exposure to fast foods worries developmentalists.

5. Discuss the state of illness and health in the world's children, including the leading cause of childhood death in the world, treatment, and prevention.

6. Define Piaget's preoperational stage and be able to give examples of behaviors that differentiate children in the symbolic functioning and intuitive thought substages.

7. Indicate what changes occur in attention, memory, and task analyses in early childhood.

8. Explain the development of theories about the mind, including the existence of a mind, its connection to the external world, inferences about mental states, separateness from the world, mental representation, and interpretation.

9. Identify observations that indicate children understand rules of morphology, syntax, semantics, and pragmatics.

10. Explain Vygotsky's theory of development, including zone of proximal development, scaffolding, language and thought, culture and society, and the educational applications of Vygotsky's theory.

11. Compare and contrast child-centered kindergarten, the Montessori approach, and the Reggio Emilia approach to early childhood education.

Explain myelination and how it is important to development.

What are the two substages of the preoperational stage? What happens in each?

Contrast the development of gross motor skills and fine motor skills for the preschool child.

Define the term "egocentrism" and explain how Piaget tested it.

Explain the development of handedness and its effects on an individual's abilities.

What is animism? Give some examples.

Define basal metabolism rate (BMR) and its relevance to children's development

Define centration and explain its limitations

What is the leading cause of childhood death around the world? How would "ORT" reverse this?

What is conservation? What are some different types of conservation?

In terms of Piaget's theory of cognitive development, explain what "operations" are.

What is short-term memory? What are its limitations in early childhood?

Symbolic function substage: 1st substage; roughly between ages 2-4; child is able to mentally represent an object that is not present
Intuitive thought substage: 2nd substage; approximately 4-7; children begin to use primitive reason & want answers to all sorts of questions; they seem sure about their knowledge but don't know how they know what they know

Myelination: a process in which nerve cells are covered & insulated with a layer of fat cells; increases speed of information traveling through the nervous system

Egocentrism: the inability to distinguish between one's own perspective & someone else's perspective
(a salient feature of preoperational thought)
The three-mountain task was used by Piaget & Inhelder to test children's egocentrism.

Gross motor skills: by 3 they hop, jump, & run; by 4, they become more adventurous & demonstrate athletic prowess & improve ability to climb up (& now down) stairs; by 5 they are even more adventurous & more active
Fine motor skills: grasping abilities & precision improve; by 5 hand, arm, body move together under better eye command

Animism: the belief that inanimate objects have "lifelike" qualities & are capable of action (e.g., the moon is following me; the tree pushed the leaf off & made it fall; I'm mad at the sidewalk because it made me fall down)

Handedness: (whether left or right is dominant) begins in infancy; while many preschoolers use both hands, by 2 years 10% are left handed
Left handers can do exceptionally well in tasks requiring imagination (e.g., art); they also do well as athletes and intellectually

Centration: focusing or centering of attention on one characteristic to the exclusion of all others; most clearly evidenced by the preoperational child's inability to conserve--a tall glass may be believed to have more water in it than a short wide glass, because the child pays attention only to the one dimension of height rather than both dimensions of height & width

Basal metabolism rate (BMR): the minimum amount of energy a person uses in a resting state;
individual variations in BMR among children may be an explanation for individual differences in children's energy levels

Conservation: a belief in the permanence of certain attributes of objects or situations in spite of superficial changes
Some dimensions of conservation: number, matter, length, volume, & area

The **leading cause** of childhood death around the world is dehydration & malnutrition as a result of diarrhea.
Oral rehydration therapy (ORT): a treatment involving a range of techniques designed to prevent dehydration during episodes of diarrhea by giving the child fluids by mouth

Short-term memory (STM): the memory system in which individuals retain information for up to 15 to 30 seconds if there is no rehearsal; 2-3 year olds typically can hold about 2 digits in STM; by 7, they can hold about 5; between 7 & 13 it increases by approximately 1-1/2 digits

Operations: internalized sets of actions that allow the child to do mentally what was done physically before

What are the components of knowledge that Flavell, Miller, & Miller (1993) noted are part of the child's developing notion of mind?

What are developmentally appropriate practices in early childhood education?

What changes in linguistic rule systems occur in early childhood?

Discuss developmentally inappropriate practices in early childhood education.

What is Vygotsky's zone of proximal development (ZPD)? What is scaffolding?

What is Project Head Start?

Explain the concept of the child-centered kindergarten.

Explain Project Follow Through.

What is the Montessori approach to education?

What activities have been suggested by the ABC Task Force to promote nonsexist early childhood education?

Describe the Reggio Emilia approach to early childhood education.

What are the characteristics of early-intervention programs that work to enhance the welfare of young children?

Developmentally appropriate practice: based on knowledge of the typical development of children within an age span (age appropriateness) as well as the uniqueness of the child (individual appropriateness)	According to Flavell, Miller, & Miller (1993), children's developing notion of the mind includes knowledge that the mind: exists, has connections to the physical world; can represent objects & events accurately or inaccurately; and actively mediates the interpretation of reality & emotions that are experienced
Developmentally inappropriate practice: ignores the concrete, hands-on approach to learning; direct teaching largely through abstract, paper-and-pencil activities presented to large groups of young children	In early childhood, children begin using plurals & possessive forms of nouns (e.g., dogs & dog's); put appropriate endings on verbs (e.g., add "ed" for past tense & "ing" for present progressive); use prepositions (e.g., "in"); articles (e.g., "the"); and forms of the verb "to be" (e.g., I was going to the store); this is evidenced in their overgeneralization (e.g., "foots" instead of "feet")
Project Head Start: a compensatory education program designed to provide children from low-income families the opportunity to acquire the skills & experiences important for success in school	***Zone of proximal development (ZPD)***: the tasks too difficult for children to master alone but that can be learned with the guidance & assistance of adults or more-skilled children ***Scaffolding***: changing support over the course of teaching session--adjust guidance to fit student's current performance level
Project Follow Through: different types of educational programs that were devised to determine which Project Head Start programs were most effective--the enriched programs were carried through the first few years of elementary school (implemented in 1967 as an adjunct to Project Head Start)	***Child-centered kindergarten***: education involves the whole child and includes concern for the child's physical, cognitive, and social development; instruction is organized around the child's needs, interests, and learning styles; the ***process*** of learning, rather than ***what*** is learned, is emphasized
ABC Task Force suggests: read books about girls & boys that contradict gender stereotypes; have children cut out pictures of males/females showing diversity; create visual displays of men & women doing same task; nonsexist role modeling; have parents with non-traditional jobs talk to students; use non-stereotyped dolls to tell stories/discuss conflict re atypical behavior	***Montessori approach***: a philosophy of education in which children are allowed considerable freedom & spontaneity in choosing activities; they are allowed to move from one activity to another as they desire; the teacher acts as a facilitator rather than a director of learning (patterned after educational philosophy of Maria Montessori, Italian physician/educator)
Characteristics of successful early intervention programs: comprehensive & intensive; staff have the time, training, & skills to build relationships of trust & respect with children & families; deal with children as part of family & family as part of community; cross long-standing professional & bureaucratic boundaries	***Reggio Emilia Approach***: an approach to early childhood education that views young children as competent, encourages them to learn by investigating & exploring topics that interest them, & uses a wide range of stimulating media & materials (developed in the northern Italian city of Reggio Emilia)

Self-Test A: Multiple Choice

1. Two important factors stated in the text that produce individual differences in height are:
   a. ethnic origin and nutrition.
   b. genetic predisposition and early behavior.
   c. standard of living and cost of living.
   d. central nervous system functioning and reduction of fat intake.

2. Which **is not** a condition the text states can produce unusually short children?
   a. physical problems
   b. congenital factors
   c. emotional difficulties
   d. ethnic origin

3. The Nortons love their son, but are concerned about his lack of height and his slow rate of growth. A medical examination would likely reveal a malfunction of the:
   a. pineal gland.
   b. adrenal gland.
   c. pituitary gland.
   d. medulla.

4. Myelination improves the efficiency of the central nervous system the way that:
   a. talking to an infant speeds his ability to produce a first word.
   b. reducing the distance between two children playing catch reduces the time it takes for a baseball to travel from one child to the other.
   c. the ingestion of certain chemicals (e.g., steroids) can improve overall muscle development.
   d. the insulation around an electrical extension cord improves its efficiency.

5. Which of the following would be considered a fine motor skill?
   a. bouncing a ball
   b. walking a straight line
   c. sorting blocks
   d. writing your name

6. Left-handedness is associated with:
   a. early maturation of motor skills.
   b. imagination and creativity.
   c. cognitive and perceptual deficits.
   d. delinquent tendencies.

7. What a child eats during the early childhood period affects all but which of the following?
   a. skeletal growth
   b. body shape
   c. susceptibility to disease
   d. basal metabolism rate

8. Your child is overweight. What is the best recommendation to help him slim down?
   a. Give him snacks only when he has been good.
   b. Put him on a diet that will help him lose weight.
   c. Encourage him to get more exercise.
   d. Punish him when you find him eating snacks.

9. The most likely cause of death in the world among children younger than five years is:
   a. birth defects.
   b. polio.
   c. diarrhea.
   d. German measles.

10. Which of the following countries has the lowest child mortality rate?
    a. the United States
    b. Sweden
    c. Afghanistan
    d. Japan

11. Wendy was listening as her mother told a friend how to get to their house. Mrs. Jones said, "Come south on Main, then turn left on Ash, then right on Cedar, and we are the second house on the right." Wendy said, "No, you turn right on Ash." She said this because from where she sat, Ash was to her right. Assuming Mrs. Jones is correct, Wendy would be demonstrating:
    a. animism.
    b. egocentrism.
    c. centration.
    d. conservation.

12. The typical "human tadpole" that preschoolers draw to represent a person probably best reflects:
    a. limited knowledge of the human body.
    b. a confusion between fantasy and reality.
    c. a symbolic representation of a human.
    d. limited perceptual motor skills.

13. Asked to sort a collection of plastic toy animals that is a mixture of black and white birds and mammals, a young child is likely to:
    a. make smaller piles of randomly chosen animals.
    b. sort them according to just one of the features.
    c. separate the mammals from the birds because they are animistic.
    d. separate the toys into the four categories of black animals, black birds, white animals, and white birds.

14. Rochel Gelman suggests that children fail conservation tasks because they:
    a. cannot think about more than one aspect of a task.
    b. do not notice important features of the tasks.
    c. cannot mentally reverse the sequence of actions in the tasks.
    d. do not understand why researchers are testing them.

15. Which of the following questions is typical of the preoperational child?
    a. "How many different piles of toys can I make from my toys?"
    b. "How much is two plus two?"
    c. "Where does the moon go when it's light out?"
    d. "Do you see the same thing I do, Daddy?"

16. Compared to that of a toddler, a preschooler's ability to pay attention enables her to:
    a. ignore unimportant but distracting details of a task.
    b. habituate more quickly to repeated stimulation.
    c. concentrate on an activity for longer periods of time.
    d. pay attention to several things simultaneously.

17. Andrew, a preschooler, was shown red and green triangles and squares and was asked to put the ones that are the same color together. What is he most likely to do?
    a. put the same-colored objects together because color is salient
    b. put the same-colored objects together because color is relevant
    c. put the same-shaped objects together because shape is relevant
    d. put the objects he likes the best together

18. According to information-processing theorists, which of the following *is not* one of the developmental steps in children's thoughts about the human mind?
    a. realizing minds exist
    b. realizing that people make cognitive connections with events and objects
    c. realizing that there is a true reality that will come to be understood
    d. understanding that the mind can represent objects and events both correctly and incorrectly

19. Lev Vygotsky said some tasks are too difficult for children to handle alone, but can be done with the help of someone more skilled. Such tasks:
    a. fall into the zone of proximal development.
    b. are difficult because they are not salient to the child.
    c. are best taught by having the child observe a skilled teacher.
    d. will be frustrating for the child and should be left to a time when the child can more easily accomplish them.

20. The zone of proximal development (ZPD) is a measure of:
    a. intelligence.
    b. potential.
    c. skill.
    d. achievement.

21. Evidence that children understand the rules of their language includes all but which of the following?
    a. observations of overgeneralizations
    b. application of rules to nonsense words
    c. correct word order placement
    d. identifying the names of objects they have never previously seen

22. Overgeneralizations of language rules indicate:
    a. a failure to apply language rules.
    b. children's guesses about language rules.
    c. the use of language rules.
    d. the imitation of language rules.

23. After racing down the street with his uncle, Peter says, "I runned very, very fast!" The use of the term "runned" exemplifies:
    a. phonological development.
    b. morphological development.
    c. syntactic development.
    d. semantic development.

24. Which of the following reflects Lev Vygotsky's beliefs about language and thought?
    a. Children who engage in high levels of private speech are usually socially incompetent.
    b. Children use internal speech earlier than they use external speech.
    c. All mental functions have external or social origins.
    d. Language and thought initially develop together and then become independent.

25. Vygotsky believed that cognitive development was most influenced by which of the following factors?
    a. biological
    b. social
    c. personality
    d. emotional

26. According to Vygostky, an institutional component that influences cognitive development is:
    a. a child's interactions with a teacher.
    b. the everyday experiences that children have with peers.
    c. the traditions of a child's ethnic group.
    d. the use of computers to teach math concepts.

27. According to David Elkind, preschool:
    a. is a critical element of the young child's socialization.
    b. is not necessary if home schooling approximates the experiences available at a competent preschool.
    c. education should not begin until the child is socially mature.
    d. can produce excessive stress and anxiety.

28. An instructor who uses developmentally inappropriate methods for teaching the alphabet would:
    a. have the children recite the alphabet three times a day every day.
    b. use music to teach the alphabet.
    c. use animal names and shapes to teach the alphabet.
    d. use the sandbox to let children draw the letters.

29. Project Head Start was designed to:
    a. provide low-income children a chance to acquire skills that would help them succeed at school.
    b. assess the advantages and disadvantages of preschool educational programs.
    c. give parents an educational day-care center.
    d. determine the feasibility of starting formal education at an earlier age.

30. Which type of approach was related to good school attendance in Project Follow Through?
    a. an academic, direct-instruction approach
    b. a Montessori-type approach
    c. a Head Start approach
    d. an affective education approach

31. Schooling for young children in Japan is most like:
    a. a developmentally appropriate kindergarten.
    b. a program of concentrated academic instruction.
    c. the kind of program most Americans want.
    d. the typical American kindergarten.

32. Which **was not** a criterion for success of early-childhood intervention presented by Lisbeth Schorr?
    a. programs that cross professional and bureaucratic boundaries
    b. programs that focus on the family and community
    c. programs that employ "tough love" discipline
    d. programs that are intensive and comprehensive

Self-Test B: Matching

Match the individuals in the left column with the appropriate descriptors in the right column.

C 1.   Lisbeth Schorr   a.   early childhood education should be part of public education on its own terms
e 2.   Jean Berko   b.   academic pressures on young children can produce stress
f 3.   Irving Lazar   c.   identified four reasons why early intervention programs work
i 4.   Maria Montessori   d.   devised the concept of MLU to measure language maturity
d 5.   Roger Brown   e.   used fictional words to test children's understanding of language rules
h 6.   Lev Vygotsky   f.   did long-term investigations of early childhood education
a 7.   David Elkind   g.   uses information-processing perspective to analyze child's inability to conserve
g 8.   Rochel Gelman   h.   language and thought, initially independent, eventually merge
b 9.   Diane Burts   i.   revolutionized teaching by allowing children freedom and spontaneity

Self-Test C: Matching Developmentally Appropriate and Inappropriate Practices

Indicate whether the early childhood education practices described below are appropriate or inappropriate.

A 1.   Experiences are provided in physical, cognitive, social, and emotional developmental areas.
I 2.   Children are evaluated only against group norms.
I 3.   Children are expected to perform the same tasks and achieve the same skills as others in their group.
A 4.   Children select many of their own activities from among a variety the teacher prepares.
A 5.   Children are expected to be mentally and physically active.
A 6.   Teachers use modeling of expected behavior.
A 7.   Teachers redirect children's inappropriate behavior to more acceptable activities.
I 8.   Children spend most of their time working individually at desks and tables.
I 9.   Teachers spend a great deal of time providing directions to the class as a whole group.
I 10.   Teachers use highly structured, teacher-directed lessons during most of the class time.

Essay Questions:

1.   Your neighbor has just become aware that his son is left-handed. He's particularly concerned because he remembers that as a child he was left-handed and was forced by his teachers and parents to use his right hand, something he believes caused him emotional problems, but he has observed that people who are left handed have problems with even simple things, like using scissors. What would you advise him about his son?

2.   You have gotten stuck in the middle of an argument among your three best friends concerning cognitive development during early childhood. One of them thinks that Piaget had the best explanations of how children develop, the second believes that Gelman and information processing demonstrate many flaws with Piaget's thinking, while the third says that Vygotsky really has a much more plausible theory. Discuss all three of these theories and state which you think makes the most sense and why.

3.   Your cousin has told you that it is not an option for her to stay home to be a full-time mother, so she needs to put her child into a day-care setting. She considers you to be a wise person, especially since you are taking this class in Life-Span Development. What would you suggest to her in terms of finding the best type of day-care option for her child?

Key to Self-Test A:

1.	a	p.	200	17.	a	p.	209-210
2.	d	p.	200	18.	c	p.	210
3.	c	p.	200	19.	a	p.	213
4.	d	p.	200	20.	b	p.	213
5.	d	p.	201	21.	d	p.	213-214
6.	b	p.	201-202	22.	c	p.	212
7.	d	p.	202	23.	b	p.	212
8.	c	p.	202	24.	c	p.	213-214
9.	c	p.	203	25.	b	p.	214
10.	b	p.	203	26	d	p.	214
11.	b	p.	204	27.	b	p.	~~215~~ 217
12.	d	p.	204	28.	a	p.	216
13.	b	p.	206	29.	a	p.	220
14.	b	p.	207	30.	d	p.	221
15.	c	p.	207	31.	a	p.	219
16.	c	p.	209	32.	c	p.	~~223~~ 225

Key to Self-Test B:

1.	c	6.	h
2.	e	7.	a
3.	f	8.	g
4.	i	9.	b
5.	d		

Key to Self-Test C:

1. appropriate
2. inappropriate
3. inappropriate
4. appropriate
5. appropriate
6. appropriate
7. appropriate
8. inappropriate
9. inappropriate
10. inappropriate

Key to Essay Questions:

1. A proper answer would acknowledge that we do, indeed, live in a "right-handed" world, but would address the positive aspects of being left-handed, particularly in terms of athletics, intelligence, and creativity.

2. To answer this question you will need to explain the three cognitive approaches that describe development at this point in time, i.e., Piaget, information processing, and Vygotsky. This will involve a discussion of the various facets of the two substages (symbolic and intuitive) of the preoperational stage (e.g., animisim, egocentrism), how Piaget arrived at his ideas, and how they have been supported; then address the criticisms of Piaget's findings (e.g., problems with his research designs, the fact that

children demonstrate certain abilities earlier than he suggested) and information-processing research concerning attention, memory, and children's theory of mind; then contrast these theories with Vygotsky's, which states that development is embedded within the sociocultural context (be sure to discuss the zone of proximal development and scaffolding). After presenting these three theories, state which makes most sense to you (or whether all three are needed together), and explain the rationale for your choice.

3. There are many issues to address here, including: the educational applications of Vygotsky's theory (e.g., use scaffolding); the various types of early childhood education programs (e.g., child-centered kindergarten, the Montessori approach, Project Head Start for educationally disadvantaged children); the developmentally appropriate and inappropriate practices (e.g., providing experiences in all developmental areas rather than narrowly focusing on cognitive development); non-sexist education; and Schorr's ideas about successful early-intervention programs. Note, too, Elkind's position that young children do need early education, whether by parents who are willing and able to provide it, or by competent preschools.

Research Project 1: Designing a Developmentally Appropriate Preschool Curriculum

Considering everything you have learned in this chapter concerning developmentally appropriate and inappropriate practices, avoiding sexist education, and creating an atmosphere that will optimize children's learning abilities while minimizing stress, design a developmentally appropriate preschool curriculum. What will you specifically include? What will you specifically omit? Describe your "dream" preschool, explaining the kinds of personnel, activities, curriculum, and physical environment you would want, and why you think these would be important. Which theories would you consider to be most relevant when designing this curriculum? How are they important and how would they be incorporated into your design?

Research Project 2: Language Development

Roger Brown has identified five stages of language development. He indicates that the mean length of utterance (MLU) is a good measure of language maturity. Using the chart below, characterize Brown's five stages of language development in terms of MLUs, age ranges, characteristics, and typical sentences.

Stage	MLUs	Age Range	Characteristics	Typical Sentences
1				
2				
3				
4				
5				

Having completed the chart, sit in a public place where you can watch children of different ages without being obvious. Listen to their conversations and assess whether what you see in "real life" is consistent with the theory you've learned in this class. What have you found by making this comparison?

Research Project 3: Early Childhood Memory

This project will assist you in understanding memory changes for young children. First, get permission from the parents of three children of the same sex, ages 2-4, 6-8, and 11-13, being sure to ask the children themselves if they are willing to help you with this project. Using the number sets below, ask the children (separately) to listen as you read each number set. Tell them you will begin each set by saying "Start," and will end by saying, "Go," at which time they should write down the numbers of each set in the order they were read. Read the numbers clearly, with four seconds between each number in the set. Record their answers in the chart below, then answer the questions that follow. After you have finished, ask the children how they were able to remember the numbers that they did remember, and what they felt were the reasons they did not remember all of the numbers.

Number Set	Child 1: Age____/Sex___	Child 2: Age____/Sex___	Child 3: Age____/Sex___
2-6			
7-4-9			
8-1-7-2			
5-3-0-9-4			
6-1-8-3-9-2			
9-2-4-3-5-7-1			
4-3-7-9-5-1-2-8			
3-9-4-6-5-1-8-0-2			

1. According to the text, what would you expect to find in terms of each child's ability to remember these numbers? Were your findings consistent with these expectations?
2. What strategies (e.g., rehearsal), if any, did each child use to try to remember these numbers? Were these behaviors consistent with what you read in the text? If so, explain how; if not, explain how they were not consistent.
3. What reasons did the children give for their ability to remember or not remember? Were these reasons consistent with the literature on cognitive development? Explain how they were or were not consistent.
4. Based on your observations of these children, which theory do you think best explains cognitive development for these age groups?
5. What similarities did you notice among the children in the way they performed? What differences did you notice?

Chapter 9   Socioemotional Development in Early Childhood

Learning Objectives

1. Understand the four major parenting styles and how parenting styles are affected by developmental changes in the child as well as culture, social class, and ethnicity.

2. Compare and contrast parent-child and sibling interactions.

3. Summarize the research that has examined birth order effects and the criticism that birth order has been overdramatized and overemphasized.

4. Describe the effects of working mothers on young children.

5. Compare and contrast the family structure model and the multiple-factors model of divorce and understand the effects of divorce regarding age, developmental changes, conflict, sex of the child, custody arrangements, income, and economic stress.

6. Indicate the role that peers play in early development and be able to differentiate peer interaction and parent-child interaction.

7. Describe the functions of play and the types of play.

8. Describe the effects of television viewing on development, including both positive and negative behavior.

9. Discuss young children's self-understanding.

10. Describe the biological, social, and cognitive factors that influence gender development.

11. Understand Piaget's theory of moral development.

Describe Baumrind's two styles of parenting that involve placing limits on children. What type of child behavior is typically associated with each?

What is play? What functions does play serve?

Describe Baumrind's two styles of permissive parenting. What type of child behavior is typically associated with each?

Describe the benefits of play therapy for a child.

How does the family structure model explain the effects of divorce on children?

Describe Parten's six categories of children's play.

How does the multiple-factor model of divorce explain the effects of divorce on children?

Compare sensorimotor play with practice play.

How has parental depression been noted to affect children?

Describe pretense/symbolic play. When does it typically occur & what is its primary function?

Explain the term "peer." What functions do peer groups serve?

Define social play & games. How is social play related to games?

Play: pleasurable activity engaged in for its own sake; it is essential to child's health
Functions include: increasing affiliation with peers, releasing tension, advancing cognitive development, increasing exploration, & providing a safe place to engage in potentially dangerous behavior

Authoritarian: restrictive, punitive; child is taught to follow directions, respect work & effort; firm limits & controls on child, little verbal exchange; associated with social incompetence

Authoritative: limits & controls but encourages independence; warm & nurturant, much verbal give & take; associated with social competence

Play therapy: allows the child to work off frustration; helps the therapist analyze the child's conflicts & ways to cope with them; children may feel less threatened and be more likely to express their true feelings in the context of play

Neglectful: the parent is uninvolved in the child's life; associated with children's social incompetence, especially lack of self-control

Indulgent: parents are highly involved with children but place few demands or controls on them; associated with social incompetence, especially lack of self-control

Parten's classifications of play: unoccupied (not engaging in play); solitary (plays alone & independently); onlooker (watches other children play); parallel (plays separately from but with toys or in similar manner of others); associative (social interaction with little or no organization); cooperative (groups social interaction with sense of group identity & organized activity)

Family structure model: differences in children from different family structures are due to family structure variations, such as the father's being absent in one set of the families

Sensorimotor play: behavior engaged in by infants to derive pleasure from exercising their existing sensorimotor schemas
Practice play: involves repetition of behavior when new skills are being learned, or physical or mental mastery & coordination of skills are required for games or sports; practice play can be engaged in throughout life

Multiple-factor model of divorce: takes account of the complexity of the divorce context; examines many influences on child's development: family structure, strengths & weaknesses of child before divorce, nature of events surrounding the divorce, custody arrangements, visitation patterns, socioeconomic status, & post-divorce family functioning

Pretense/symbolic play: occurs when the child transforms the physical environment into a symbol (make-believe, pretend play)
Between 9 & 30 months
Vygotsky: pretending helps develop children's imagination

Depression in parents is associated with children's problems of adjustment & disorders, especially depression in children.

Social play: involves social interaction with peers
Games: activities engaged in for pleasure; include rules & often competition with one or more individuals
Social games involve social play since they involve interacting with others.

Peers: children of about the same age or maturity level
Peer groups provide a source of information & comparison about the world outside the family; important for normal socioemotional development

Describe constructive play.

Explain the
cognitive developmental theory of
gender.

Explain the concept of
self-understanding.

Define the terms "schema" and
"gender schema."
What does gender schema theory
say about gender development?

Differentiate among:
gender, gender identity, and
gender roles.

What is moral development?

What are the main classes of
male and female hormones?

Describe Piaget's two stages of
moral development.

Explain Freud's identification theory
of gender development.

Explain the notion of
immanent justice.

How does social learning theory
explain gender development?

What is empathy and
how does it relate to
moral development?

Cognitive developmental theory: children's gender typing occurs after they have developed a concept of gender; once they consistently conceive of themselves as male or female, children often organize their world on the basis of gender

Constructive play: combines sensorimotor/practice of repetitive activity with symbolic representation of ideas; occurs when children engage in self-regulated creation or construction of a product or a problem solution

Schema: cognitive structure/network of associations that organize/guide perceptions
Gender schema: organizes the world in terms of male/female
Gender schema theory: individual's attention & behavior guided by internal motivation to conform to gender-based sociocultural standards & stereotypes

Self-understanding: the child's cognitive representation of self, the substance and content of the child's self-conceptions
Begins with self-recognition (around age 18 months)

Moral development: concerns rules & conventions about what people should do in their interactions with other people

Gender: the social dimension of being male or female
Gender identity: the sense of being male or female (usually acquired by age 3 years)
Gender role: a set of expectations that prescribe how females & males should think, act, & feel

Heteronomous: Piaget's 1st stage of moral development, from approximately age 4 to 7; justice & rules seen as unchangeable properties of the world, removed from personal control
Autonomous: 2nd stage, from about age 10 and older; child becomes aware that rules & laws are created by people; in judging actions consider the actor's intentions & the consequences

Androgen: the main class of male sex hormones
Estrogen: the main class of female sex hormones
Differentiation of sex organs begins after first few weeks of gestation when XY chromosomes in the male embryo trigger secretion of androgen

Immanent justice: in heteronomous thinking, the concept that if a rule is broken, punishment will be meted out immediately

Identification theory: Freudian theory that preschool children develop a sexual attraction to opposite-sex parent; by approximately age 5 or 6 the child renounces this attraction because of anxious feelings; subsequently the child identifies with the same-sex parent, unconsciously adopting same-sex parent's characteristics

Empathy: reacting to another's feelings with an emotional response similar to the other's feelings; has emotional & cognitive aspects; positive feelings (e.g., empathy, sympathy, self-esteem, & admiration) and negative feelings (anger, outrage, shame, guilt) contribute to a child's moral development & influence children to act according to standards of right & wrong

Social learning theory of gender: emphasizes that children's gender development occurs through observation & imitation of gender behavior, & through rewards & punishments children experience for gender appropriate and inappropriate behavior

Self-Test A: Multiple Choice

1. What "basic truth" have investigators found about effective parenting around the world?
   a. Children's socioemotional development is best promoted by love and at least some moderate parental control.
   b. Children's behavioral and cognitive development is best promoted when parents exert control, especially in early childhood and adolescence.
   c. Children's intellectual competence is best enhanced when parents provide little control but at least moderate love.
   d. There is no universal "basic truth."

2. All of the following characterizes children of authoritarian parents **except** they:
   a. fail to initiate activity.
   b. have poor communication skills.
   c. are anxious about social comparison.
   d. lack self-control.

3. Parenting style and disciplinary action change in which of the following ways as children approach their elementary school years?
   a. Physical punishment increases.
   b. Reasoning with the child increases.
   c. Physical affection increases.
   d. Withholding special privileges decreases.

4. Competent parents should _____ children's developmental changes.
   a. moderate
   b. adapt to
   c. manipulate
   d. ignore

5. It is more common for working-class families than middle-class families to use:
   a. verbal praise.
   b. criticism.
   c. reasoning.
   d. asking questions.

6. Siblings can be a _____ socializing influence than parents.
   a. weaker
   b. stressful
   c. stronger
   d. better

7. Compared with White American families, ethnic minority families:
   a. have more problems with their children.
   b. differ in their reliance on kinship networks.
   c. have fewer children surviving into adulthood.
   d. have stronger family values, which leads to fewer single-parent families.

8. Parents are likely to treat their firstborns differently than their later-born children in that they:
   a. have higher expectations for later-born children.
   b. put more pressure on the firstborn to succeed.
   c. interfere less with the firstborn's activities.
   d. give the firstborn more attention than later-born children.

9. Compared to later-born children, firstborn children's relationships with their siblings tend to be:
   a. more positive.
   b. more negative.
   c. more positive and more negative.
   d. about the same.

   pg 234

10. Compared to historical times, children today are growing up in _____ family structures.
    a. about the same kinds of
    b. entirely different
    c. a smaller variety of
    d. a greater variety of

11. Which of the following **is not** a good defense of the assertion that having a working mother is good for the child?
    a. The extra income will improve the standard of living for the child.
    b. Rigid sex-stereotyping is perpetrated by the division of labor in the traditional family.
    c. The mother will present a broader range of emotions and skills.
    d. The additional source of identity and self-esteem will make it easier for the mother to loosen her hold on the growing child.

12. Which of the following is true about the effects of the age of children on the ability to adjust to the divorce of parents?
   a. Younger children remember the conflicts surrounding the divorce longer than older children.
   b. Older children blame themselves more than younger children.
   c. Younger and older children express a desire to have grown up in an intact family.
   d. Older children fear abandonment more than younger children.

13. Sarah and Tina's parents have recently divorced. Sarah now lives with their father, and Tina now lives with their mother. Based on the research in this area, which of the following might we expect?
   a. Sarah will adjust better than Tina.
   b. Tina will adjust better than Sarah.
   c. Both girls will adjust well in time.
   d. Neither girl will adjust well since they've been separated from each other.

14. With respect to conflict in divorce:
   a. children in divorced families that are high in conflict function better than children in intact, never-divorced families that are high in conflict.
   b. the escape from conflict divorce provides is seen immediately for the children.
   c. while the escape from conflict that divorce provides may benefit the children, for the first year after the divorce the conflict increases.
   d. once the parents have separated, the children begin to benefit because the custodial parent now has the energy to devote to the children, not the conflict.

15. You are going through a divorce and must talk to your children about it. Which of the following is a good recommendation?
   a. Do not explain the separation because no matter what you say, the children are likely to believe it's somehow their fault.
   b. Explain that it may take time to feel better.
   c. Help them understand the divorce by being honest about your ex-spouse's shortcomings as well as your own.
   d. Make a "clean break" by starting fresh and getting rid of as many reminders of the marriage as possible.

16. Research on the children of depressed parents suggests that these children:
   a. learn to become more nurturing than others.
   b. are generally not greatly affected by their parents' depression.
   c. are more likely to become schizophrenic than depressed.
   d. are at greater risk for problems of adjustment and psychological disorders.

17. The main function of the peer group is to:
   a. foster love and understanding.
   b. act as a surrogate for the parents.
   c. teach the importance of friendship.
   d. teach about the world outside the family.

18. Experimental studies of monkeys and case studies of humans support all of the following conclusions *except*:
   a. peer relationships are not necessary for normal social development in children.
   b. peer relationships contribute to the normal social development of children.
   c. attachment to peers produces different effects than does attachment to adults.
   d. isolation from peers can produce social maladjustment.

19. Play therapy is based on the notion that:
   a. play relaxes children and acts as a calming influence.
   b. if the child feels less threatened, true feelings will be displayed.
   c. the child will model adaptive behavior during play.
   d. the increase in cognitive functioning during play allows the child to understand whatever problem is being experienced.

20. Parten's play categories are examples of increasingly complex and interactive:
   a. pretense/symbolic play.
   b. social play.
   c. instructional play.
   d. academic play.

21. Practice play differs from sensorimotor play in that practice play:
   a. is common in the infancy stage of development.
   b. involves coordination of skills.
   c. revolves around the use of symbols.
   d. is done for its own sake.

22. One conclusion that is evident about watching television is that:
    a. children should not be allowed to watch television unless supervised by an adult.
    b. there is no relationship between watching violence on television and aggressive behavior.
    c. children who watch violence on television get it out of their systems and are actually less likely to fight.
    d. children who view violence on television are more likely to engage in aggressive behavior.

23. Aimee Leifer (1973) found television viewing to be associated with young children's:
    a. hostile behavior.
    b. prosocial behavior. *Pg. 246*
    c. capacity to use their imaginations.
    d. cognitive functioning.

24. Oscar's parents openly value Oscar's participation in family conversations. Although he frequently misunderstands the topic, they answer his questions, help him to join in, or simply enjoy Oscar's sometimes fantastic ideas. According to Erik Erikson, these parents are encouraging:
    a. initiative.
    b. conscience.
    c. identification.
    d. self-concept.

25. Preschoolers most often describe themselves in terms of their:
    a. thoughts.
    b. physical characteristics.
    c. emotions.
    d. relationships to other people.

26. Gender identity refers to the:
    a. biological dimension of being male or female.
    b. social dimension of being male or female.
    c. sense of being male or female.
    d. set of expectations that prescribe how males or females should think, act, or feel.

27. Female sex hormones are called _____; male sex hormones are called _____.
    a. estrogen; androgen
    b. testosterone; estrogen
    c. androgen; testosterone
    d. androgen; estrogen

28. The Freudian belief that anatomy is destiny has been criticized because it:
    a. overlooks social and cognitive factors that influence gender role.
    b. gives instinct a place in the development of gender role.
    c. ignores the connection between hormones and behavior.
    d. transcends biological heritage.

29. Which of the following statements is most accurate about identification theory and social learning theory with respect to gender-role development? *Pg. 248*
    a. Both assume that children adopt the characteristics of their parents.
    b. Both assume that rewards directly shape gender-role development.
    c. Both assume that children actively acquire gender roles.
    d. Identification theory rejects the idea that anatomy is destiny, while social learning theory accepts it.

30. In which way do the media continue to discriminate between men and women?
    a. Women do not occupy high-status roles in television shows.
    b. Women appear only as housewives or lovers.
    c. Women are less competent than men in the roles they play.
    d. Women are cast primarily as sex objects.

31. A major distinction between autonomous morality and heteronomous morality is that autonomous moral thinkers focus on the:
    a. consequences of behavior.
    b. intentions of someone who breaks a rule.
    c. way a specific behavior makes them feel.
    d. rewards moral behavior will bring.

32. Which of the following **is not** a suggestion made in the text for improving young children's socioemotional development?
    a. Be an authoritarian parent.
    b. Adapt to the child's developmental changes.
    c. Provide the child with many opportunities for play.
    d. Monitor the child's TV viewing.

33. According to social learning theorists, the ability to resist temptation is closely tied to the development of:
    a. empathic behavior.
    b. spontaneity.
    c. abstract reasoning.
    (d.) self-control.

34. Which cognitive ability is essential to the capacity for empathy?
    a. conservation
    b. logical reasoning
    c. decentration
    (d.) perspective-taking

35. Which of the following **is not** a recommendation by Ellen Galinsky and Judy David for working parents who encounter work/family interference?
    a. Select one problem at a time rather than tackling everything at once.
    b. Understand expectations and determine if they are realistic.
    (c.) Avoid the temptation to escape from the routines of everyday life.
    d. Form a variety of interpersonal support networks.

Self-Test B: Matching

Match the individuals in the left column with the appropriate descriptors in the right column.

i	1. Lawrence Kohlberg	a.	pretend play allows children to try out different roles
f	2. Anna Freud	b.	play satisfies an exploratory drive in each of us
g	3. Hugh Hartstone/Mark May	c.	parenting style is related to child's socioemotional development
b	4. Daniel Berlyne	d.	offered solutions to parents with conflicts between work and family
d	5. Ellen Galinsky/Judy David	e.	analyzed & categorized children's play
e	6. Mildred Parten	f.	psychiatrist who showed peers are important for social development
a	7. Catherine Garvey	g.	determined that moral development depends on the situation
j	8. E. Mavis Hetherington	h.	stated that maternal employment is a part of modern life
h	9. Lois Hoffman	i.	gender constancy develops about 6-7 in concert with conservation
c	10. Diana Baumrind	j.	saw negative effects on boys living with mothers who didn't remarry

Self-Test C: Matching Types of Play

Match the types of play in the left column with their descriptions in the right column.

h	1. unoccupied	a.	child watches other children play
f	2. solitary	b.	organized social interaction in a group with a sense of group identity
a	3. onlooker	c.	child derives pleasure from exercising existing sensorimotor schemas
g	4. parallel	d.	repetition of behaviors as new skills are learned, coordination develops
j	5. associative	e.	child transforms physical environment into a symbol
b	6. cooperative	f.	child plays independently of others
c	7. sensorimotor	g.	child plays separately but with similar toys/activities as others
d	8. practice	h.	child stands in one spot, looks around, or performs random movements
e	9. pretense/symbolic	i.	child engages in self-regulated creation/construction of product/solution
i	10. constructive	j.	children engage in social interaction with little or no organization

Self-Test D: Matching Parenting Styles with Child Outcomes

Match the parenting styles in the left column with the descriptions and predicted child outcomes in the right column.

d 1.   authoritarian   a.   highly involved/few demands; social incompetence, lack of self-control
c 2.   authoritative   b.   uninvolved in the child's life; social incompetence, lack of self-control
b 3.   neglectful   c.   limits/controls, warm/nurturant, verbal give & take; social competence
a 4.   indulgent   d.   restrictive/punitive; child follows directions but develops social incompetence

Essay Questions:

1.   Being almost half-way through your Life-Span Development course, you are seriously considering opening a child-care center after you complete your education and get the appropriate degrees and certification. Your center will accept children who have been potty-trained, including toddlers, preschoolers, and children in the primary grades (for after-school care). You anticipate opening in an area that is ethnically, culturally, and/or racially diverse, and expect that the parents of these children will come from diverse educational and socioeconomic backgrounds as well. You want to incorporate the parents as partners in providing an optimal developmental context for the children. Based on the information in this chapter: (a) What kinds of facilities/activities would you need to provide for the children? and (b) What kinds of training might you provide to the parents?

2.   Your best friend's child has just celebrated her fourth birthday and now your friend is thinking about preparing her daughter for the school years ahead. Although she hates to part with her daughter, she nonetheless thinks it's in the girl's best interests to begin attending a preschool. Based on what you have learned in this life-span development class, what advice would you give your friend about how to select a good preschool

Key to Self-Test A:

1.	a	p.	227	19.	b	p.	238
2.	d	p.	228	20.	b	p.	239
3.	b	p.	229-230	21.	b	p.	240
4.	b	p.	229-230	22.	d	p.	242-243
5.	b	p.	230	23.	b	p.	244
6.	c	p.	231-232	24.	a	p.	245
7.	b	p.	230-231	25.	b	p.	245
8.	b	p.	234	26.	c	p.	246
9.	c	p.	232	27.	a	p.	246
10.	d	p.	235	28.	a	p.	246
11.	a	p.	233-234 235	29.	a	p.	246-247
12.	c	p.	235	30.	c	p.	249
13.	b	p.	235	31.	b	p.	250
14.	a	p.	235	32.	a	p.	251
15.	b	p.	235-236	33.	d	p.	252
16.	d	p.	236-237	34.	d	p.	253
17.	d	p.	237	35.	c	p.	255
18.	a	p.	237				

Key to Self-Test B:

1. i
2. f
3. g
4. b
5. d

6. e
7. a
8. j
9. h
10. c

Key to Self-Test C:

1. h
2. f
3. a
4. g
5. j

6. b
7. c
8. d
9. e
10. i

Key to Self-Test D:

1. d
2. c
3. b
4. a

Key to Essay Questions:

1. In answering this question you would want to look at the types of facilities that would encourage age-appropriate play, so you would need to discuss the purpose of play and the different categories of play that children engage in as they develop, being sensitive to what are and what are not age-appropriate social interactions with peers and adults. You would also want to consider the issue of television, and how its use can be both useful and harmful; and look at the types of caregiver-to-child activities that would be appropriate for these children, listing the strategies for enriching quality of children's play outlined in the text (e.g., allowing uninterrupted time for sociodramatic and constructive play; providing adequate space to play effectively); be sensitive to gender differences (e.g., boys get more attention than girls while girls' learning deficits are not identified as often as boys'); and incorporate activities that will assist the children in developing empathy. With respect to parents, it would be helpful to teach them about Baumrind's parenting styles and the effect each style has on children, and provide them with guidelines for improving their children's socioemotional development (authoritative parenting, adapting to the child's developmental changes); provide information concerning the effects of divorce on children and how to minimize the negative effects; and discuss with them the research concerning the most effective ways to use television (as well as its problems).

2. First, you might want to put your friend's mind at ease about placing her child in preschool, since many mothers feel guilty about this. Further, as noted by Lois Hoffman, working mothers are more realistic models for the socialization of today's child than are full-time mothers, especially in the case of daughters. In the United States, it is often necessary for both parents to work, so the question isn't whether the mother should stay home to care for her children, but rather, how to find the best placement possible. Consider the cognitive and socioemotional needs of the young child (e.g., development of peer relationships), and discuss how placement in preschool could facilitate the child's growth (e.g., through play, peer interactions, development of empathy, etc.).

Research Project 1: Sibling Birth Order

The text provides interesting findings concerning the effects of birth order on later development, but notes that these effects may be "overdramatized and overemphasized." Using the chart below as a starting point, track as many of your friends and relatives as you practically can, indicating each person's birth order (e.g., only child, second of four, etc.), sex, their personal characteristics (per those indicated in the text or otherwise), their job title/position, and other information that you believe is relevant. Then answer the questions that follow.

Person	Birth Order	Sex	Characteristics	Job Title/ Position	Other

1. Looking at your data overall, understanding that there will be individual differences, were your observations consistent with what you might expect from the research described? Explain your response.

2. What patterns did you notice when comparing persons of similar birth order in terms of the material discussed in this chapter?

3. What differences did you notice when comparing persons of similar birth order in terms of the material discussed in this chapter?

4. What differences did you notice when comparing persons of different birth order in terms of the material discussed in this chapter?

5. What might you conclude about the effects of birth order based on your observations?

Research Project 2: Developing   Parental   Guidelines   for Children's Television Viewing

Apply the Life-Span Developmental concepts in this chapter to devise guidelines that would assist parents in using television as a positive influence on their children's lives. Consider the different roles that television plays, the types of influence that it has on children, the characteristics of children that are attracted to specific types of programs, how the amount of television watching may affect children, and how parents can most effectively use television as a positive factor for their children's socioemotional development. Suggest possible guidelines and how parents might interact with their children to discuss what they view on television.

Research Project 3: Observing Gender Differences

As pointed out in the text, and as has been publicized on various television "news magazine" programs, boys and girls are treated differently, even by the best of teachers (who are typically unaware of this differential treatment). Select two or three different locations for observation (your own Life-Span Development class, a child-care center, public or private school classroom, park, etc.) and observe how adults interact with boys and girls (or, in a college classroom, men and women).

1. Describe these interactions. Are adults more active with boys than with girls? Are they more nurturant with girls than with boys? Do they pay more attention to the boys than to the girls? How much time is spent talking with females who respond to questions in class versus time spent with males? What types of responses are given to males compared with the types of responses given to females (is one or the other given more nods, more "yes, that's right," "good point," smiles, etc.)? What other differences do you notice?

2. Do your observations fit with the research presented in the text? Explain how they do or do not.

3. Assuming there are differences in the way adults respond to females and males, how do you think this affects gender socialization/gender development?

Section V   Middle and Late Childhood

Chapter 10 Physical and Cognitive Development in Middle and Late Childhood

Learning Objectives

1.   Describe advances in gross and fine motor skills during childhood.

2.   Identify the pros and cons of children's participation in sports.

3.   Describe cognitive appraisal and indicate its role in the experience of stress.

4.   Describe what is known about acculturative and socioeconomic stress.

5.   Know the causes of and treatments for attention-deficit hyperactivity disorder.

6.   Understand Piaget's concrete operational stage and summarize the contributions and criticisms of Piaget's theory.

7.   Explain how memory develops and how children use schemes and scripts.

8.   Define metacognition, cognitive monitoring, and critical thinking.

9.   Explain why intelligence is probably both a general ability and a number of specific abilities, and describe the relevant theories of intelligence.

10.   Compare approaches to learning, cognitive development, and intelligence.

11.   Describe what is known about the extremes of intelligence.

12.   Identify the main ways children are taught to read.

13.   Understand intrinsic and extrinsic motivation and discuss research concerning achievement in ethnic minority children.

What is stress and how does it relate to the child's development?

How does neo-Piagetian theory differ from traditional Piagetian theory?

Explain cognitive appraisal. Contrast primary appraisal with secondary appraisal.

Explain the process of long-term memory as it relates to middle and late childhood.

How does acculturation relate to issues of stress?

Explain how control processes work.

What is the purpose of Public Law 94-142?

Describe the notion of "scripts" in regard to behavior.

Explain the notion of inclusion and how it relates to children with learning disabilities.

Explain what metacognitive knowledge is. How does that relate to cognitive monitoring?

Describe the characteristics of attention-deficit hyperactivity disorder.

How does reciprocal teaching work?

Neo-Piagetians: developmentalists who have elaborated on Piaget's theory; they believe children's cognitive development is more specific in many respects than believed by Piaget; less focus on grand stages, more emphasis on the roles of strategies, skills, how fast & automatically children can process information

Stress: the response of individuals to the circumstances and events (called "stressors") that threaten them & tax their coping abilities
Children need to have the time/space, and a well rounded life that lets them develop skills to cope with stress

Long-term memory: a relatively permanent & unlimited type of memory that increases with age during middle & late childhood, particularly due to improvements in control processes and learner characteristics

Cognitive appraisal: interpreting events as harmful, threatening, or challenging; assessing if one has the resources to cope effectively; **Primary appraisal**: assessing if an event involves harm/loss already occurred, a future threat, or a challenge to be overcome; **Secondary appraisal**: evaluating one's resources & coping ability

Control processes: cognitive processes that do not occur automatically, but require work & effort; they are under the learner's conscious control & can be used to improve memory; also called "strategies" Control processes include rehearsal & imagery.

Acculturation: cultural change that results from continuous, firsthand contact between two distinctive cultural groups
Acculturative stress: the negative consequence of acculturation

Scripts: schemas for an event, such as what a child should do and what is typically expected to occur in any given situation (e.g., in a restaurant there will be tables where the child will sit to eat, servers to take food orders, a check at the end of dinner, etc.)

Public Law 94-142: the federal government's mandate to provide a free and appropriate education for all children; a key provision is to develop individualized education programs for children with special needs

Metacognitive knowledge: knowledge about cognition, mind, & its workings (e.g., insights such as "there is a limit to how much information I can process"); needed for: **Cognitive monitoring**: the process of taking stock of what you are currently doing, what you will do next, and how effectively the mental activity is unfolding

Inclusion: educating children with disabilities in regular schooling environments, such as regular kindergarten and elementary school classrooms; some education for children with disabilities, however, takes place in a resource room as well

Reciprocal teaching: an instructional procedure used by Brown & Palincsar to develop cognitive monitoring; requires students to take turns leading a study group in the use of strategies for comprehending & remembering text content

Attention-deficit hyperactivity disorder (ADHD): characterized by a short attention span, distractibility, and high levels of physical activity

What is critical thinking and where should it take place? How is it facilitated by the Jasper Project?

How is the term "gifted" used when discussing a child's intellectual abilities?

How do mental age (MA) & chronological age (CA) relate to the intelligence quotient (IQ) & intelligence?

Contrast convergent thinking and divergent thinking.

What is the relationship between IQs and the "normal distribution"?

Explain the notion of creativity.

Describe triarchic theory.

Compare the whole-language approach with the basic-skills-approach and the phonetics approach to learning.

What are culture-fair tests? Are they truly "culture fair"?

What is bilingual education? What does the research say concerning the use of more than one language by children?

Define mental retardation. How does organic retardation differ from cultural-familial retardation?

Differentiate intrinsic motivation from extrinsic motivation.

Giftedness: above-average intelligence (IQ of 120 or higher) and/or superior talent for something
Characteristics include: precocity, marching to one's own drummer, and a passion to master

Convergent thinking: produces one correct answer and is characteristic of the kind of thinking on standardized intelligence tests
Divergent thinking: produces many answers to the same question & is more characteristic of creativity

Creativity: the ability to think about something in novel and unusual ways and to come up with unique solutions to problems
Circumstances that may destroy a child's creativity include: surveillance, rewards, overcontrol, restricting choices, & pressure

Whole-language approach: reading instruction should parallel children's natural language learning; reading materials should be whole & meaningful
Basic-skills-and-phonetics approach: reading instruction should stress phonetics & its basic rules for translating written symbols into sounds; early reading instruction should involve simplified materials

Bilingual education: programs for students with limited proficiency in English that instruct students in their own language part of the time while they learn English
Evaluation research indicates that bilingualism does not interfere with performance in either language

Intrinsic motivation: the internal desire to be competent and do something for its own sake
Extrinsic motivation: the influence of external rewards and punishments on an individual's performance of a task

Critical thinking: ability to grasp the deeper meaning of problems, keep an open mind about different approaches & perspectives, think reflectively not just accept statements without understanding & evaluation; used in & out of classroom
Jasper Project: 12 videodisc-based adventures focusing on real-world math

Intelligence: verbal ability, problem-solving skills, & ability to learn from & adapt to experiences of everyday life; inferred from IQ, a test score based on the formula where mental age (MA) is divided by chronological age (CA) & multiplied by 100
$IQ = MA/CA \times 100$

Normal distribution: symmetrical pattern of scores as seen in a normal curve; a majority of cases fall in the middle of the possible range of scores and few scores appear toward the extreme range
The pattern of distribution for IQ scores approximates a normal curve, with most of the population falling in the middle range.

Triarchic theory: Sternberg's theory that intelligence consists of componential intelligence (analytical thinking/abstract reasoning), experiential intelligence (insightful/creative thinking), and contextual intelligence (street smarts & practical know-how)

Culture-fair tests: tests designed not to be culturally biased, e.g., those with items familiar to individuals from all socioeconomic/ethnic backgrounds and those in which verbal items are removed
No test is completely culture-fair--people with more education score higher and cannot rule out differences in experience.

Mental retardation: individual has limited mental ability; IQ usually below 70 on traditional intelligence tests, & individual has difficulty adapting to everyday life; **Organic retardation**: from genetic disorder or brain damage; **Cultural-familial retardation**: no evidence of organic brain damage, IQ of 50-70, normal variation + individual grew up in a below-average intellectual environment

Self-Test A: Multiple Choice

1. The story related in the text about Jessica Dubroff suggests that:
   a. parents need to be sensitive to and encourage the special talents and desires of their children.
   b. parents can gently guide their children in a way that the parents are able to fulfill their own desires.
   c. children should be allowed to have a well-rounded life.
   d. parents need to restrict their children's activities to prevent them from injuring themselves.

2. During middle and late childhood, body changes occur:
   a. at close to the same rate as they occurred during early childhood.
   b. much more rapidly than they did during early childhood.
   c. in the skeletal and muscular systems and in motor skills.
   d. most significantly in the dermal and subdermal systems.

3. The middle and late childhood period of development is characterized by which of the following kinds of changes in the body?
   a. slow, consistent growth
   b. rapid, consistent growth
   c. rapid spurts of growth
   d. moderate growth with occasional spurts

4. Which pattern best portrays changes in gross and fine motor skills in middle and late childhood?
   a. Girls outperform boys in gross motor skills.
   b. Boys outperform girls in gross motor skills.
   c. There are no sex differences in the development of gross and fine motor skills.
   d. Boys outperform girls in fine motor skills.

5. Circumstances and events that threaten individuals and tax their coping abilities are called:
   a. hassle factors.
   b. stresses.
   c. stressors.
   d. secondary factors.

6. All of the following are evaluated in primary appraisal *except* potential:
   a. harm.
   b. threat.
   c. challenge.
   d. coping.

7. Whenever Roseanne plays or talks with her parents, her brother Tom interrupts. Tom's attention-seeking behavior is _____ for Roseanne.
   a. a daily hassle
   b. an acculturative stress
   c. a conflict
   d. a life event

8. As a member of a minority, Sunny has had many uncomfortable experiences. For example, there is a great deal of poverty and a high rate of unemployment among her family and neighbors, and all through school people have called her offensive names. As a result, Sunny has felt a sense of isolation and alienation most of her life. This is indicative of _____ stress.
   a. acculturative
   b. sociocultural
   c. status
   d. socioeconomic

9. A characteristic of individuals that helps to buffer them from adverse developmental consequences is:
   a. adaptation.
   b. reciprocity.
   c. resilience.
   d. temperament.

10. The most frequent handicap among school children in the United States is:
    a. visual impairment.
    b. emotional disturbance.
    c. mental retardation.
    d. speech handicap.

11. The Education for All Handicapped Children Act mandated that all states provide which of the following for all handicapped children?
    a. free health care and free health education
    b. educational programs for their parents
    c. free testing programs
    d. individualized educational programs

12. Mainstreaming or inclusion refers to:
    a. teaching handicapped children in public schools.
    b. assigning handicapped children to regular classrooms.
    c. giving handicapped children as high an educational priority as nonhandicapped children receive.
    d. assuring that handicapped children interact with nonhandicapped children whenever possible in school.

13. Jack, a second grader, has no trouble with math, science, or art, but he cannot spell, read, or write. Jack is likely to be found to have:
    a. a vision impairment.
    b. a speech handicap.
    c. a learning disability.
    d. an attention deficit.

14. Timothy is suffering from attention-deficit hyperactivity disorder. He is most likely to be experiencing all but which of the following symptoms?
    a. He has a short attention span.
    b. He is easily distracted.
    c. His intelligence is below normal for his age.
    d. He engages in high levels of physical activity.

15. Which of the following class of drugs is most likely to be given to a child to control attention-deficit hyperactivity disorder?
    a. stimulants
    b. depressants
    c. tranquilizers
    d. relaxants

16. A child who can separate playing cards by suit and number is in which Piagetian stage?
    a. sensorimotor
    b. preoperational thought
    c. concrete operational thought
    d. symbolic thought

17. Reversible mental actions are called:
    a. focal points.
    b. symbolic thought.
    c. abstractions.
    d. operations.

18. Which of the following is an application of Jean Piaget's ideas to education?
    a. We need to know how children understand the world to teach them effectively.
    b. Children's illogical or distorted ideas about the world make it hard for them to learn.
    c. The pattern of mental development is universal, so one curriculum could be developed to be used for all students.
    d. By the third or fourth grade, children are ready for abstract learning.

19. All but which of the following criticisms have been applied to Piaget's work?
    a. Not all aspects of a cognitive stage develop at the same time.
    b. Changing the tasks that measure cognitive development changes skills children can exhibit.
    c. Children can be trained to do tasks that they should not be able to do given the cognitive stage they are in.
    d. Some of the skills Piaget identified appear much later than he suggested.

20. All of the following control processes are involved in children's memory abilities *except*:
    a. rehearsal.
    b. perception.
    c. organization.
    d. imagery.

21. Susan and her family are going to a restaurant for dinner. She knows that not only can she expect to sit down and eat, but also knows someone will take their order, serve them, and give them a check to pay. This demonstrates the use of:
    a. cognitive monitoring.
    b. organization.
    c. scripts.
    d. metacognition.

22. Schemas are used in all but which of the following circumstances?
    a. making inferences about information
    b. receiving information in long-term memory
    c. encoding information into long-term memory
    d. receiving sensations from the environment

23. Katie and her grandfather are reading a book about dinosaurs. Katie has been learning about dinosaurs in her second-grade class, but her grandfather is learning about them for the first time. When they are finished, we expect that:
    a. Katie will remember more about dinosaurs because she has had more to relate the information to.
    b. her grandfather will remember more because he is older and processes information better.
    c. their memory for what they learned will be about equal.
    d. each will remember different things about dinosaurs.

24. Teachers can use reciprocal teaching to improve:
    a. learning.
    b. memory.
    c. cognitive monitoring.
    d. problem solving.

25. Sarah, who is reflectively reading a book of essays on politics in various societies, is open to different approaches and perspectives. She is exhibiting:
    a. global thought.
    b. critical thinking.
    c. reflective thinking.
    d. conscious thought.

26. Compared to Piaget's approach to intelligence, Binet's approach was especially concerned with:
    a. finding a way to describe how thought itself changes with age.
    b. developing ways to measure differences in ability.
    c. revealing how the mind works.
    d. identifying universals in cognitive growth.

27. The purpose of the first intelligence test designed by Alfred Binet and Theophile Simon was to:
    a. identify students who should be placed in special classes.
    b. identify gifted students who should be placed in accelerated training programs.
    c. measure intelligence so that future success could be predicted.
    d. form a basic definition of intelligence and find definitive answers to what intelligence is.

28. A person who has a mental age of 13 and a chronological age of 10 has an intelligence quotient of:
    a. 130.
    b. 10.
    c. 13.
    d. 100.

29. Jeffrey grew up in poverty and first learned to care for himself and his sister by selling newspapers and developing "street smarts." Although he never did well in school, and did not test well on intelligence tests, he has become a successful businessman. In terms of Robert Sternberg's triarchic theory, which type(s) of intelligence does Jeffrey have?
    a. componential
    b. experiential
    c. contextual
    d. all three factors of intelligence

30. Many of the early intelligence tests favored urban, middle-income, White individuals. These tests are considered to be:
    a. culture-fair.
    b. culture-biased.
    c. culturally differentiating.
    d. normative.

31. Why does it seem to be impossible to devise a universal, culture-fair intelligence test?
    a. We cannot establish norms for the different populations of people who take the test.
    b. Languages are so different that some languages cannot express what other languages can.
    c. Different cultures appear to encourage the development of different intellectual skills or knowledge.
    d. We are beginning to doubt that IQ tests actually measure intelligence.

32. Information about the causes of mental retardation suggests that:
    a. the causes are primarily organic.
    b. environment is more important than biology.
    c. most retardation is due to genetic factors.
    (d.) both biological and environmental factors are involved.

33. Gary is asked to come up with as many possible uses of a paper clip as possible. This task requires Gary's:
    a. verbal comprehension.
    b. convergent thinking.
    (c.) divergent thinking.
    d. critical thinking.

34. Bilingual education programs allow students whose native language is not English and who are not proficient in English to:
    a. speak both their native language and English in classes.
    b. use their native language at school when they are not in classes.
    c. have remedial classes taught in their native language.
    (d.) learn most coursework in their native language.

35. Daniel has been working on a science project for the past two months. He wants it to be perfect not just because he would like to win first prize in the Science Fair, but also because he enjoys making things and takes great pride in seeing his creations work. Daniel is exhibiting:
    (a.) intrinsic motivation.
    b. extrinsic motivation.
    c. cognitive monitoring.
    d. convergent thinking.

36. Dr. Sacks and her colleagues want to predict the achievement motivation of a group of African American children they have been working with for the past month. As psychologists, Dr. Sacks and her colleagues would use the children's _____ as a predictor.
    a. mastery orientation
    (b.) socioeconomic status
    c. race
    d. intelligence

37. The Bogalusa, Louisiana school system has implemented a program aimed at improving its students':
    a. cognitive skills.
    (b.) health.
    c. math scores.
    d. verbal and math skills.

Self-Test B: Matching

Match the individuals in the left column with the appropriate descriptors in the right column.

1. Alfred Binet
2. Howard Gardner
3. John Flavell
4. Richard Lazarus
5. Lewis Terman
6. David Wechsler
7. David McClellan
8. Sandra Graham
9. William Stern
10. Robert Sternberg

a. a pioneer in providing insights into the ways in which children think
b. favors interpreting achievement of minority children as general motivation
c. created the major alternative to the Stanford-Binet intelligence test
d. proposed the view that stress depends on one's cognitive appraisals
e. created the first test to determine which children would do well in school
f. proposed a theory of seven kinds of intelligence
g. devised the concept of intelligence quotient or IQ score
h. developed the triarchic theory of intelligence
i. performed a longitudinal study of gifted individuals
j. assessed achievement motivation by presenting individuals with ambiguous stimuli

Self Test C: Matching Critical Thinking Skills

Match the critical thinking skills in the left column with their appropriate example in the right column.

c 1. open mindedness

a 2. intellectual curiosity

d 3. planning & strategy

b 4. intellectual carefulness

a. Adam read British & American books about the American Revolution

b. Sarah wrote a paper on Piaget then checked the facts for accuracy

c. After reading *Uncle Tom's Cabin,* Aisha read several critiques of it

d. Alex's group met each week to plan and study for the triathalon

Essay Questions

1. In Chapter 1 of this text the author began with a story of Theodore Kaczynski and Alice Walker, comparing their early childhood experiences and their later adult "accomplishments." The author asks how Kaczynski became the infamous Unabomber, killing and maiming so many people, while Walker became a famous writer, whose work has had a positive effect on so many. In Chapter 10, the author looks at the different kinds of stress children experience, the possible effects of stress on children, how to minimize the negative effects of stress on children, and the relatively new, but potent, research on resilience. Discuss these various elements of stress and dealing with stress, and describe how you would design a classroom and curriculum to maximize the positive effects of stress while minimizing its harmful consequences.

2. You have been approached by your favorite elementary school teacher, who has asked you for your ideas on creating a health, holistic atmosphere for his students. He wants to address their physical, emotional, and cognitive needs. Bearing inmind all of the developmental isssues you have studeied in this chapter, what would you suggest?

3. Your roommates are arguing about whose ideas were more appropriate for application to education, Piaget's or Sternberg's. Knowing that you are taking this classs in Life-Span Development, they turn to you for your wise counsel. How would you settle this dispute using the theories and applications of both Piaget and Sternberg?

Key to Self Test A:

1. c p. 265
2. c. p. 266
3. a. p. 266
4. b. p. 266
5. c. p. 268
6. d. p. 268
7. a. p. 268
8. a. p. 269
9. c. p. 270
10. d. p. 271-272
11. d. 271
12. b. 271
13. c. p. 272-273
14. c. p. 272
15. a. p. 272
16. c. p. 273
17. d. p. 273
18. a. p. 275
19. d. p. 275-276
20. b. p. 277
21. c. p. 277
22. a. p. 277
23. d. p. 277
24. c. p. 278
25. b. p. 279
26. b. p. 281
27. a. p. 281
28. a. p. 281-282
29. b. p. 285
30. c. p. 286
31. c. p. 283
32. d. p. 288
33. c. p. 290
34. d. p. 293
35. a. p. 294
36. b. p. 296
37. b. p. 299

Key to Self-Test B:

1. c
2. a
3. d
4. b

Key to Self-Test C:

1. b
2. e
3. g
4. h

5. f
6. a
7. d
8. c

Key to Essay Questions:

1. Here you will need to define stress, then explore Lazarus' research on cognitive factors, including an explanation of cognitive appraisal, as well as primary and secondary appraisal, and what you think would affect how a child makes such an appraisal. Also explain the effects of life events and daily hassles, sociocultural factors such as acculturative stress and socioeconomic status. Explain what resilience is and the three factors that Garmezy concludes are important to help children become resilient. Use the material in this chapter to explain how you would design a classroom and a curriculum that would use the positive aspects of stress (remember, we need some stress in our lives to challenge us to grow) and minimize its negative effects.

2. Your answer here should encompass the entire chapter, including physical changes in the skeletal and muscular systems and increased motor skills (gross and fine) and how that relates to their need for exercise, as well as the positive and negative consequences of participation in sports; the various components of stress, what to be sensitive to, and how to use it to improve children's functioning while avoiding the negative effects it can have; sensitivity to various issues of children's disabilities (e.g., speech handicaps, ADHD) and socioeconomic issues; then move on to the developmental changes in children's cognitive abilities (they are now in the concrete operational stage), addressing application of Piaget's theory to education, what information-processing theory says about memory, use of scripts, metacognition, cognitive monitoring, scientific reasoning, and critical thinking. You will also need to address the issues of intelligence, creativity, language skills, and achievement motivation. Then, after addressing all of these components of development, suggest how you would use this information to assist your teacher in creating a model classroom with a developmentally appropriate curriculum to achieve optimal outcomes for all of the students.

3. Here, of course, you will need to lay out the theories of both Piaget and Sternberg, discussing what Piaget said about children's abilities in the concrete operational stage and how that information can be applied to education (e.g., assuming the constructivist approach, children need to be actively involved in seeking solutions for themselves) and the criticisms of his theory (e.g., some cognitive abilities emerge earlier than he thought). Then you will need to address Sternberg's triarchic theory of intelligence with its three separate components and explain how each of those can be incorporated into the teaching/learning process, discussing what he believes is important in teaching (i.e., balance instruction related to the three types of intelligence in additional to traditional memorization). Bringing in any of the other theories you wish to consider, state which approach you think works best and explain your rationale.

Research Project 1: Resilience

Review what the text says about resilience, then research the topic (e.g., on the Internet, in your campus library) being sure to look at the work by Garmezy and Emmy Werner (see the reference section of the text for some of their work). After you have some idea of what has already been done in this area, check around your local area to see if there are organizations that help children develop resilience. Consider what you learned earlier about children's temperament--do you think that is related to resilience? Are there certain children that might be predisposed to finding a mentor to take them "under wing" and help them through difficult times? On the basis of what you have learned through your library research and your search of local resources, design a mentoring program that you believe would provide children with the help they need to become resilient, explaining exactly which characteristics would be enhanced and/or developed through your program. How would you reach the most needy children--those who do not have the inherent skills to seek out a mentor? Present your ideas to your class.

Research Project 2: Fine and Gross Motor Activity

This is a way to see developmental changes in fine and gross motor activity over time. Ask five children from five different age groups (ranging from 2 through 10) to write (or print, as appropriate) their first name and their age and to draw a picture of themselves (note that only one chart is provided--be sure to make four more copies before using this one). Compare the handwriting and the drawings in terms of what you have learned so far. Then answer the questions below.

Name:
Age:
Self-Portrait:

1. What similarities and what differences did you notice in how the children held their writing/drawing utensil (pencil, crayon, etc.)?
2. What patterns of development did you notice when comparing the writing and drawing of the children in terms of the material discussed in this chapter?
3. Were your observations consistent with what you might expect from the research described? Explain your response.
4. What might you conclude about development of these skills based on your observations?

Research Project 3: Conservation Tasks

Work with two children, one between the ages of 4 and 5, the other between 6 and 7. Be sure to obtain written consent from the parents; it is also appropriate to have the children sign (or print, as the case may be) the consent form as well--even if they do not sign the consent form, you should be sure to ask them for permission to work with them. Usually if you tell them that you are working on a project for your class and ask if they would be willing to help you out, they are more than willing to do so. In the event parent and/or child wishes to have the parent present while you are doing these tasks, instruct the parent to say nothing, merely to observe. Also, be sure that you do not have both of these children present and observing each other since that might influence the outcome.

Referring back to Chapter 8 of the text, look at Figures 8.4 and 8.5, which contain conservation tasks. You may administer any or all of these to the children to demonstrate differences in conservation ability. For example, to do the conservation of liquid (volume) task, you will need a pitcher of colored water (use a couple of drops of food coloring), two glasses (glasses A and B) that are the same size, and one glass (glass C) that is taller and thinner than the other two. In the presence of the child, pour water into glass A; then, as you pour water into glass B, ask the child to tell you when there is exactly the same amount of water in glass B as in glass A. When the child is sure they're the same, ask: "Do both of these glasses have the same amount of water?" If the child says yes, then pour water from glass B into glass C, saying: "I'm pouring the water from this glass into this glass. I'm not adding any, I'm not taking any away." After you have poured all the water into glass C, ask the child: "Do both glasses have the same amount of water, or does one have more?" Typically, the younger child will say one has more. If so, ask: "Which has more?" In either case, whether the child says one has more or they're the same, ask: "How do you know?" Then pour the water back into glass B and ask: "Are they both the same, or does one have more?" Unless you've spilled some in the process, the child will almost always say they're the same. Repeat the entire process again.

You can do a similar task for conservation of number using twelve objects of the same size, shape, and color (pennies, the plastic tops of water bottles, whatever). Lay them out in two rows of six, being sure that they are completely aligned with each other. Ask the child whether there are the same amount (don't say "number") of pennies (or whatever) in the top row as in the bottom row. Then spread out the bottom row and ask the child again if there are the same amount in the top row as the bottom row. Whatever the answer, ask: "How do you know?" Then put the items back into aligned rows and repeat the process.

You can do similar tasks with all of the forms of conservation discussed in Figure 8.5. You may also wish to look at the children's degree of animism--whether they consider inanimate objects to be alive. A well used question is: "Have you ever watched the moon at night when you're riding in a car? What does it do?" The typical animistic (preoperational) response is "It follows me."

Using the charts below (or one that you devise), record the two children's responses. Then answer the questions that follow.

Task	Child 1 (age:___/sex:__) Response 1	Reason for Response	Child 1 (age:__sex:__) Response 2	Reason for Response
Conservation of Liquid				
Conservation of Number				

Task	Child 2 (age:___/sex:__) Response 1	Reason for Response	Child 2 (age:__sex:__) Response 2	Reason for Response
Conservation of Liquid				
Conservation of Number				

1. What similarities and what differences did you notice in how the children responded?
2. What patterns of development did you notice when comparing the responses of the children in terms of the material discussed in Chapters 8 and 10?
3. Were your observations consistent with what you might expect from the research described? Explain your response.
4. What might you conclude about development of these skills based on your observations?

Chapter 11 Socioemotional Development in Middle and Late Childhood

Learning Objectives

1. Explain how cognitive development during middle childhood may make parenting easier than it was or will be during other times in children's lives.

2. Define boundary ambiguity, and describe patterns of adjustment in stepfamilies.

3. Define and distinguish among popular children, neglected children, rejected children, and controversial children.

4. Identify Dodge's five steps in social cognition and explain their role in aggressive boys' behavior.

5. Discuss the functions that friendships serve in childhood.

6. Discuss the effects on children of teachers, SES, and ethnicity in schools.

7. Describe the development of self-understanding and perspective taking.

8. Provide a definition of self-esteem and self-concept and be able to describe the factors that contribute to the development of strong esteem in children.

9. Define gender-role stereotyping and summarize the research regarding gender similarities and differences.

10. Explain gender-role classification and gender-role transcendence.

11. Understand Kohlberg's theory of moral development and related criticisms.

Explain the potential problems
inherent in boundary
ambiguities.

Describe the characteristics of
intimacy in friendships.

Describe the term "latchkey
children."
What special problems
do they face?

What is aptitude-treatment
interaction?

Contrast the characteristics and
experiences of popular children with
those of average children.

Explain Aronson's notion of
the jigsaw classroom and
how it works.

Contrast the behaviors and
experiences of rejected
children with those of
neglected children.

Describe perspective taking, how
it develops, and its
behavioral benefits.

Explain what
controversial children are.

Differentiate between
self-esteem and
self-concept.

What are the major
functions of friendship?

What are the categories in
Susan Harter's
Self-Perception Profile for
Children?

Intimacy in friendships: refers to self-disclosure and the sharing of private thoughts
True intimate friendships may not appear until early adolescence.

Boundary ambiguity: the uncertainty in stepfamilies about who is in or out of the family & who is performing or responsible for certain tasks in the family system
This increases stress for the family system & the probability of behavior problems in children.

Aptitude-treatment interaction (ATI) stresses the importance of children's aptitudes or characteristics & the treatments or experiences they are given in classrooms.
Aptitude: characteristics such as academic potential & personality characteristics
Treatment: educational techniques such as structured versus flexible classrooms

Latchkey children: children who are given the key to their home, take the key to school, then use it to let themselves into the home while their parents are still at work
They are largely unsupervised 2 to 4 hours a day during the school week; for the entire day--5 days/week during summer; they have greater responsibility/greater likelihood to get in trouble

Jigsaw classroom: students from different cultural backgrounds are placed in a cooperative group in which they have to construct different parts of a project to reach a common goal (Elliot Aronson, 1986)
Lessons divided so each student in the group gets a part to study, then teach to the other members of the group.

Popular children: liked by peers & often nominated as best friend; high rates of positive behaviors, low rates of negative behaviors
Average children: moderately liked by peers & moderately often nominated as best friend; moderate levels of both positive & negative behaviors

Perspective taking: the ability to assume another person's perspective & understand his or her thoughts & feelings
Selman (1980) believes there are five stages, from age 3 through adolescence.
Perspective taking increases self-understanding & peer group relations/friendships; important for growth of moral development.

Rejected children: actively disliked by peers, infrequently nominated as best friend; high rates of negative behaviors, low rates of positive behaviors; most serious long-term adjustment problems
Neglected children: not disliked by peers, but infrequently nominated as best friend; low levels of both positive & negative behaviors

Self-esteem: the global evaluative dimension of the self; also, self-worth or self-image
Self-concept: domain-specific evaluations of the self, such as in academics, athletics, appearance, etc.
Self-esteem refers to global self-evaluations, self-concept to domain-specific evaluations.

Controversial children: frequently disliked by peers, but often nominated as best friend; high rates of both positive & negative behaviors

Self-Perception Profile for Children (Harter, 1985) taps five specific domains of self-concept (scholastic competence, athletic competence, social acceptance, physical appearance, & behavioral conduct) plus general self-worth.

Major functions of friendship: companionship, stimulation, physical support, ego support, social comparison, and intimacy/affection

What are gender-role stereotypes?
How universal are they?

What is Kohlberg's second level of
moral development?
What are the two stages in this
second level?

Differentiate between
rapport talk and
report talk.

What is Kohlberg's highest level of
moral development?
What are the two stages in this
highest level?

What are
gender-role classifications?

Differentiate between the justice
perspective and the
care perspective.

Explain the term androgyny.
What is
gender-role transcendence?
How does it occur?

What is altruism?
How does it relate to survival?

Describe the term
internalization.

Explain Goleman's position
concerning
emotional intelligence (EQ).

What is Kohlberg's lowest level of
moral development?
What are the two stages in this
lowest level?

Describe the six strategies
listed for supporting
children's socioemotional
development.

Conventional reasoning: the individual's internalization is intermediate; the person abides by certain standards (internal), but they are standards of others (external), e.g., parents, laws
Interpersonal norms: person values trust, caring, loyalty as basis of moral judgments
Social system morality: moral judgments based on understanding social order, law, justice, duty

Gender-role stereotypes: broad categories that reflect impressions & beliefs about females & males
A 30-country study: males believed to be dominant, independent, aggressive, achievement oriented, enduring; females to be nurturant, affiliative, less esteemed, more helpful; greater similarity seen in more highly developed nations

Postconventional reasoning: morality completely internalized, not based on others' standards
Community rights vs. individual rights: person understands that values & laws are relative & standards vary from one person to another
Universal ethical principles: persons have developed moral standard based on universal human rights

Rapport talk: the language of conversation & a way of establishing connections & negotiating relationships
Report talk: talk that gives information (e.g., public speaking)
Males hold center stage through report talk; females prefer rapport talk
(Tannen, 1990).

Both are moral perspectives
Justice: focusing on the rights of the individual; individuals stand alone & independently make moral decisions (Kohlberg's is justice perspective)
Care: views people in terms of connectedness with others; emphasizes interpersonal communication, relationships with & concern for others (Gilligan's is care perspective)

Gender-role classification: classifying an individual in terms of masculine, feminine, androgynous, or undifferentiated, rather than using traditional gender-role stereotypes
(Bem, 1977)

Altruism: an unselfish interest in helping someone else
Reciprocity & exchange are involved in altruism; "Do unto others. . ."

Androgyny: refers to the presence of desirable masculine and feminine characteristics in the same person; ("andro" = male; "gyno" = female)
Gender-role transcendence: when personal competence is at issue, it should be conceptualized on a personal basis rather than the basis of masculinity, femininity, or androgyny; occurs through rearing competent children

Goleman argues in _Emotional Intelligence_ (1995): "when it comes to predicting a person's success, IQ . . . might matter less than emotional intelligence. . . . Self-awareness. . . . The idea is not to repress feelings, but to become aware of them so we can cope effectively. . . .Use anxiety wisely; Most visible emotional skills: empathy, graciousness, ability to read social situations"

Internalization: the developmental change from behavior that is externally controlled to behavior that is internally controlled (Kohlberg, 1986)

Strategies to support children's socioemotional development: adapt to developmental changes in children; improve children's peer & friendship skills; create schools that support the child's socioemotional development; improve children's self-esteem; nurture children's moral development; improve the child's emotional intelligence

Preconventional reasoning: the child shows no internalization of moral values; moral reasoning controlled by external rewards/punishments
Punishment & obedience orientation: moral thinking based on fear of punishment
Individualism & purpose: moral thinking based on rewards & self-interest

Self-Test A: Multiple Choice

1. Which parent-child topic will most likely occur in the middle and late childhood period?
   a. getting dressed
   b. getting the chores done
   c. attention-seeking behavior
   d. bedtime

2. During the elementary school years, coregulation results in:
   a. more control taken by parents.
   b. moment-to-moment self-regulation by children, but general parental supervision.
   c. transfer of control to children.
   d. no change from early childhood in the amount of control exercised by parents.

3. Which of the following is a good example of boundary ambiguity?
   a. parents in a blended family deciding on who should discipline the children
   b. children of divorce who are deciding which parent they will stay with
   c. fighting parents who are unsure if they should divorce or separate
   d. children from a blended stepfamily attending a birthday party

4. Hetherington demonstrated that whether children cope effectively with living in a divorced or stepfamily is associated with:
   a. the degree of conflict between the child's biological parents.
   b. parenting techniques and school environment.
   c. whether the child lives in a single-parent or two-parent family.
   d. the age and sex of the child.

5. Marlene, a single parent, works full time so 11-year-old daughter Beth is an after-school latchkey child. To minimize the negative impact of this situation, Marlene should:
   a. use authoritative parenting and monitor Beth's activities.
   b. encourage Beth to make friends that she can hang out with after school.
   c. explain the importance of independence and provide at-home responsibilities so she learns independent living.
   d. hire a baby-sitter.

6. Which statement about peer interactions **is false**?
   a. They usually occur at one of the children's homes.
   b. They occur more often in private places than public places.
   c. They are most often with members of the same sex.
   d. They usually involve play, socializing, or going places.

7. All of the following children will be popular with their peers **except**:
   a. those who give out lots of reinforcement.
   b. those who listen carefully to what others have to say.
   c. those who try to please others even if it means compromising themselves.
   d. those who are self-confident.

8. Samantha has few friends at school. Other children pay little attention to her and no one invites her home. Samantha is probably a:
   a. rejected child.
   b. neglected child.
   c. latchkey child.
   d. controversial child.

9. When teaching a rejected child how to gain popularity with peers, a counselor should encourage the child to:
   a. avoid asking his peers questions.
   b. gain status by talking about items of personal interest, even if they are of no interest to others.
   c. get peers to pay attention to her through some positive activity (e.g., giving everyone in class a cookie).
   d. listen to what other children are saying without trying to change what is taking place.

10. The correct order of Kenneth Dodge's (1983) stages of processing of social information is:
    a. enacting, searching for a response, decoding social cues, interpreting, selecting an optimal response.
    b. decoding social cues, interpreting, searching for a response, selecting an optimal response, enacting.
    c. searching for a response, decoding social cues, selecting an optimal response, enacting, interpreting.
    d. interpreting, selecting an optimal response, decoding social cues, enacting, searching for a response.

11. Friendships from ages 6 to 12 are most frequently based on which of the following?
    a. one-way assistance
    b. proximity
    c. similarity
    d. intimacy

12. Tamara's friend Shelly is someone she can confide in and get good advice from, and her friend Tanya is interesting and introduces her to many new things to do. The functions each of these friendships serve, respectively, are:
    a. companionship and social comparison.
    b. intimacy/affection and stimulation.
    c. ego support and physical support.
    d. intimacy and similarity.

13. The school environment forces children to do all but which of the following?
    a. develop new relationships with new significant others
    b. adopt new reference groups
    c. develop new standards by which to judge themselves
    d. adjust to increasing self-esteem

14. Teachers who implement an aptitude-treatment interaction approach in their teaching rely on their:
    a. ability to plan.
    b. awareness of individual differences.
    c. adaptability.
    d. flexibility.

15. According to Jacqueline Jackson (1977), the United States maintains:
    a. a high quality of education for students of all races and ethnicities.
    b. smaller class sizes for ethnic minorities.
    c. lousy conditions for African Americans.
    d. the lowest levels of education of all the major industrialized nations.

16. James Comer's (1993) program for improving the quality of education for poor inner-city youths is based on the premise:
    a. "all for one and one for all."
    b. "Black power."
    c. "money makes the world go 'round."
    d. "what's good for business is good for America."

17. As children mature, their self-descriptions are likely to include more of all of the following *except*:
    a. psychological characteristics.
    b. physical characteristics.
    c. social aspects of self.
    d. social comparison.

18. In Chapter 10, your author indicates that handicapped children are increasingly aware of the deficits they suffer compared to nonhandicapped children. Which new process involved in self-understanding probably generates this sensitivity?
    a. perspective taking
    b. use of abstractions to describe the self
    c. awareness of social aspects of the self
    d. social comparison

19. A child who has a sense of differentiation of self and others, but cannot distinguish between the thoughts and feelings of others and self would be in which of Selman's stages of perspective taking?
    a. egocentric viewpoint
    b. social-informational perspective taking
    c. self-reflective perspective taking
    d. mutual perspective taking

20. The parenting attributes that are associated with high self-esteem are characteristic of a parenting style called:
    a. protective.
    b. indulgent.
    c. authoritarian.
    d. authoritative.

21. Which of the following *is not* one of the ways the text suggested for increasing a child's self-esteem?
    a. setting high goals with a need to succeed
    b. identifying the causes of low self-esteem and the domains of competence important to the self
    c. providing emotional support and social approval
    d. achievement and effective coping

22. Amara is a single mother with one child, 15-year-old Aslam. Amara decides to enroll Aslam in a local Boy's Club program. In doing so, Amara is attempting to raise her son's self-esteem through:
    a. achievement.
    b. coping.
    c. emotional support.
    d. ethnocentrism.

23. Children in the middle and late childhood period of development are also in which of Erikson's psychosocial stages?
    a. trust versus mistrust
    b. autonomy versus shame and doubt
    c. industry versus inferiority
    d. identity versus identity confusion

24. J. O. Halliwell's (1844) poem in which he describes girls as being made of "Sugar and spice and all that's nice" provides a good example of:
    a. gender-role transcendence.
    b. androgyny.
    c. gender-role stereotyping.
    d. gender-based prejudice.

25. When reviewing research comparing males versus females, it is important to keep in mind that:
    a. even when differences are found, most of the individuals in the groups are virtually identical.
    b. it is unfair to compare the groups since almost all gender differences are a result of uncontrollable biological factors.
    c. it is only when statistically significant scores are found that you can conclude there is little overlap between male and female scores.
    d. even when differences are reported, there is considerable overlap between the sexes.

26. Which of the following has been found in terms of the physical comparisons of males and females?
    a. Females are more vulnerable than males.
    b. Females are more likely than males to develop physical or mental disorders.
    c. Analyses of metabolic activity in the brain show females to demonstrate greater emotionality than males.
    d. Analyses of metabolic activity in the brain show females to demonstrate greater physical expressiveness than males.

27. For which of the following do investigators continue to find gender differences?
    a. verbal skills
    b. math skills
    c. social skills
    d. suggestibility

28. Tess met Tasha and engaged her in a personal conversation. They discussed mutual feelings about boys, parents, and other friends through which they strengthened their already tight friendship. In terms of socioemotional development, they were engaging in:
    a. rapport talk.
    b. report talk.
    c. girl talk.
    d. gossip.

29. The term "androgyny" refers to a gender role that is:
    a. highly masculine.
    b. highly feminine.
    c. both highly masculine and highly feminine.
    d. neither masculine nor feminine.

30. Researchers have found that high-masculinity adolescent boys:
    a. often engage in problem behaviors.
    b. do exceptionally well in school.
    c. are highly protective and nurturing of others.
    d. are more flexible, competent, and mentally healthy than other adolescent boys.

31. Which of the following ethnic groups would most likely expect a woman to carry on domestic duties, marry, become an obedient helper of her mother-in-law, and bear sons?
    a. African American
    b. Anglo
    c. Asian
    d. Hispanic

32. Lawrence Kohlberg's theory of moral development stresses that a child's moral level is determined by:
    a. how well the child defends the correct answer to a moral dilemma.
    b. the nature of the child's ideas about morality.
    c. how a child processes information about moral problems.
    d. the child's reasoning about moral decisions.

33. "Heinz should steal the drug. It isn't like it really cost $2,000, and he'll be really unhappy if his wife dies." This statement is characteristic of a stage of morality called:
    a. punishment and obedience orientation to morality.
    b. individualism and purpose morality.
    c. interpersonal norms morality.
    d. social system morality.

34. A pacifist who is thrown in jail for refusing to obey the draft laws because he believes that killing is morally wrong is at what stage of moral development?
    a. community rights versus individual rights
    b. punishment and obedience
    c. interpersonal norms
    d. universal ethical principles

35. Carol Gilligan argues that Lawrence Kohlberg's theory is limited because it **_does not_**:
    a. indicate how moral reasoning relates to moral behavior.
    b. include a role for reasoning about relationships between people in evaluating moral decisions.
    c. capture the moral thinking of all cultures; some moral systems do not "fit" Kohlberg's theory.
    d. indicate how moral reasoning relates to moral feeling.

36. Carol Gilligan has found that as girls reach adolescence, they:
    a. become increasingly moral.
    b. adopt a justice perspective of morality.
    c. increasingly silence their "distinctive voice."
    d. become more outspoken about their inner feelings.

37. William Damon (1988) has found that by the time children enter elementary school, they share with others:
    a. for the fun of the social play ritual.
    b. out of imitation of older people.
    c. out of obligation, but don't think they need to be as generous to others as they are to themselves.
    d. from a sense of fairness involving principles of equality, merit, and benevolence.

38. An important aspect of self-control, as stated by Daniel Goleman, is the ability to:
    a. reduce anxiety.
    b. delay gratification.
    c. be gracious.
    d. demonstrate altruism.

39. When Madeline Cartwright was principal of North Philadelphia's James G. Blaine public school, located in a low-income neighborhood, she changed children's lives by:
    a. protecting them from abusive parents.
    b. having police stand guard at the school.
    c. increasing their positive role models.
    d. encouraging a local laundry to provide low-cost facilities for poor families.

Self-Test B: Matching

Match the individuals in the left column with the appropriate descriptors in the right column.

h 1. Robert Selman
j 2. Carol Gilligan
b 3. Sandra Bem
a 4. Lynette Long
c 5. Madeline Cartwright
d 6. Susan Harter
e 7. William Damon
f 8. Lawrence Kohlberg
k 9. Kenneth Dodge
i 10. E. Mavis Hetherington
j 11. Harry Stack Sullivan

a. interviewed latchkey children
b. developmentalist who devised an inventory to measure gender orientation
c. inner-city school principal who built a model school & got parents involved
d. her self-perception profile measures children's self-esteem in many domains
e. described a developmental model of children's altruism
f. stressed that moral development is based on moral reasoning
g. emphasized the importance of friendships for children's well-being
h. proposed a developmental theory of perspective taking
i. demonstrated effects of parenting style on children's coping in stepfamilies
j. a critic of Kohlberg; distinguished between justice & care perspectives
k. analyzed how children process information about peer relations

Self-Test C: Matching Stages of Perspective Taking

Match the stages of perspective taking in the left column with some of their descriptions in the right column.

c 1. egocentric viewpoint (stage 0)
a 2. social-informational (stage 1)
d 3. self-reflective (stage 2)
e 4. mutual (stage 3)
b 5. social & conventional system (stage 4)

a. aware other has social perspective based on own reasoning
b. mutual perspective taking doesn't always lead to understanding
c. sense of differentiation of self/other but not social perspective
d. each aware of other's perspective & that it influences views
e. self/other view each other mutually/simultaneously as subjects

Essay Questions:

1. One of your best friends has given you the great news that she is planning to remarry after having been divorced for two years. Her major concern, though, is the effect this will have on her 12-year-old daughter. Your friend's fiancé has a daughter about the same age, who is very different from your friend's daughter; he also has a 10-year-old son. She has a secondary concern about the fact that both she and her fiancé have full-time jobs that neither can afford to quit, which means the children will be left home alone for several hours after school. What advice would you give her about providing the optimum environment for the children's safety and most risk-free development?

2. Assume you have decided to open a day-care center for elementary school children to provide an optimum environment for them between the hours that school lets out and their parents finish working. You've already talked to some of the parents and, while they may not tell you *their* child has problems, each has been quite open about some of the other children's problems. The parents have also asked if you would be willing to help their children develop in a morally appropriate manner, but they come from different religious perspectives, so they want to keep religion out of the picture in your center. Further, it appears that among the children who will participate in your center, there are all five types: popular, average, neglected, rejected, and controversial. How would you help all of these children have the best possible growth experience in your day-care facility? How would you assist them in developing perspective taking, altruism, and a solid foundation for moral development?

Key to Self-Test A:

1.	b	p.	301	21.	a	p.	312-313
2.	b	p.	302	22.	c	p.	312
3.	a	p.	302	23.	c	p.	313
4.	b	p.	302-303	24.	c	p.	313
5.	a	p.	303	25.	d	p.	313-314
6.	a	p.	304	26.	c	p.	314
7.	c	p.	304	27.	b	p.	314-315
8.	b	p.	304	28.	a	p.	315
9.	d	p.	304	29.	c	p.	316
10.	b	p.	304	30.	a	p.	317
11.	c	p.	305	31.	c	p.	318-319
12.	b	p.	305	32.	d	p.	319
13.	d	p.	306	33.	c	p.	319
14.	b	p.	307	34.	d	p.	320
15.	c	p.	307	35.	b	p.	321
16.	a	p.	309	36.	c	p.	321
17.	c	p.	310-311	37.	c	p.	322
18.	d	p.	311	38.	b	p.	324
19.	a	p.	311	39.	c	p.	327
20.	d	p.	312				

Key to Self-Test B:

1.	h	7.	e	
2.	j	8.	f	
3.	b	9.	k	
4.	a	10.	i	
5.	c	11.	g	
6.	d			

Key to Self-Test C:

1. c
2. a
3. d
4. e
5. b

Key to Essay Questions:

1. Here you will need to look at the relationship between custodial parents and their children; the issue of boundary ambiguity and who will make which decisions; the need to use effective parenting techniques (noting that the authoritative parenting style is the most effective for stepfamilies); how to get the children communicating and working together; and finally, the issues of dealing with latchkey children, such as carefully monitoring their activities and getting them involved in academically, socially, and emotionally supportive after-school activities.

2. You will need to describe the five types of children, explain the stages of perspective taking and moral development, and how these can be facilitated in children. You will also need to address self-esteem building, and the various domains where a child can learn to acquire skills.

Research Project 1: The Bem Sex-Role Inventory

Table 11.2 of the text sets out sixty items taken from Sandra Bem's Sex-Role Inventory. First, assess your own score on the scale. Then administer the items to other people--your friends, family, classmates--to assess how they score. Note that there is a fourth category not included, "undifferentiated," which is low on both masculinity and femininity. You may also wish to locate a self-esteem scale (you might check out Stanley Coopersmith's, which is relatively short and easy to administer, or Harter's scales for adolescents (*Self-Perception Profile for Adolescents*, 1988) or adults (Messer, B., & Harter, S. [1986] *Adult Self-Perception Profile*). (If you can't find these, you might write to Dr. Harter at the University of Denver.) If you do both the sex-role inventory and the self-esteem assessment, you could then do a correlational analysis to see if there is any particular relationship between the sex role statuses and self-esteem. Based on the research, which status (masculine, feminine, androgynous, undifferentiated) do you think would rank highest on self-esteem? Why?

Research Project 2: Helping "Challenged" Children

Consider the problems of the rejected, neglected, and controversial children discussed in this chapter. Understand that these children may be the bane of society in years to come, so it would benefit us all to have some early intervention. Design a program that looks at the underlying factors that lead to these children adopting such a status, and presents appropriate interventions to teach them to interact effectively with other children and with adults. This will need to include development of friendships, perspective taking, altruism, and morality. Present your ideas to your professor for critique and streamlining, then present it to your local school districts to see if they would be willing to put it into action.

1. When designing this program, what do you believe are the underlying factors that will lead a child to attain a status of: rejected; neglected; controversial?

2. Will the same types of interventions help all three types of children? What will work for each?

3. Considering their current level of development (ignoring their peer status, based on the research, what could reasonably be expected from them in terms of perspective taking, altruism, and moral development?

4. How can you teach these children to develop friendships? perspective taking? altruism? morality?

Research Project 3: The Jigsaw Classroom

Elliot Aronson (1986) developed the jigsaw classroom in response to a major crisis in the education system in Austin, Texas. As described in your text, "students from different cultural backgrounds are placed in a cooperative group in which they have to construct different parts of a project to reach a common goal" (p.). Each student is responsible for one part of a project (e.g., learning about ways to improve relations among ethnically diverse students), each student learns his or her part, then all of the students in the group come back and teach their respective parts to the entire group. There is a great deal of research to indicate that the best way to smooth out relations among persons of diverse views is to have them cooperate with each other on a project where they have a common goal. Try this technique either with your classmates or with a group of children from different cultural orientations.

Take note of: (a) how the individuals interact with each other **before** the intervention; (b) their scores on tests/quizzes **before** the intervention; (c) how they interact with each other **after** the intervention; and (d) their scores on tests/quizzes **after** the intervention. What differences do you notice? Did the results of your intervention coincide with those found in the literature? If they are different, what do you think would explain the difference?

Chapter 12 Physical and Cognitive Development in Adolescence

Learning Objectives

1.   Describe the psychological and physical changes that accompany puberty.

2.   Define and distinguish among early, late, and on-time maturation.

3.   Characterize Piaget's formal operational stage and explain some of the challenges to Piaget's ideas.

4.   Explain how social cognition (adolescent egocentrism, imaginary audience, and personal fable) affects adolescent behavior.

5.   Explain why the transition to middle or junior high school can be stressful. Include a definition of the top-dog phenomenon.

6.   Summarize the Carnegie report's recommendations for middle schools.

7.   Evaluate the claim that dropout rates are comparable for ethnic majority and minority students.

8.   Define juvenile delinquency and identify some of the possible causes of delinquency.

9.   Indicate the incidence and consequences of adolescent pregnancy.

What is menarche?
How has it changed over the
past 100 to 150 years?

Explain the concept of
hypothetical-deductive
reasoning.

Explain the process
of puberty.

Describe Elkind's notion of
adolescent egocentrism.

What is testosterone
and what does it do?

Define and give examples of
the imaginary audience.

What is estradiol
and what does it do?

Define and give examples of
the personal fable.

Describe the psychological
accompaniments of
physical changes in
adolescence.

Discuss the major concerns of
educators & psychologists
concerning junior high and middle
schools.

What are the characteristics
of formal operational thought?
When does formal operational
thought occur?

Explain the top-dog
phenomenon.

Hypothetical-deductive reasoning: Piaget's formal operational concept that adolescents have the cognitive ability to develop hypotheses, or best guesses, about ways to solve problems, such as an algebraic equation; they then systematically deduce, or conclude, which is the best path to follow in solving the problem

Menarche: first menstruation
The age of menarche has been declining at an average of about 4 months per decade for the past century (Petersen, 1979).

Adolescent egocentrism consists of imaginary audience & a personal fable.
Attention-getting behavior is common & reflects egocentrism & desire to be on stage, noticed, & visible.

Puberty: a period of rapid skeletal and sexual maturation that occurs mainly in early adolescence
It is part of a gradual process.

Imaginary audience: the adolescent's belief that others are as preoccupied with the adolescent as the adolescent is
Example: an 8th grade boy who thinks everyone is noticing the small spot on his trousers, or the 7th grade girl who thinks everyone is looking at the tiny blemish on her complexion

Testosterone: a hormone associated in boys with the development of genitals, an increase in height, and a change in voice

Personal fable: the part of adolescent egocentrism that involves an adolescent's sense of uniqueness--so unique no one can understand him/her
Example: adolescent girl thinks her mother is totally incapable of sensing how hurt she is because her boyfriend broke up with her

Estradiol: a hormone associated in girls with breast, uterine, and skeletal development

One major concern of educators & psychologists about middle/junior high school is that they have become watered down versions of high schools.

Psychological accompaniments of physical change include: preoccupation with bodies, development of individual images of what the body is like; early-maturing boys perceive selves more positively & have better peer relations than late maturers; early maturation is mixed blessing for girls--more problems in school but more independence & popularity with boys

Top-dog phenomenon: the circumstance of moving from the top position (in elementary school, being the oldest, biggest, and most powerful students in the school) to the lowest position (in middle or junior high school, being the youngest, smallest, and least powerful stuents in the school)
The transition to middle/jr. high can be hard.

Formal operational thought: thought is more abstract, no longer limited to concrete experiences; conjure up make-believe situations, hypothetical possibilities; purely abstact propositions, increased interest in thought itself & abstractness of thought; more idealistic & more logical; emerges between 11 and 15

What has Joan Lipsitz (1984) decided makes a successful middle school?

How does adolescent pregnancy differ now from adolescent pregnancy in the 1950s and 1960s?

What does the Carnegie report (1989) recommend for improving our middle schools?

What are the consequences of adolescent pregnancy?

Which students are most likely to drop out of high school?

What social policies have been recommended to improve the lives of adolescent mothers?

Which drugs have been particularly abused by middle school and high school students?

Define anorexia nervosa. What are its potential consequences?

What is juvenile delinquency?

What is bulimia?

What are the antecedents of delinquency?

What strategies does the author suggest for improving the lives of adolescents?

Adolescent pregnancy: despite the rise in teen birth rate in the late 1980s, the rate was lower than in the 1950s & 1960s; the difference is the steady rise in nonmarital teen births; 40% of pregnant teens have abortions; because the stigma of illegitimacy is less severe; only 5% give the baby up for adoption (compared with 35% in the 1960s)

Joan Lipsitz (1984) found the following make middle schools outstanding for their ability to education youth: a willingness & ability to adapt school practices to the individual differences in physical, cognitive, & social development of the students

Consequences of adolescent pregnancy: increased health risks to child and mother (higher rate of low birthweights, neurological problems, & childhood illnesses); high rate of school drop outs, failure to gain employment; dependence on welfare; adolescent parents are more likely to have low-paying, low-status jobs or to be unemployed

For improving middle schools, the Carnegie report (1989) recommended: develop small "communities" so schools are less impersonal; student-counselor ratios of 10:1; involve parents & community leaders in schools; curricula that produce literate students; team teaching in flexible time blocks; boost students' health & fitness

Social policy recommendations for improving lives of adolescent mothers: different types of programs for different types of adolescent mothers; expand service to include elementary-age children; coordinate services & family systems; use of family systems perspective (evaluate the effect of the system & provide intervention where necessary

High school dropouts: rates are highest for Latinos and Native Americans
Reasons for dropping out include school-related issues (e.g., not like school, being suspended or expelled); economic reasons; or personal reasons (e.g., pregnancy, marriage)

Anorexia nervosa: an eating disorder that involves the relentless pursuit of thinness through starvation
Among the many debilitating health consequences, the most critical is that anorexia nervosa can eventually lead to death.

Drug use/abuse: alcohol is the most widely used drug by U. S. adolescents; marijuana had the sharpest increase in use by adolescents from 1992 to 1995; other drugs include cigarettes, cocaine, LSD, amphetamines, stimulants, & inhalants; the U.S. has the highest rate of adolescent drug use among the industrialized nations

Bulimia: an eating disorder in which the individual consistently follows a binge-and-purge eating pattern (purging typically involves induced vomiting and/or use of laxatives)

Juvenile delinquency: a variety of behaviors, ranging from socially unacceptable behavior (such as acting out in school) to status offenses (such as running away) to criminal acts (such as burglary)

Strategies for improving the lives of adolescents: develop positive expectations for adolescents; create better schools; reduce adolescent pregnancy rate & provide better coordination of services for mothers & children; expand successful programs for high-risk youth

Antecedents of delinquency: negative identity, low degree of self-control, age (early initiation), being male, low expectations for education & little commitment, low achievement in early grades, heavy peer influence with low resistance, low socioeconomic status, lack of parental monitoring with low support & ineffective discipline, & urban high-crime/high-mobility neighborhood

Self-Test A: Multiple Choice

1. The age at which puberty arrives is _____ with each passing decade.
   a. increasing
   b. decreasing
   c. staying the same
   d. approaching a plateau

2. Wet dreams, first menstruation, skeletal growth, and changing body shape are events that occur in:
   a. late childhood.
   b. puberty.
   c. menarche.
   d. climacteric.

3. Whereas _____ is responsible for development of genitals, increase in height, and changes in boys' voices, _____ is a hormone associated with breast, uterine, and skeletal development in girls.
   a. testosterone; estradiol
   b. estradiol; testosterone
   c. estrogen; progesterone
   d. serotonin; dopamine

4. The most noticeable changes in body growth for females include all of the following *except*:
   a. height spurt.
   b. tendencies toward obesity.
   c. breast growth.
   d. menarche.

5. Recent research about puberty suggests all but which of the following?
   a. Early puberty is better than late puberty during the adolescent period.
   b. Pubertal variations are less dramatic than commonly thought.
   c. Adolescents are affected by puberty as well as by cognitive and social changes.
   d. The onset of puberty is related to self-esteem throughout adolescence and into early adulthood.

6. At age 13, Sheila still has not entered puberty. What is she likely to experience by the time she reaches tenth grade?
   a. an increase in popularity and self-esteem
   b. a sharp drop in self-confidence because boys will be attracted primarily to the more mature girls
   c. a strong sense of identity
   d. an increase in problems at school

7. In recent years developmental researchers have begun to view the effects of puberty as:
   a. overrated.
   b. identical for early- and late-maturing individuals.
   c. positive for males and negative for females.
   d. more dramatic than they had expected.

8. A child in the formal operational thought stage of cognitive development is most likely to engage in which of the following activities?
   a. using building blocks to determine how houses are constructed
   b. writing a story about a clown who wants to leave the circus
   c. drawing pictures of a family using stick figures
   d. writing an essay about patriotism

9. Jean Piaget's ideas on formal operational thought are being challenged in all but which of the following ways?
   a. Not all adolescents are capable of formal operational thought.
   b. Not all adults in every culture are formal operational thinkers.
   c. There is more individual variation in the development of formal operations than Piaget thought.
   d. Only those with scientific training use hypothetical-deductive reasoning.

10. Jennifer, who is having unprotected sex with her boyfriend, comments to her best friend, Anne, "Did you hear about Barbara? You know how she fools around so much. I heard she's pregnant. That would never happen to me!" This is an example of the:
a. imaginary audience.
b. false-belief syndrome.
c. personal fable.
d. adolescent denial syndrome.

11. Sydney calls her best friend Aisha in a panic. She has a date with Jason, someone she has wanted to date for months, but now she has a blemish on her forehead, which she knows Jason (and everyone else) will notice. This is an example of the:
a. imaginary audience.
b. false-belief syndrome.
c. personal fable.
d. personal absorption syndrome.

12. Unlike children, adolescents who interpret personality information concerning another person:
a. rely heavily on the current situation and ignore past experiences with the individual.
b. realize that personality traits are highly consistent.
c. tend to incorporate traditional sex-role stereotypes into their analysis.
d. often attempt to identify the "hidden cause" of the person's behavior.

13. In the 1970s, experts on education found that high schools:
a. need to focus more on basic intellectual skills.
b. interfere with the transition from adolescence to adulthood.
c. allow adolescents to spend too many hours in part-time work.
d. are too concerned with the social and emotional lives of students.

14. Which movement has gained increasing momentum in the 1990s?
a. the socioemotional approach
b. the holistic child approach
c. the back-to-basics movement
d. the disciplinary movement

15. A trend in adolescent development that has stimulated the creation of middle schools is:
a. an increase in formal operational thinking among early adolescents.
b. the appearance of greater autonomy from adults.
c. the earlier and highly variable beginning of puberty.
d. the fact that today's teens spend more time with peers than with parents or adults.

16. Students experiencing the top-dog phenomenon are most likely to exhibit which of the following?
a. high achievement motivation
b. little satisfaction with school
c. good relations with peers
d. power over other students

17. Joan Lipsitz (1984) said that the common thread among schools that have been successful in diminishing the trauma often associated with the middle-school experience is that they all emphasized:
a. gender equity.
b. curricular flexibility.
c. discipline.
d. the importance of high academic standards.

18. The Carnegie (1989) recommendations for improving middle schools in the United States included all the following *except*:
a. lower the student counselor ratio to 10:1.
b. get parents involved.
c. integrate physical health into the curriculum.
d. promote continuity by keeping all class sessions the same length.

19. During the last 40 years, the high school dropout rate among American school children has:
a. increased significantly.
b. increased slightly.
c. decreased slightly.
d. decreased significantly.

20. Which of the following *was not* one of the reasons cited in the text for leaving school?
a. family pressures
b. economic reasons
c. marriage
d. not liking school

21. The frequency of marijuana use by teenagers _____ from 1991 to 1995.
    a. increased
    b. decreased
    c. remained the same
    d. was almost eradicated

22. The most widely used drug by adolecents is:
    a. cocaine.
    b. marijuana.
    c. alcohol.
    d. speed.

23. Cheryl Perry and her colleagues (1988) developed three programs to curb adolescent smoking ("Keep It Clean," "Health Olympics," and "Shifting Gears"). A follow-up study found that five years later:
    a. students who participated in the programs smoked less than their peers, but there were no differences in their use of alcohol or marijuana.
    b. there were no differences between students who did and did not participate with respect to use of cigarettes, alcohol, or marijuana.
    c. students who participated in the programs were much less likely than their peers to smoke cigarettes, use marijuana, or drink alcohol.
    d. students who participated in the programs actually smoked more cigarettes, drank more alcohol, and had higher marijuana use than their peers.

24. A study by Kandel (1974) found that adolescents are most likely to use drugs:
    a. when their parents use drugs, but peers do not.
    b. when their peers use drugs, but parents do not.
    c. in rebellion against their parents who do not use drugs.
    d. when their parents and their peers use drugs.

25. The causes of juvenile delinquency include all of the following *except*:
    a. heredity.
    b. identity problems.
    c. family experiences.
    d. boredom.

26. A parenting practice that is associated with an adolescent becoming delinquent is:
    a. disciplining adolescents for antisocial behavior.
    b. indulgence of a child's wants.
    c. lazy supervision of a teen's whereabouts.
    d. restrictively controlling an adolescent's behavior.

27. Which of the following *has not been* successful in reducing violence in youth?
    a. early intervention
    b. slogan campaigns and scare tactics
    c. anger management programs
    d. encouragement from positive adult role models

28. When comparing the overall pregnancy rates of American teenagers with the rates in other industrialized nations, the rate of pregnancy in the United States is:
    a. much higher.
    b. higher than some, lower than others.
    c. pretty much the same.
    d. much lower.

29. Which method of suicide is more likely to be used by a male?
    a. sleeping pills
    b. guns
    c. knives
    d. carbon monoxide poisoning

30. Which of the following *is not* a recommendation for dealing with a suicidal adolescent?
    a. Ask if the person has a plan for killing himself.
    b. Heed warning signs and take them seriously.
    c. Assure the person everything is under control.
    d. Help the person find appropriate counseling.

31. Anorexics are likely to have all of the following characteristics *except*:
    a. they are male.
    b. they are white.
    c. they are well edcuated.
    d. they come from the middle or upper class.

32. Teenagers who suffer from anorexia nervosa:
    a. have a distorted need to be sexually desirable.
    b. suffer from an abnormal function of the hypothalamus.
    (c.) strive to gain control of their lives.
    d. know they are too thin but think they look good anyway.

33. Areas of special concern that make up a large portion of at-risk youth include all of the following *except*:
    a. delinquency.
    (b.) engaging in sexual intercourse.
    c. substance abuse.
    d. school-related problems.

34. Ruby Takanishi (1993) has suggested that the most productive way to deal with adolescent risk factors is to:
    a. determine which is the most high-risk behavior, then begin with that one and move on to the others in terms of danger.
    b. use a tough-love approach, telling the teen to straighten up or get out.
    c. provide adolescents with sufficient information and teaching skills, understanding that the teen must now learn to make decisions for himself or herself.
    (d.) promote clusters of health-enhancing behaviors with networks of support.

35. Laurence Steinberg and Ann Levine say parents should send their child to a professional:
    a. only after they have identified the basic problem.
    b. whenever a child experiences any traumatic event (e.g., the death of a grandparent).
    c. only after they have attempted to "treat" the problem on their own.
    (d.) whenever a child is displaying a severe problem (e.g., depression, drug addiction).

Self-Test B: Matching

Match the individuals in the left column with the appropriate descriptors in the right column.

e 1. David Elkind   a. identified the best middle schools in the United States
a 2. Joan Lipsitz   b. one of the researchers who surveyed adolescents about their drug use
c 3. Joy Dryfoos   c. identified possibilities for preventing juvenile delinquency
g 4. Laurence Steinberg   d. developed programs to curb adolescent smoking
f 5. Ruby Takanishi   e. the imaginary audience & personal fable are part of adolescent egocentrism
b 6. Lloyd Johnston   f. described the importance of improving the opportunity side of risk-taking
d 7. Cheryl Perry   g. developed guidelines to determine when to get professional help for a teen

Essay Questions:

1. Your former high school counselor has invited you to speak to the students at your old high school. She has asked you to talk to them about high-risk behaviors--what they are, how kids get involved with them, the consequences, and how to avoid getting involved. Which issues would be important for you to address, what would you tell them about each of these, and what suggestions would you have for avoiding them?

2. Your favorite aunt and uncle have come to you because they say they cannot understand their teen-age daughter. One minute she's loving and adoring, the next she's a total monster. They try to comfort her when she's upset, but she screams, "You can't possibly understand how I feel"; if she is having a "bad hair day," she refuses to go out in public, even to accompany them to religious services. How would you explain these behaviors to your aunt and uncle, and what would you suggest for helping them to work with their daughter?

Key to Self-Test A:

1.	b	p.	336	19.	d	p.	343
2.	b	p.	336	20.	a	p.	343
3.	a	p.	336	21.	a	p.	343-344
4.	b	p.	336	22.	c	p.	344
5.	d	p.	337	23.	c	p.	344
6.	a	p.	337	24.	d	p.	345
7.	a	p.	337	25.	d	p.	345
8.	d	p.	337-338	26.	c	p.	345
9.	d	p.	338	27.	b	p.	346
10.	c	p.	339	28.	a	p.	346-347
11.	a	p.	339	29.	b	p.	348
12.	d	p.	339	30.	c	p.	349
13.	b	p.	339	31.	a	p.	349
14.	c	p.	340	32.	c	p.	349
15.	c	p.	341	33.	b	p.	350
16.	b	p.	342	34.	d	p.	351
17.	b	p.	342	35.	d	p.	353
18.	d	p.	342				

Key to Self-Test B:

1.	e	5.	f
2.	a	6.	b
3.	c	7.	d
4.	g		

Key to Essay Questions:

1. You would need to address the issues of dropping out of school, drugs, juvenile delinquency, adolescent pregnancy, suicide, and eating disorders. As a backdrop to understanding the issues, briefly present physiological changes in adolescence, Piaget's notion of formal operations (abstract thought and metacognition--i.e., thinking about thinking), Elkind's adolescent egocentrism, and Erikson's fifth stage, identity versus role confusion. Then present ways to avoid these problems, such as developing effective ways to cope rather than turning to drugs, learning about conflict management, working on ways to increase self-esteem, choosing friends wisely, etc. Be sure to discuss the factors (distal and proximal) associated with suicide, as well as what to do and what not to do if you suspect someone is likely to commit suicide.

2. To answer this question you will need to discuss Elkind's notion of adolescent egocentrism with its two components of the imaginary audience and the personal fable. Then present the strategies for improving an adolescent's life (e.g., developing more positive expectations), but also be sensitive to the guidelines for determining when an adolescent may need therapy for problem behaviors.

Research Project 1: Cross-Cultural Comparisons of Secondary Schools

The text presents a cross-cultural comparison of secondary schools. Using that information, as well as information you can gather from the Internet, library research, and/or interviews of students or educators from other countries, compare and contrast the following aspects of secondary schools around the world with the United States.

Country	Mandatory Age	No. of Levels	Entrance/ Exit Exams	Sports	Content & Philosophy	Foreign Languages
United States						

1. What similarities do you see between these countries and the United States? What differences?
2. What effect do you think the differences have on children's intellectual education? What effect do these differences have on social and/or behavioral outcomes?
3. Some educators believe that students in the United States should spend more time in school (i.e., the school year and/or school day should be longer so students in the United States can catch up with those in other countries academically). What do you think about this suggestion? Explain your rationale.

Research Project 2: Helping Youth Avoid Problem Behaviors

Consider all of the problem behaviors presented in this chapter. What do you believe are the antecedents of such behaviors? What are the consequences? What can be done to avoid each of these problem behaviors? What type of interventions would be useful?

Behavior	Antecedents	Consequences	Prevention/Interventions
Dropping out of School			
Drug Use/ Abuse			
Juvenile Delinquency			
Adolescent Pregnancy			
Suicide			
Eating Disorders			

On the basis of what you have learned about these problems, design a program that could be implemented in middle schools, junior high schools, and/or high schools to help confront and eliminate these problems. Meet with a local high school counselor and/or principal to discuss your ideas, then report your findings and your revised (or not revised) program to your class.

Also you can prepare a resource guide that can be distributed to teens and pre-teens to offer them help with various problems they may face. For example, there are many toll-free numbers for organizations, such as Covenant House (crisis intervention, referral, and information services for troubled teens and their families: 1-800-999-9999); Youth Crisis Hotline (counseling and referrals for teens in crisis: 1-800-448-4663); National Clearinghouse for Alcohol and Drug Information (alcohol and drug information and referrals: 1-800-729-6686); and National Runaway Switchboard (24-hour hot line for runaway and homeless youth and their families: 1-800-621-4000). Alcoholics Anonymous (AA), AlAnon, AlaTeen, and Narcotics Anonymous (NA) are all listed in local phone books, too. There are also Internet resources, such as: Mental Health Net (general guide to online mental health topics: www.cmhc.com); and National Clearinghouse for Alcohol and Drug Information: www.health.org.

Chapter 13 Socioemotional Development in Adolescence

Learning Objectives

1. Contrast the old model of parent-adolescent relationships with the new model of parent-adolescent relationships.

2. Explain how changes regarding biology, cognition, social relationships, and personality each could cause increased conflict between adolescents and parents.

3. Describe the developmental progression of peer pressure and conformity.

4. Describe how peer groups differ for children and adolescents.

5. Describe how peer groups are similar for children and adolescents.

6. Discuss the two ways peers can be used to improve social policy and adolescent development.

7. Explain how cross-cultural studies expand our knowledge about adolescence and guard against overgeneralizations.

8. Explain the idea that social class confounds ethnic explanations for adolescent development.

9. Define and distinguish between assimilation and pluralism.

10. Identify important considerations about the process of identity formation suggested by contemporary views of adolescence.

11. Define and distinguish among identity diffusion, identity foreclosure, identity moratorium, and identity achievement.

12. Discuss the role of individuality and connectedness in identity formation.

13. Describe cultural and ethnic aspects of identity development.

14. Describe the six stages of James Fowler's theory of religious development and indicate concerns about this theory.

Explain how the "old" and "new" models of parent-adolescent relationships describe autonomy and attachment in adolescence.

What purpose do dating scripts serve?

Describe the maturational changes of adolescents and their parents as the child proceeds through adolescence.

What is the purpose of cross-cultural studies?

What are the parental characteristics most likely to promote competent adolescent development?

What is the primary purpose of rites of passage? What is involved in rites of passage?

Explain how peer pressure in adolescence can have both positive and negative outcomes.

What role does ethnicity play in adolescent development?

What is the relationship between self-esteem and clique membership?

What is the Quantum Opportunities Program?

What is the progression of stages that Dunphy describes for peer group relations in adolescence?

Contrast assimilation with pluralism.

Dating scripts: the cognitive models that guide individuals' dating interactions Rose & Frieze (1993): males follow proactive script (e.g., initiating the date, controlling public domain, initiating sexual interaction); females are reactive (e.g., focus on private domain, respond to male-set structure/sexual overtures)

Old model of parent-adolescent relationships: as teens mature they detach from parents & become increasingly autonomous from them; the conflict between them is intense & stressful throughout adolescence; **New model**: parents are important attachment figures/support systems as teens explore the world; conflict is moderate & helps teen move to independence

Cross-cultural studies involve the comparison of a culture with one or more other cultures; they provide information about the degree to which development is similar, or universal, across cultures, or the degree to which it is culture-specific

Adolescent changes: puberty, expanded logical reasoning & increased idealistic & egocentric thought, violated expectations, changes in schooling, peers, friendships, & dating, movement toward independence
Parental changes: marital dissatisfaction, economic burdens, career reevaluation, time perspective, & health & body concerns

Rites of passage: ceremonies or rituals that mark an individual's transition from one status to another; the most interest in rites of passage focuses on the transition to adult status (some societies have elaborate ceremonies that signal the adolescent's move to maturity & achievement of adult status)

Parental characteristics likely to produce competent adolescents: display warmth & mutual respect; sustained interest in their lives; recognize/adapt to cognitive/socioemotional development; communicate expectations for high standards of conduct/achievement; display authoritative, constructive ways to deal with problems & conflict

Even middle-class ethnic minority youth may face prejudice/discrimination/bias associated with being a member of an ethnic minority; many ethnic minority adolescents also live in poverty & have a double disadvantage: prejudice/discrimination/bias from minority status & stressful effects of poverty

Conformity to peer pressure can be negative by encouraging inappropriate behaviors (e.g., stealing, vandalizing, making fun of parents & teachers); it can be positive by encouraging teens to engage in prosocial activities (e.g., clubs that raise money for worthy causes, cleaning up the beaches, mentoring younger children, etc.).

Quantum Opportunities Program: a 4-year, year-round mentoring effort; every day for 4 years, mentors provide sustained support, guidance, & concrete assistance to these students; students participate in academic activities outside school; community service projects; cultural/personal enrichment

Jocks (athletically oriented), **populars** (well-known students/lead social activities), & those not in cliques: highest self-esteem; **nobodies** (low in social skills/intellectual abilities): lowest self-esteem; self-esteem level not noted for **normals** (middle-of-the-road/masses) & **druggies or toughs** (drug users/delinquents)

Assimilation: the absorption of ethnic minority groups into the dominant group; this often means the loss of some or virtually all of the behavior & values of the ethnic minority group
Pluralism: the coexistence of distinct ethnic & cultural groups in the same society; cultural differences are maintained & appreciated

Dunphy's Stages: 1: precrowd, isolated, unisexual groups; 2: begin crowd, unisexual groups start group-group interaction; 3: crowd in structural transition, unisexual groups form heterosexual groups; 4: fully developed crowd, closely associated heterosexual groups; 5: crowd disintegration, loosely associated couples groups

Which of Erikson's eight stages of psychosocial development takes place during adolescence?	Which typess of parenting styles are likely to be related to which types of adolescent characteristics?
Contrast the concepts of crisis & commitment as used by James Marcia (1980, 1994).	Explain the two dimensions of individuality.
Explain Marcia's status of identity diffusion.	Explain the two dimensions of connectedness.
Explain Marcia's status of identity foreclosure.	What relationship did Phinney & Alipuria (1990) find between ethnic identity and self-esteem?
Explain Marcia's status of identity moratorium.	What strategies are suggested in the text for supporting adolescents' socioemotional development?
Explain Marcia's status of identity achievement.	What are Fowler's (1981) six stages of religious development?

Democratic parents encourage adolescents to participate in family decision making & foster identity achievement; ***authoritarian parents*** control the adolescent's behavior, do not allow opportunities to express opinions, & encourage identity foreclosure; ***permissive parents*** provide little guidance, allow adolescents to make their own decisions, & promote identity diffusion.

Erikson's 5ᵗʰ stage: identity achievement versus identity confusion; youth who successfully cope with conflicting identities (gap between security of childhood & autonomy of adulthood) develop a new, acceptable sense of self; those who don't either withdraw & isolate themselves or lose their identity in the crowd

Individuality consists of two dimensions: self-assertion, the ability to have and communicate a point of view; and separateness, the use of communication patterns to express how one is different from others.

Crisis: the period of identity development during which the adolescent is choosing among meaningful alternatives
Commitment: the part of identity development in which adolescents show a personal investment in what they are going to do

Connectedness consists of two dimensions: mutuality, sensitivity to and respect for others' views; and permeability, openness to others' views.

Identity diffusion: Marcia's term for the status of adolescents who have not yet experienced a crisis (i.e., they have not yet explored meaningful alternatives) or made any commitments; they are undecided about occupational & ideological choices, and are likely to show little interest in such matters

Phinney & Alipuria (1990): ethnic identity exploration was higher among ethnic minority than among White American college students; the ethnic minority students who had thought about & resolved issues involving their ethnicity had higher self-esteem than their ethnic minority counterparts who had not.

Identity foreclosure: Marcia's term for the status of adolescents who have made a commitment but have not experienced a crisis; usually occurs when parents hand down commitments to adolescents, often in an authoritarian manner so adolescents have not had adequate opportunities to explore different approaches, ideologies, & vocations on their own

Supporting adolescents' socioemotional development: understand the importance of autonomy & attachment; keep parent-adolescent conflict from being turbulent; use good communication skills; recognize importance of peers, youth organizations, & mentors; help adolescents understand diversity & value conflicts; let them explore their identity

Identity moratorium: Marcia's term for the status of adolescents who are in the midst of a crisis, but their commitments are either absent or only vaguely defined; these adolescents are still attempting to define their specific ideologies, vocations, etc.

Fowler's stages: 1: intuitive-projective faith (early childhood); 2: mythical-literal faith (middle & late childhood); 3: synthetic-conventional faith (childhood-adolescence transition, adolescence); 4: individuating-reflexive faith (transition between adolescence-adulthood, early adulthood); 5: conjunctive faith (middle adulthood); 6: universalizing faith (middle or late adulthood)

Identity achievement: Marcia's term for the status of adolescents who have undergone a crisis and have made a commitment; they are clear about their ideologies, vocations, etc.

Self-Test A: Multiple Choice

1. Parents who want their adolescents to make the smoothest transition into adulthood should:
   a. relinquish control in all areas and let the adolescent take over.
   b. maintain control in as many areas as possible for as long as possible.
   c. relinquish control in areas where the adolescent has shown competence and maintain control in those areas where the adolescent's knowledge is limited.
   d. maintain control of issues dealing with family and relinquish control for those issues having to do with peer relations.

2. Talia, a16-year-old, has a secure attachment with her parents; one might expect she will:
   a. have trouble breaking away from her parents to form relationships with age-peers.
   b. tend to be more dependent in her relationship with her best friend.
   c. have a lower sense of her self-worth.
   d. have a secure relationship with her spouse once she marries.

3. Conflicts between parents and adolescents are most likely to revolve around all of the following *except*:
   a. keeping bedrooms clean.
   b. getting home on time.
   c. taking drugs.
   d. talking on the phone.

4. Which of the following best characterizes the new model of parent-adolescent relationships?
   a. As adolescents mature, they detach themselves from parents and move into a world of autonomy apart from parents.
   b. Parent-adolescent conflict is intense and stressful throughout adolescence.
   c. Everyday negotiations and minor disputes between parents and adolescents have a harmful effect on developmental functions.
   d. Serious, highly stressful parent-adolescent conflict is associated with juvenile delinquency, school dropout, pregnancy, and drug abuse.

5. As adolescents mature, so, too, do their parents. Which of the following *has not been* noted as a parental change that takes place as adolescents are maturing?
   a. lower levels of religious affiliation
   b. increased marital dissatisfaction
   c. greater economic burdens
   d. more concern about health and body

6. Competent adolescent development is most likely to happen when adolescents have parents who:
   a. display authoritative ways of dealing with problems and conflict.
   b. display authoritarian ways of dealing with problems and conflict.
   c. insist that their adolescents learn to resolve problems and conflict on their own.
   d. develop more flexible boundaries and learn to become friends with their children.

7. Which of the following children is most likely to conform to peer pressure to engage in antisocial acts such as shoplifting or drawing graffiti?
   a. Andrew, who is in seventh grade
   b. Brandon, who is in ninth grade
   c. Charles, who is a high school sophomore
   d. Dale, who is a high school senior

8. Compared to children's cliques, adolescents' cliques are more likely to:
   a. be made up of many types of individuals.
   b. have both male and female members.
   c. contain individuals who are not friends.
   d. be smaller.

9. A study of clique membership by Brown and Lohr (1987) revealed that the individuals with the lowest self-esteem were the:
   a. jocks.
   b. populars.
   c. druggies.
   d. nobodies.

10. Which of the following school groups appears to enjoy the highest self-esteem?
    a. normals
    b. druggies
    c. brains
    d. independents

11. Children's groups differ from those formed by adolescents in that they:
    a. are more informal.
    b. rely more on the leaders of the groups.
    c. have more interests in common.
    d. include a greater diversity of individuals.

12. Researchers have found that adolescents who join youth organizations are likely to experience all of the following **except**:
    a. have higher self-esteem.
    b. be better educated.
    c. practice skills important for adult success.
    d. develop counseling and mentoring skills.

13. Which of the following is most likely to reduce the onset of smoking in adolescence?
    a. peer-led programs on smoking
    b. fear-inducing ad campaigns
    c. programs on smoking led by high school counselors
    d. informational pamphlets sent home to parents requesting they discuss smoking with their adolescents

14. Sandra, a junior in high school, has become a peer-tutor. She has gone through the necessary training and has been tutoring Nelson, a tenth-grader who is having trouble with his math. From what you have learned about peer-tutoring, you might expect that:
    a. Nelson would be more likely to improve his math skills working with a professional tutor.
    b. Nelson would be more likely to improve his math skills if his math teacher gave him extra assignments to complete after school.
    c. Nelson is unlikely to improve his math skills because it's difficult to learn from someone who is close to your own age.
    d. while Nelson is likely to improve his math skills, Sandra will benefit from the experience as well.

15. Feiring's (1996) study of 15-year-olds' romantic relationships found that:
    a. over half of the respondents were currently involved in a steady relationship.
    b. at least 25% of the respondents had had relationships that lasted a year or longer.
    c. although the length of a relationship may have been brief, contact was very frequent.
    d. tenth-graders experienced less conflict in their relationships than did twelfth-graders.

16. John and Mary, juniors in high school, have been dating for the past two months and are in love with each other. According to research by Rose and Frieze (1993), which of the following is **least likely** to occur?
    a. John calls Mary to ask her out, she accepts.
    b. John invites Mary out to dinner, and she drives to the restaurant.
    c. John asks Mary what she would like to eat and she says, "Why don't you order for me?"
    d. John kisses Mary goodnight and she responds accordingly.

17. Which of the following best reflects societal attitudes toward sex in adolescence?
    a. Over the past century, attitudes toward sexuality for females have become more permissive in the United States.
    b. The Mangaian culture in the South Sea Islands has more restrictive attitudes toward adolescent sexuality than the United States.
    c. The Ines Beag culture off the coast of Ireland has more permissive attitudes toward adolescent sexuality than the United States.
    d. With only a few exceptions (i.e., cultures that are either extremely permissive or extremely conservative), attitudes toward adolescent sexuality are relatively universal.

18. A ceremony that marks an individual's transition from one status to another (such as adolescence to adulthood) is called a:
    a. rite of passage.
    b. transitory stage.
    c. period of transition.
    d. ritualistic transition.

19. Rituals that provide a forceful and discontinuous entry into the adult world, forging a bond between the individual and his or her instructors, typically take place:
    a. by the end of childhood to ensure commitment.
    b. early in adolescence.
    c. late in adolescence.
    d. when the adolescent is perceived to be ready for the change.

20. Which of the following is true regarding the rite of passage from adolescence to adulthood in American culture?
    a. There are many points of transition to adulthood in American culture.
    b. There is an abrupt entry into adulthood in American culture.
    c. The end of adolescence in American culture is more clearly marked by biological change than by social milestones.
    d. No specific event marks the end of adolescence in American culture.

21. One of the major limitations of studies on the effects of ethnicity is that the factor of _____ may play a larger causal role than ethnic heritage, but it is difficult to tease the two variables apart.
    a. race
    b. innate physical variation
    c. social class
    d. language

22. Which of the following would best fit the term "model minority"?
    a. Carlos, who is Mexican
    b. Mitsuyo, who is Japanese
    c. Marinella, who is Italian
    d. Sandrine, who is French

23. If a government decided to incorporate a new ethnic-minority group through assimilation, one of the first laws passed might be to:
    a. require that several museums dedicated to that culture be set up in major cities.
    b. make racially motivated crimes punishable by death.
    c. ban use of that minority's language in schools.
    d. select at least one of the minority group's celebrations and make it a national holiday.

24. Which would you likely find in a country driven by ethnic pluralism?
    a. high schools being required to teach courses in the history of minority cultures
    b. tremendous internal racism
    c. great consensus on what the "average" person within that country is like
    d. virtually no foreign characters on prime-time television shows

25. Stanley Sue (1990) suggests we resolve value conflicts about sociocultural issues if we:
    a. restrict immigration for a period of time.
    b. design a national referendum to determine what the majority of individuals within a culture believe is appropriate.
    c. eliminate all culturally specific institutions.
    d. conceptualize or redefine them in innovative ways.

26. Henry Gaskins (1983) has designed an effective minority program based on:
    a. one-on-one tutoring with adult and peer volunteers.
    b. emphasizing the importance of being proud of one's ethnic heritage.
    c. the principles of Head Start.
    d. pairing troubled minority youths with high-functioning White youths during an intensive summer camp experience.

27. The adolescent identity crisis refers to a period:
    a. of confusion during which youth are choosing between attachment and autonomy.
    b. when adolescents are actively making decisions about who they want to be.
    c. when adolescents actively avoid commitment to ideas or occupations.
    d. of intense turmoil and stress that lasts a short time and determines an adolescent's identity status.

28. When Erikson said "[It] is never established in the form of a personality armor, or anything static and unchangeable," he was describing:
    a. psychological moratorium.
    b. the nature of identity.
    c. the nature of crisis.
    d. the influence of culture on identity.

29. According to Erikson, the individual who is caught between the security of childhood and the autonomy of adulthood is in:
a. adolescence.
b. a diffused state.
c. psychological moratorium.
d. early adulthood.

30. The term that James Marcia (1966, 1991) uses to refer to the amount of personal investment a person has about an idea or issue is:
a. value.
b. desire.
c. commitment.
d. involvement.

31. Asked whether they ever had doubts about their religion, four students gave the following answers. Which of these students has arrived at identity achievement?
a. Kristin: "Oh, I don't know. It really doesn't bother me. I figure one's about as good as another."
b. Joe: "No, not really. Our family is pretty much in agreement about these things."
c. Alicia: "Yes, I guess I'm going through that right now. How can there be a god with so much evil in the world?"
d. Phil: "Yeah, I even started wondering if God existed. I've pretty much resolved that, though."

32. A high school student who has explored all potential employment and educational options and has chosen to attend the state college near home is experiencing identity:
a. achievement.
b. moratorium.
c. foreclosure.
d. diffusion.

33. Authoritarian parents are most likely to have adolescents experiencing identity:
a. achievement.
b. moratorium.
c. foreclosure.
d. diffusion.

34. Jessica's parents have never "forced" their opinions on her, and have always allowed her to try anything she wanted to because they did not want to put any limits on her development. Based on the research, we would expect Jessica to experience identity:
a. achievement.
b. moratorium.
c. foreclosure.
d. diffusion.

35. Another way of stating Cooper and Grotevant's point about the need for connectedness and individuation in adolescent identity development is that identity development requires:
a. separation and conflict.
b. obedience and self-regulation.
c. family and peer relations.
d. attachment and autonomy.

36. Which statement best reflects Erik Erikson's (1968) belief about the relationship between culture and identity development?
a. Culture plays a critical role in identity development.
b. In some individuals, cultural factors may play a role in identity development.
c. For all individuals, cultural factors play a minor role in identity development.
d. Cultural factors have no influence on identity development.

37. Most ethnic minorities first consciously confront their ethnicity in:
a. early childhood.
b. middle childhood.
c. adolescence.
d. young adulthood.

38. What relationship did Phinney and Alipuria (1990) find between ethnic identity and self-esteem for ethnic minority college students?
   a. Those who had thought about and resolved issues involving their ethnicity had lower self-esteem than their counterparts who had not.
   b. Those who had thought about and resolved issues involving their ethnicity had higher self-esteem than their counterparts who had not.
   c. There were no differences in self-esteem between those who had thought about and resolved issues involving their ethnicity and their counterparts who had not.
   d. They found no relationship between ethnic identity an self-esteem.

39. Gilligan (1990), investigating gender and identity development, has found:
   a. relationships and emotional bonds are more important concerns of females, while autonomy and achievement are more important concerns of males.
   b. relationships and emotional bonds are more important concerns of males, while autonomy and achievement are more important concerns of females.
   c. the differences in focus toward relationships and autonomy that were noted by Erikson are now so minimal that they barely exist today.
   d. because of the women's liberation movement, males and females are now both focusing more on relationships and emotional bonds.

40. Eighteen-year-old Jeremiah's belief in God is consistent with what he has been taught by his parents and in religious school. He just heard someone robbed a store owned by family friends, and believes this person should be punished both in Heaven and on Earth for the harm he has done. Jeremiah is probably in which of Fowler's stages of religious development?
   a. mythical-literal faith
   b. synthetic-conventional faith
   c. individuating-reflexive faith
   d. conjunctive faith

41. A technique that is currently being used around the country, for example, by the Valued Youth Program, to improve adolescents' feelings about themselves and their education is to:
   a. involve them in sports.
   b. have them tutor younger children.
   c. have them tutored by adult volunteers.
   d. give them additional remedial training.

Self-Test B: Matching

Match the individuals in the left column with the appropriate descriptors in the right column.

b 1. Stanley Sue   a. developed an effective minority program based on volunteer tutors
e 2. James Marcia   b. contends that value conflicts often occur in response to ethnic issues
a 3. Henry Gaskins   c. developed the idea of an identity crisis during adolescence
c 4. Erik Erikson   d. developed a model of the progression of peer group relations in adolescence
f 5. James Fowler   e. further developed Erikson's identity crisis into four identity statuses
d 6. Dexter Dunphy   f. proposed a theory of religious development focused on the motivation to discover meaning in life

Self-Test C: Matching Fowler's Stages of Religious Development

Match the stages of religious development in the left column with the appropriate descriptors in the right column.

C 1. intuitive-projective faith   a. being open to paradox & opposing viewpoints

f 2. mythical-literal faith   b. accepting full responsibility for one's religious beliefs

e 3. synthetic-conventional faith   c. inventing one's own intuitive images of good & evil

b 4. individuating-reflexive faith   d. transcending specific belief systems; achieving oneness with all being

a 5. conjunctive faith   e. integration of beliefs; abstract but conforming to views of others

d 6. universalizing faith   f. literal interpretations; God is seen as a parent figure; good people are rewarded, the bad are punished

Self-Test D: Matching Dunphy's Progression of Peer Group Relations

Match the stages in the left column with the appropriate descriptors in the right column.

C 1. Stage 1   a. beginning of the crowd; unisexual groups start group-group interaction

a 2. Stage 2   b. beginning of crowd disintegration; loosely associated groups of couples

e 3. Stage 3   c. precrowd; isolated, unisexual groups

d 4. Stage 4   d. fully developed crowd; heterosexual groups are closely associated

b 5. Stage 5   e. crowd is in structural transition; unisexual groups are forming heterosexual groups

Essay Questions:

1. You are giving a talk to a group of parents about adolescent development. One of the mothers asks you, "What do you do if your teenager is going to parties where alcohol is served and you know your teen is drinking? I know that if I tell him he can't go, he'll go anyway."[1] How would you respond to her question?

2. The principal and school counselor of your former high school have asked for your advice on dealing with issues of diversity they are facing at school. The diversity is being noticed in terms of the cliques that are forming, as well as racial and ethnic conflict that seems to be a growing problem. What advice could you give them?

---

[1]Special thanks to Danielle Williams, one of my Introductory Psychology students at DeVry/Pomona, for posing this intriguing question.

Key to Self Test A:

1.	c p. 360	22.	b p. 369	
2.	d p. 360	23.	c p. 370	
3.	c p. 361	24.	a p. 370	
4.	d p. 361	25.	d p. 370	
5	a p. 362	26.	a p. 371	
6.	a p. 362	27.	b p. 372	
7.	b p. 363	28.	b p. 372	
8.	b p. 364	29.	c p. 372	
9.	d p. 363	30.	c p. 372	
10.	d p. 363	31.	d p. 372-373	
11.	a p. 364	32.	a p. 372-373	
12.	d p. 364	33.	c p. 373	
13.	a p. 364	34.	d p. 373	
14.	d p. 365	35.	d p. 373	
15.	c p. 366	36.	a p. 373	
16.	b p. 366	37.	c p. 374	
17.	a p. 367	38.	b p. 374	
18.	a p. 368	39.	a p. 375	
19.	d p. 368	40.	a p. 374	
20.	d p. 368	41.	b p. 379	
21.	c p. 368			

Key to Self Test B:

1. b
2. e
3. a
4. c
5. f
6. d

Key to Self Test C:

1. c
2. f
3. e
4. b
5. a
6. d

Key to Self Test D:

1. c
2. a
3. e
4. d
5. b

Key to Essay Questions:

1. Included in your answer should be a discussion of Erikson's and Marcia's ideas about the identity crisis and the different statuses an adolescent may be in with respect to different areas of her or his life; also critically important to this are Elkind's notion of adolescent egocentrism discussed in Chapter 12, and the extension of Baumrind's work on parenting styles, noting that adolescents whose parents use an authoritative parenting style are more socially competent, socially responsible, and cognitively competent than adolescents whose parents use other parenting styles (the authoritative parenting style encourages children to make choices and understand the consequences of their choices, an important issue in terms of engaging in potentially harmful activities). Also, throughout Chapter 13 the author has interspersed information about various activities (e.g., peer-tutoring) that have been effective for increasing adolescents' self-esteem and keeping them engaged in prosocial activities. You might note, however, that some behaviors (such as drinking alcohol) may be both illegal and detrimental, but they are not outside the norm in terms of exploring the adolescent's identity.

2. Explore with them the notions of ethnicity and social class to understand whether they are dealing with one or both of these issues, so they know how to proceed. It is important to discuss the stigmas associated with minority status, as well as the cultural differences (e.g., different customs and different values) that may or may not exist, including parenting practices and how they affect the adolescents' behavior. Note Stanley Sue's contention that value conflicts are often involved when individuals respond to ethnic issues, thus it would be important to teach the students to conceptualize or redefine these conflicts in innovative ways. Also important here is the work (for example, by Phinney & Alipuria) where those students who had explored their ethnic identity had higher self-esteem. Based on the research, make your suggestions for ways to reduce the conflict that is becoming a problem as "requested" by your former principal and high school counselor.

Research Project 1: Peer-Tutoring

In several places throughout this chapter the author discusses various prosocial activities such as peer-tutoring and mentoring. Organize your classmates into a peer-tutoring group. Decide which topics each of you will tutor, then approach the appropriate person at your college (e.g., dean of students, learning resources center, etc.) or at local high schools (e.g., principal, counselor, etc.) and offer your services. Before beginning the tutoring it is helpful to get assistance on effective ways to teach both your peers and younger students; also, at the beginning of this project, chart each group member's grades to use for comparison purposes after you have begun tutoring. Keep track of grades (e.g., midterms and papers throughout the semester or, if you continue to tutor throughout your college career, each term) to see if they are going up. For most of you they probably will. Also, see which grades in particular are getting better--are they related to the topics you are teaching to someone else? Is this consistent with what you have learned about peer tutoring? Explain.

Tutor (Name)		
Course	Grade	Grade Point Average
Introductory Psychology		
Life-Span Development		

Research Project 2: Exploring Your Identity

Note the author's "Adventures for the Mind" concerning "Exploring Your Identity." Note that he asks you to think about the experiences you have had so far as a college student. "What experiences have stimulated you to think about your identity? Have your classmates, friends, or instructors challenged your view of yourself?" He suggests that you do not reject someone else's views just because they differ from yours. "Think about the ideas. Massage them. Bounce your own thoughts and feelings off others. Don't be afraid of criticism." He also suggests that you "Think about your identity in many domains of your life: career, religious, achievement, intellectual, political, sexual, gender, lifestyle, and ethnic/ cultural. What is your identity status in these different areas--diffused, foreclosed, moratorium, or achieved? If it is diffused or foreclosed, take some time to think about what you need to do to move into a moratorium or achieved status in those areas." Use the chart below to explore your identity status in each of the areas mentioned, explaining how you determined you are in that status; then state how you might move to moratorium or achieved status if you are not there.

Area	Status	Explanation	Plan for Changing Status
Career			
Religious			
Achievement			
Intellectual			
Political			
Sexual			
Gender			
Lifestyle			
Ethnic/Cultural			

1. As you look over the chart, are you in different statuses for different areas of your life? What does this tell you about yourself? What does it tell you about how Erikson's and Marcia's theories fit into adolescent development?
2. Santrock suggests that you work on moving from diffused or foreclosed to moratorium or identity achieved. Do you believe this is appropriate for you? Is there some reason why it may be more appropriate for you to be in any particular status at this point in your life? Explain your reasons.

Section VII Early Adulthood

Chapter 14 Physical and Cognitive Development in Early Adulthood

Learning Objectives

1. Describe and give examples of the criteria for adulthood.

2. Indicate when adulthood functioning is at its peak and how health habits help determine development.

3. Describe how nutrition and exercise affect physical and psychological well-being in early adulthood.

4. Compare homosexual and heterosexual sexual attitudes and behaviors.

5. Explain how reactions to sexual issues such as AIDS, hormonal fluctuations, and rape influence sexual attitudes and behavior.

6. Discuss what is known about forcible sexual behavior and sexual harassment.

7. Discuss Schaie's cognitive stages.

8. Understand the theories that help to explain career choices.

9. Explain the life contour of work in adulthood. In addition, pay attention to the research on women and work.

Differentiate between
youth and
adulthood.

Explain the importance of
aerobic exercise for health

What "markers" are noted
in the text that
signify entry into adulthood?

What is a
psychoactive drug?

What problems have been
associated
with binge drinking
among college students?

Explain the term
tolerance with respect
to drug use.

Explain the relation of
"set point" to
weight.

Contrast physical dependence
with psychological dependence
in terms of drug use.

Explain what relationship
basal metabolism rate
(BMR) has with weight.

Describe how alcohol
acts on the body.

How effective is dieting
for losing weight?

Explain what it is to be
bisexual.

Aerobic exercise: sustained exercise (e.g., jogging, swimming, cycling) that stimulates heart & lung activity

Youth: sociologist Kenneth Kenniston's term for the transitional period between adolescence & adulthood that is a time of extended economic & personal temporariness

Psychoactive drug: any drug that acts on the nervous system to alter states of consciousness, modify perceptions, and change moods

The most widely recognized **marker of entry into adulthood** is when an individual first takes a more or less permanent, full-time job (Scheer & Unger, 1994); a second study (Arnette, 1995) found accepting responsibility for the consequences of one's actions, deciding on one's own beliefs & values, & establishing a relationship with parents as an equal adult

Tolerance: as a person continues to take a psychoactive drug, a greater amount of the drug is needed to produce the same effect

Problems associated with binge drinking for college students include: missing classes, physical injuries, troubles with policy, & having unprotected sex

Physical dependence: the physical need for a drug that is accompanied by unpleasant withdrawal symptoms when the drug is discontinued
Psychological dependence: the subjective feeling of craving & perceived need for a drug

Set point: the weight maintained when no effort is made to gain or lose weight; when people gain weight, the number of fat cells increases & they might not be able to get rid of them

Alcohol acts on the body primarily as a depressant & slows down the brain's activities; the areas in the brain involved in controlling inhibition & judgment slow down; with increased drinking, judgments, skill, & intellectual functioning become increasingly impaired, the drinker becomes drowsy/falls asleep; extreme intoxication may lead to coma & death

Basal metabolism rate (BMR): the amount of energy an individual uses in a resting state; BMR varies with age & sex; weight gain with age may, to some degree, be due to declining BMR, underscoring the importance of reducing food intake as we grow older if we want to maintain our weight

Bisexual: being sexually attracted to people of both sexes (Kinsey et al. [1948] found about 1% of the population to be bisexual)
Sexual orientation is currently viewed along a continuum from exclusive heterosexuality to exclusive homosexuality, rather than as an either/or proposition.

While some individuals lose weight and maintain the loss when they **diet**, how often this occurs & whether some programs are better at achieving weight loss are open questions.

What factors are
considered to determine
an individual's sexual orientation?

Describe Schaie's
executive and reintegrative stages.

How does psychologist
Laura Brown (1989) describe
the way gays & lesbians
experience life?
How do they adapt?

What is Eli Ginzberg's
developmental theory
of career choice?

What are STDs and AIDS?
In what ways can AIDS
be transmitted?

Explain Donald Super's
career self-concept theory.

How can you reduce the likelihood
that you will contract
an STD?

What is John Holland's
personality type theory?
What are the six personality
types?

Define the term "rape."
What is date or acquaintance rape?

What do employers typically look
for to determine
whether a candidate
has the skills to succeed
at a job?

Describe K. Warner Schaie's
achieving and responsibility stages.

What are the four stages of
the occupational cycle?

Executive stage: middle adulthood; people are responsible for societal systems/organizations (e.g., government); the individual develops an understanding of how societal organizations work & the complex relationships that are involved
Reintegrative stage: involves older adults' choosing to focus their energy on tasks & activities that have meaning for them

Factors most likely to determine sexual orientation: a combination of genetic, hormonal, cognitive, and environmental factors

Developmental theory of career choice: Eli Ginzberg's view that individuals go through three career choice stages: fantasy (childhood), tentative (early adolescence), & realistic (from about 17 or 18 through early 20s)

Laura Brown (1989): gays & lesbians experience life as a minority in a dominant, majority culture; developing a **bicultural identity** creates new ways of defining themselves

Career self-concept theory: Donald Super's view that the individual's self-concept plays a central role in career choice; a number of developmental changes in vocational self-concept take place during the adolescent & young adulthood years (from crystallization to specification to implementation to stabilization to consolidation)

STDs: sexually transmitted diseases
AIDS: acquired immuno deficiency syndrome, a sexually transmitted disease caused by the human immuno deficiency virus (HIV), which destroys the body's immune system; AIDS can be transmitted by sexual contact, sharing needles, contaminated blood transfusions, & contact with infected blood, semen, vaginal fluids

Personality type theory: John Holland's view that it is important to develop a match or fit between an individual's personality type & the selection of a particular career
Realistic, investigative, artistic, social, enterprising, & conventional

The likelihood of contracting an STD can be reduced by: assessing your & your partner's risk status; obtaining prior medical examinations; using condoms; not having sex with multiple partners

To determine whether a candidate has the skills to succeed at the job, employers look for evidence in the candidate's accomplsihments & experiences including: leadership positions, involvement in campus organizations & extracurricular activities, relevant experience in internships, part-time work, or co-ops, good grades, & communication skills

Rape: forcible sexual intercouse with a person who does not give consent (exact legal definitions vary from state to state)
Date/acquaintance rape: coercive sexual activity directed at someone with whom the perpetrator is at least casually acquainted

Stages of the occupational cycle: selection & entry, adjustment, maintenance, & retirement

Achieving stage: Schaie's early adulthood stage that involves application of intelligenc to situations that have profound consequences for achieving long-term goals, such as those involving careers & knowledge
Responsibility stage: occurs when a family is established & attention is given to the needs of a spouse & offspring

Self-Test A: Multiple Choice

1. According to Kenneth Kenniston, which of the following questions *is least likely* to be asked by young adults?
   a. How do I relate to society?
   b. What should my vocation be?
   c. How do I define myself?
   d. What lifestyle should I choose?

2. In what way does the move from high school to college differ from the move from elementary school to junior high school?
   a. Junior high school students experience the top-dog phenomenon, but college freshmen do not.
   b. College freshmen experience increased achievement pressure, but junior high school students do not.
   c. College freshmen have opportunities to explore lifestyles, but junior high school students do not.
   d. Junior high school students are challenged by academic work, but college freshmen are not.

3. In comparison to their counterparts in the 1980s, college students today indicate that they feel:
   a. more excited about their opportunities.
   b. more depressed.
   c. a lack of preparation for college.
   d. more prepared for college.

4. Peak physical performance is reached:
   a. in early adolescence.
   b. in late adolescence.
   c. in early adulthood.
   d. at different times, depending on the type of activity.

5. How well do college students use their knowledge about health?
   a. They are well informed and a majority use the information to live healthy lifestyles.
   b. Surveys indicate that most of them are aware of what it takes to be healthy and almost 50% practice what they know.
   c. Those who are well-informed also tend to practice what they know.
   d. Although most of them know what it takes to be healthy, most don't apply it.

6. Now in her middle twenties, Harriet exercises rarely, skips breakfast to get to work early, and parties hard on weekends to compensate for the long hours of hard work she must put in to support her ambitious career plans. Late in life, when she has achieved success and retired, Harriet will be:
   a. relatively healthy, because in her youth peak resources protected her against the stress she experienced.
   b. in satisfactory health, because her stressful living makes up for early success.
   c. vigorous, because she has trained herself for the demands of a successful career.
   d. relatively less healthy and dissatisfied with her life.

7. Which of the following is most accurate concerning the behavior of individuals in their twenties?
   a. College students drink more than youths who end their education after high school.
   b. College students smoke more than youths who end their education after high school.
   c. Married individuals are more likely than singles to smoke marijuana.
   d. Individuals who become engaged tend to show an increase in their alcohol consumption.

8. Which of the following might be expected to occur when an individual reaches age 30?
   a. greater muscle tone and strength
   b. radical changes in the sensory systems
   c. sagging chins and protruding abdomens
   d. decrease in the body's fatty tissues

9. With increasing age, basal metabolism rate:
   a. increases steadily.
   b. reaches a peak and levels off.
   c. declines steadily.
   d. does not change.

10. All of the following are environmental influences on body weight *except*:
    a. basal metabolism rate.
    b. declining physical activity.
    c. energy saving devices.
    d. greater availability of food.

11. The main focus of research on the effects of exercise on health has involved:
    a. reducing weight.
    b. preventing cancer.
    c. staying young.
    d. preventing heart disease.

12. At age 30 you find you are a successful, hardworking executive, but you are also slightly overweight and have increasing difficulty coping with the tension in your life. What can you do to help with both problems and possibly improve your job performance?
    a. lose weight
    b. start a program of weight lifting and stretching exercises
    c. begin walking or jogging at a moderate pace three to five times a week
    d. push yourself to jog fast three to five times a week

13. Experts recommend that American adults engage in at least _____ minutes of exercise or more on a _____ basis.
    a. 15; daily
    b. 30; daily
    c. 30; every other day
    d. 60; weekly

14. Which of the following *is not* a criterion for a psychoactive drug?
    a. acts on the nervous system to create an altered state of consciousness
    b. modifies perceptions
    c. is physically addicting
    d. changes mood

15. Which individual provides the best example of a drug-related psychological dependence?
    a. Charles uses drugs because he can't cope with everyday stressors without them.
    b. Benjamin uses drugs because when he stops he becomes ill.
    c. Margaret has decided she needs to start taking drugs to make her feel better.
    d. Francis is concerned because his wife is addicted to painkillers and her behavior is threatening to destroy their family.

16. Alcohol is a:
    a. stimulant.
    b. depressant.
    c. hallucinogen.
    d. antipsychotic agent.

17. Who would most likely have a philosophical disagreement with the approach emphasized by Alcoholics Anonymous?
    a. Artie, who is poor
    b. Dan, who is an atheist
    c. Goldie, who is a strong feminist
    d. Dick, who believes in the power of abstinence

18. A study of sexual activity by Michael et al. (1994) found all of the following *except*:
    a. married couples have sex more than single people.
    b. the favorite sexual act was oral sex.
    c. adultery is clearly the exception rather than the rule.
    d. men think about sex far more than women do.

19. Which statement concerning homosexuality *is false*?
    a. The increase in homosexual behavior increases in individuals denied access to the opposite sex.
    b. An early, positive homosexual relationship will generally predict that a homosexual preference will remain for life.
    c. The percentage of the population practicing exclusively homosexual behavior has remained constant during most of this century.
    d. Male homosexuals tend to be more sexually active than lesbians.

20. AIDS cannot be transmitted by:
    a. intimate sexual contact.
    b. sharing needles.
    c. blood transfusions.
    d. contact with urine.

21. You cannot contract AIDS from:
    a. a kiss.
    b. heterosexual intercourse.
    c. contact with AIDS-infected blood.
    d. oral sex.

22. Which of the following *is not* a characteristic of rapists?
    a. They use aggression to enhance their sense of power.
    b. They have an abnormal need for sexual pleasure.
    c. They are generally angry at women
    d. they want to hurt their victims

-170-

23. Which of the following *is true* concerning rape?
    a. A man cannot rape his wife.
    b. Rape is a traumatic experience for the victim and those close to her.
    c. Men cannot be raped.
    d. Many women actually want to be raped.

24. Sexual harassment is:
    a. a manifestation of power and domination of one person over another.
    b. always so blatant that it is hard to miss.
    c. becoming less prevalent because of awareness.
    d. less prevalent than the media would have us believe.

25. Gisela Labouvie-Vief believes that, when compared to those in adolescence, thought processes of individuals in early adulthood are more:
    a. pragmatic.
    b. logical.
    c. idealistic.
    d. optimistic.

26. Introductory psychology students often complain, "Why do we have to learn all of these theories? Why don't you just teach us the right one?" According to William Perry, this complaint reflects _____ thinking.
    a. dualistic
    b. multiple
    c. relative subordinate
    d. full relativistic

27. Jan Sinnott believes that advances in cognitive development occur during the adult years:
    a. only if the adult achieved a sense of identity in adolescence.
    b. as adults become more relativistic in their thinking.
    c. as a consequence of facing the multiple realities of work and intimate relationships.
    d. as the adult becomes more efficient in processing new information.

28. Dr. Lopez, a new psychology professor in the university's graduate program, has established a research program and is comfortable with her teaching responsibilities. Now she is concentrating on helping her advisees and training her graduate students. Dr. Lopez is in which of Schaie's stages?
    a. achieving
    b. responsibility
    c. executive
    d. reintegration

29. The first two stages of work in adulthood, selection/entry and adjustment, appear to require Schaie's stage of cognitive development called:
    a. achieving.
    b. responsibility.
    c. executive.
    d. reintegration.

30. Which of the following disciplines shows the earliest decline in productivity?
    a. art
    b. humanities
    c. social science
    d. business

31. When children say they want to grow up to be a doctor, they are in Eli Ginzberg's ____ stage of career choice.
    a. tentative
    b. fantasy
    c. realistic
    d. imaginative

32. Matt is in his last year of college and is now doing a teaching internship. He is also preparing letters for fourth-grade teaching positions. Matt is in Donald Super's vocational phase called:
    a. crystallization.
    b. specification.
    c. implementation.
    d. stabilization.

33. According to John Holland, the person with a conventional personality is most likely to be:
    a. a bank teller.
    b. an artist.
    c. a social worker.
    d. a carpenter.

34. The subtle barrier that is virtually transparent, yet is so strong it prevents females from moving up in the management hierarchy, is called the:
   a. glass ceiling.
   b. pink curtain.
   c. lace curtain.
   d. masculine barrier.

35. Advantages of dual-career marriages include all of the following *except*:
   a. financial benefits.
   b. increased self-esteem for men.
   c. a more equal relationship between men and women.
   d. more commitment to work by women.

36. Faye Crosby (1991) has described the "jugglers," women who have multiple roles of career, home, and family. She has concluded that:
   a. the high stress levels will undoubtedly create major problems in at least one of the "juggled" areas.
   b. women with multiple roles provide a chance to fashion social worlds that promote healthy communities, families, and individuals.
   c. while juggling may be beneficial for communities, it is a hardship on families and the individual.
   d. working from home will allow women to handle multiple roles more easily.

Self-Test B: Matching

Match the individuals in the left column with the appropriate descriptors in the right column.

k 1. Kenneth Kenniston
f 2. Alfred Kinsey
i 3. Robert Michael
b 4. William Perry
a 5. John Holland
d 6. K. Warner Schaie
e 7. Donald Super
j 8. Eli Ginzberg
g 9. Laura Brown
c 10. Jan Sinott
h 11. Faye Crosby

a. proposed the personality type theory of career development
b. believes how we view the world evolves from dualistic to fully relativistic
c. cognitive advances develop through facing work/relationship realities
d. how adults use intellect, not how they acquire information, progresses
e. believes that self-concept plays a central role in career choice
f. sex researcher whose studies caused a scandal in the 1940s and 1950s
g. gays & lesbians experience life as a minority in a dominant, majority culture
h. described the advantages of multiple roles ("juggling") for women
i. primary investigator who surveyed American sexual patterns in 1994
j. adults go through three career choice stages: fantasy, tentative, & realistic
k. sociologist whose term "youth" refers to transition from adolescence to adulthood

Self-Test C: Matching Cognitive Stages

Match the cognitive stages in the left column with some of their descriptions in the right column.

h 1. dualistic thinking
a 2. multiple thinking
b 3. relative subordinate thinking
f 4. full relativism
c 5. achieving stage
g 6. responsibility stage
e 7. executive stage
d 8. reintegrative stage

a. individuals understand that authorities may not have all the answers
b. an analytical, evaluative approach to knowledge is consciously & actively pursued
c. apply intelligence to situations with consequences for long-term goals
d. persons choose to focus energy on activities that have meaning for them
e. people are responsible for societal systems & organizations
f. truth is relative; meaning is related to context & knower's framework
g. occurs when family is established; attention given to family's needs
h. the world is viewed in terms of polarities, e.g., right/wrong, good/bad

Sample Test D: Matching Holland's Personality Type with Careers

Match the personality type in the left column with the careers in the right column.

c 1. realistic   a.   bank tellers, secretaries, file clerks
f 2. investigative   b.   teaching, social work, counseling
e 3. artistic   c.   farming, truck driving, construction
b 4. social   d.   sales, management, politics
d 5. enterprising   e.   sculptors, photographers
a 6. conventional   f.   scientist, researcher

Essay Questions:

1. Imagine that you have been offered the position of a career counselor at your college, but have been told that you may also need to offer advice to young adults about other life choices in areas such as sexuality and drug use. What specific things will you need to know so you can help these students?

2. You have been asked to talk to a group of college students about sex. While you know many have probably been sexually active, you are advised that since you are their peer, they may be more open and honest with you in what they say and the questions they ask. You need to be prepared to discuss the whole range of topics including sexual orientation, physiological changes, sexually transmitted diseases and ways to prevent them, sexual harassment, and rape. What can you say about each of these topics?

Key to Self Test A:

1.	c p. 387	19.	b p. 394-395
2.	c p. 388	20.	d p. 396
3.	b p. 388	21.	a p. 396
4.	c p. 388	22.	b p. 397
5.	d p. 389	23.	b p. 397
6.	d p. 389	24.	a p. 398
7.	a p. 389	25.	a p. 399
8.	c p. 390	26.	a p. 399
9.	c p. 391	27.	c p. 399
10.	a p. 391	28.	b p. 399
11.	d p. 391	29.	a p. 399
12.	c p. 392	30.	c p. 400
13.	b p. 392	31.	b p. 401
14.	c p. 392	32.	c p. 402
15.	a p. 392	33.	a p. 403
16.	b p. 393	34.	a p. 406-407
17.	b p. 393	35.	b p. 407
18.	b p. 393	36.	b p. 408

Key to Self-Test B:

1.	k		7.	e
2.	f		8.	j
3.	i		9.	g
4.	b		10.	c
5.	a		11.	h
6.	d			

Key to Self-Test C:

1.	h		5.	c
2.	a		6.	g
3.	b		7.	e
4.	f		8.	d

Key to Self-Test D:

1. c
2. f
3. e
4. b
5. d
6. a

Key to Essay Questions:

1. First, you will have to discuss the theories of Eli Ginzberg (i.e., developmental theory of career choice), Donald Super (career self-concept theory), and John Holland (personality type theory) so you can assess the students' level of development and interests. You will also need to look at occupational outlook, how to find the right match between student and career, how to interview, the occupational work cycle, and women's issues in the work force (e.g., changing roles, dual-career marriages, and juggling roles, etc.). Then you will need to look at the basic health issues of alcohol and other drug use and how that might affect the students' current school performance as well as their ability to find and hold a job. Often times students will look to school counselors as someone to talk to about their sexuality, sexual practices, and sexual orientation; thus, you will need to be familiar with the information concerning these areas of sexuality, but do know when to send a troubled student to the college psychologist.

2. Here you will need to discuss the wide range of sexual orientation (from heterosexuality to homosexuality and all points in between), physiological changes that occur in young adulthood, sexually transmitted diseases and AIDS and ways to prevent each of them (e.g., abstinence, use of condoms, monogamy, etc.), sexual harassment (e.g., what behaviors would constitute harassment, what are the consequences of harassment for victim and perpetrator), and rape (e.g., the definition of rape, understanding this is an issue of power and control, not of sex, etc.).

Research Project 1: College Drinking Patterns

This project will assist you in understanding the drinking patterns of college students. You may wish to look at surveys that have been used by other researchers (see Figure 14.1 in the text for useful questions), and you may need to have your research project approved by an Internal Review Board at any college where you administer the survey. Gather basic demographic data, such as student's sex, age, years of education, etc., then ask about the students' drinking patterns (e.g., how often they consume alcohol, how much they consume at any given time, when they consume it, when they first started drinking, etc.) and the problems they encounter from consuming alcohol (see Figure 14.1). Do a statistical analysis of your data to see what patterns emerge. What is the prevalence of alcohol consumption on campus? Who is most likely to abstain from drinking? Who is most likely to engage in moderate or heavy drinking? Is alcohol consumption primarily a social activity, or are many students drinking alone? What specific problems do the students encounter from drinking alcohol? Prepare a chart that indicates who has the problems and specifically what types of problems they have.

1.   What did you notice in terms of the specific problems that drinkers have?
2.   What patterns of drinking did you notice?
3.   Were your observations consistent with what you might expect from the research described? Explain your response.
4.   Based on your observations, what might you conclude about drinking patterns on college campuses and the problems that may be incurred?

Research Project 2: Avoiding Sexually Risky Behaviors

Consider the risk factors that young adults face when engaging in sexual activities. Design a public awareness program for your class, your campus, or your community that will assist young adults in viewing their sexual behaviors realistically. Be specific in stating the potential consequences of various forms of sexual interactions, ranging from kissing (minimal risk) to engaging in vaginal or anal intercourse without a condom (high risk). Include in your presentation a discussion of the range of sexual orientations (heterosexual to homosexual--you may wish to use Figure 14.4); rape (e.g., it is a matter of power and control, not sexual gratification; talk about marital rape and date rape, and concerns about whether a person has the mental capacity to consent); and sexual harassment. Relying on the text and the professional literature, provide a good outline of ways to reduce the risks involved in engaging in sexual activities. It's important to remember to keep one's own value judgments out of such a presentation, and rely instead on the heavy body of research in this field; however, the members of your audience will be sure to have strong emotional responses to what you say. (Note that if you get asked a question for which you don't have an answer, you can always respond with something like: "That's an excellent/interesting question. I don't have the answer right now, but if you'd like, I'll research it and get back to you." Or, "That's an interesting question. What do you think?")

Allow for a question-and-answer period, keeping track of the questions. What types of questions are asked? Are they consistent with the type of information provided in the text? Were questions raised that weren't discussed in the text that you think would be appropriate for inclusion? What were they? Were there questions you couldn't answer? What were they?

Chapter 15 Socioemotional Development in Early Adulthood

Learning Objectives

1. Describe the different types of love postulated by Berscheid and be able to compare them with Sternberg's three forms of love.

2. Discuss the stages of the family life cycle.

3. Discuss how marital expectations and myths may influence the course of marriage.

4. Discuss gender, intimacy, and family work in marriage.

5. Discuss the advantages and disadvantages of being single.

6. Describe the consequences of divorce for both men and women.

7. Describe and give examples of the five styles of intimacy, and the levels of relationship maturity.

8. Explain how women and men balance their need for intimacy with their need for independence.

9. Review the potential problems women face in contemporary society.

10. Discuss male role strain and the areas where men's roles can cause strain.

Explain the notion of
consensual validation.

What factors are
associated with
loneliness?

What are the four
forms of love
described by Berscheid (1988)?

State the five skills
described for developing
adaptive relationships?

Explain the
term "friendship."

Explain the first stage
in the family life cycle.
How does that relate to
launching?

What is romantic love?
What other terms are used for
romantic love?

What is the second stage
in the family life cycle?

Describe
affectionate love.

What is the third stage
in the family life cycle?

What is Sternberg's theory
of triangular love?
How do the parts intertwine
to determine specific types of love?

What is the fourth stage
in the family life cycle?

Loneliness: associated with an individual's gender, attachment history, self-esteem, and social skills; lack of time spent with families; the social transition to college

Consensual validation: explains why individuals are attracted to people who are similar to them; our attitudes & behavior are supported when someone else's attitudes & behavior are similar to ours; their attitudes & behavior validate ours; also, dissimilar others are unlike us & more unknown, so we may be able to gain more control over similar others & predict their behavior

Five skills for developing adaptive relationships: have one or more good friends; develop a satisfying love relationship with a partner; develop good communication skills; be assertive, not aggressive; reduce loneliness (e.g., become involved in activities; recognize warning signs of loneliness early; think about people you see now & those you would like to meet)

Ellen Berscheid (1988) describes four forms of love: altruism, friendship, romantic or passionate love, and affectionate or companionate love.

Leaving home & becoming a single adult: 1st stage in family life cycle; accepting emotional & financial responsibility for self--involves **launching**, the process in which youths move into adulthood & exit their family of origin

Friendship is a form of close relationship involving enjoyment, acceptance, trust, respect, mutual assistance, confiding, understanding, & spontaneity.

New couple: 2nd stage of family life cycle; in which two individuals from separate families of origin unite to form a new family system (commitment to new system)

Romantic love: also called "passionate love" or "Eros"; it has strong sexual & infatuation components, and it often predominates in the early part of a love relationship

Becoming parents & a family with children: 3rd stage of family life cycle; entering this stage requires that adults now move up a generation & become caregivers to the younger generation; accepting new members into the system

Affectionate love: also called "companionate love"; the type of love that occurs when individuals desire to have the other person near and have a deep, caring affection for the person

Family with adolescents: 4th stage of family life cycle; adolescence is a period of development in which individuals push for autonomy & seek to develop their own identity; increasing flexibility of family boundaries to include children's independence & grandparents' frailties

The triangular theory of love: Sternberg's (1993) theory that love has three main forms: passion, intimacy, and commitment
Infatuation: if only passion is present;
Companionate/affectionate love: intimacy & commitment present, passion low or absent
Fatuous love: passion & commitment present
Consummate love: all three are present

What is the fifth stage in the family life cycle?	Contrast the stereotyped style of intimate interaction with the pseudointimate style and the isolated style.
What is the sixth stage in the family life cycle?	According to the model developed by Kathleen White et al. (1987), what are the three levels of relationship maturity?
Describe Jeffrey Larson's (1988) findings concerning marital myths.	Describe the relationship between intimacy and independence.
What myths did Okun & Rappaport (1980) report about parenting?	Describe Joseph Pleck's (1981, 1995) role-strain view.
What crisis did Erikson believe occurs in early adulthood? What are the consequences of not resolving that crisis?	Differentiate between women's and men's conversation as discussed by Deborah Tannen (1990).
Contrast the intimate style of intimate interaction with the preintimate style.	Explain the problem of using the term "the male experience."

Stereotyped style: superficial relationships that tend to be dominated by friendship ties with same-sex, not opposite-sex, friends
Pseudointimate style: long-lasting sexual attachment with little or no depth or closeness
Isolated style: the individual withdraws from social encounters & has little or no attachment to same- or opposite-sex individuals

Family at midlife: the 5th stage of family life cycle; it is a time of launching children, playing an important role in linking generations, & adapting to midlife changes in development; accepting a multitude of exits from & entries into the family system

White's levels of relationship maturity: *self-focused* (one's perspective on another person or relationship is concerned with how it affects oneself); *role-focused* (perceive others as individuals in their own right, but perspective is stereotypical; emphasizes social acceptability); & *individuated-connected* (understand oneself & have consideration for others' motivations & anticipate their needs; concern/caring involve emotional support/individualized interest

Family in later life: the 6th & final stage of family life cycle; retirement alters a couple's lifestyle, requiring adaptation; grandparenting also characterizes many families in this stage; accepting the shifting of generational roles

Intimacy/independence relationship: as individuals are trying to establish an identity, they are faced with increasing independence from parents, developing intimate relationships with another person, & increasing friendship commitments; delicate balance between intimacy & commitment with independence & freedom

Jeffrey Larson (1988) constructed a marriage quiz to measure college students' information about marriage; college students responded incorrectly to almost half the items; males missed more than females & students with less romantic perceptions missed fewer than romantically inclined students

Joseph Pleck's (1981, 1995) role-strain view: the male role is contradictory & inconsistent; men not only experience stress when they violate men's roles, they also are harmed when they *do* act in accord with men's roles

Okun & Rappaport (1980) reported myths about parenting: having a baby will save a failing marriage; as their parents' possession, children think, feel, behave like their parents did as children; children will care for parents in old age; children will respect/obey/love parents; parents can mold children into what they want; it's the parents' fault when children fail; mothers are naturally better parents than fathers; parenting is instinctive & needs no training

Deborah Tannen (1990): wives complain about lack of communication; husbands see their wives as making unreasonable demands or manipulatively attempting to do what he wants to do; she refers to **rapport talk**, a way of establishing connections & negotiating relationships, & **report talk**, public speaking

Erik Erikson: the 6th stage/crisis that takes place in early adulthood is intimacy versus isolation; if intimacy is not developed in early adulthood, the individual may be left with isolation; individuals face the task of forming intimate relationships with others--Erikson described intimacy as finding oneself yet losing oneself in another person

"The male experience": it is important to consider variations in male experiences; many men are becoming responsible fathers, share household duties, relinquish their drive to wield power over others; experiences may also vary according to ethnicity & culture

Intimate style: the individual forms & maintains one or more deep & long-lasting love relationships
Preintimate style: the individual shows mixed emotions about commitment, an ambivalence reflected in the strategy of offering love without obligations or long-lasting bonds

Self-Test A: Multiple Choice

1. Which of the following statements is consistent with the research findings on close relationships?
   a. People who live in glass houses shouldn't throw stones.
   b. Birds of a feather flock together.
   c. Distance makes the heart grow fonder.
   d. A rose by any other name will smell as sweetly.

2. Consensual validation refers to:
   a. the adolescent's first experience of sexual intercourse.
   b. a high level of agreement among members of a social group.
   c. parental acceptance of their offspring as independent adults.
   d. attraction among similar individuals.

3. Which of the following *is not* one of the forms of love described by Ellen Berscheid (1988)?
   a. altruism
   b. friendship
   c. infatuation
   d. affectionate love

4. In what way are friends different from romantic partners?
   a. Relationships with romantic partners are more likely to involve fascination and exclusiveness.
   b. Relationships with friends are more likely to involve fascination and exclusiveness.
   c. Relationships with romantic partners are more likely to involve trust and spontaneity.
   d. Relationships with romantic partners are more likely to involve acceptance and mutual assistance.

5. According to Ellen Berscheid (1988), when we say we are in love, we are most likely referring to _____ love.
   a. affectionate
   b. compassionate
   c. romantic
   d. consummate

6. When unattached college students identified their closest relationship, most named:
   a. a friend.
   b. their parents.
   c. a close, but nonparent, relative.
   d. a romantic partner.

7. According to Ellen Berscheid, romantic love cannot be experienced without:
   a. sexual desire.
   b. a strong sense of personal identity.
   c. consensual validation.
   d. trust.

8. A desire to have a partner who is adored and will be near is the basis of:
   a. affectionate love.
   b. consummate love.
   c. friendship.
   d. romantic love.

9. If the only real attraction that Richard and Jamie feel toward each other is sexual, Robert Sternberg would argue that they are:
   a. experiencing infatuation.
   b. experiencing companionate love.
   c. experiencing fatuous love.
   d. not experiencing love.

10. Research has shown that people feel lonely for all of the following reasons *except*:
    a. society's emphasis on self-fulfillment.
    b. the importance attached to relationships.
    c. a decline in stable, close relationships.
    d. the rising divorce rate.

11. Which of the following statements regarding loneliness and college is *most* accurate?
    a. Loneliness is likely to develop during the social transition from high school to college.
    b. Loneliness remains of little concern for college students.
    c. A lonely high school student is likely to be a lonely college student.
    d. Males are more likely to be lonesome than females.

12. The textbook suggests that one way an individual may try to reduce loneliness is by:
    a. changing his or her social needs or desires.
    b. going to a lot of dances.
    c. placing an ad in the singles section of the campus newspaper.
    d. becoming a workaholic.

13. Which process in the "family life cycle" is related to launching?
    a. birth
    b. leaving home and becoming a single adult
    c. taking one's first job and entering the workforce
    d. expecting that, upon reaching the age of 18, the teenager leave home

14. Which phrase would many individuals begin to hear during the sixth stage of the "family life cycle"?
    a. "How come I have to clean my room? I'm almost in the fifth grade!"
    b. "I now pronounce you husband and wife."
    c. "Hi, Grandpa; hi, Grandma."
    d. "Honey, I'm pregnant!"

15. Which of the following best reflects the changes that have occurred in marital relations over the past 60 years?
    a. They have become more fragile due to the changing norm of male-female equality.
    b. They have become more stable because women are now more satisfied with their lives.
    c. The proportion of women who never marry has increased dramatically.
    d. There have been no major changes in terms of stability, only in terms of structure.

16. The developmental course of marriage is:
    a. varied both within and across cultures.
    b. the same across cultures.
    c. easy to predict once a couple falls in love.
    d. determined by the individuals involved.

17. In a cross-cultural study of marriage around the world, Buss et al. (1990) found which of the following countries considered chastity to be the most important factor in marital selection?
    a. China
    b. Ireland
    c. Germany
    d. the United States

18. In a study of beliefs in marriage myths among college students, Jeffrey Larson found that:
    a. college students' beliefs about marriage are surprisingly realistic.
    b. females tended to approach the subject of marriage more realistically than males.
    c. highly romantic students are likely to experience more marital stability.
    d. the low participation rate in the study indicates that low interest in the subject of marriage seems characteristic among college students generally.

19. When looking at gender differences and marital satisfaction, researchers have found all of the following *except*:
    a. women are more expressive and affectionate than men.
    b. men do not understand what their wives want from them.
    c. the type of family work women do is unrelenting, repetitive, and routine when compared with the work that men do.
    d. women find their family work highly rewarding.

20. Men working around the house are most likely to:
    a. do the dishes.
    b. take out the garbage.
    c. vacuum.
    d. go shopping.

21. Which statement *is not* a myth about parenting?
    a. The birth of a child will save a failing marriage.
    b. Children will take care of parents in their old age.
    c. When children fail, the parent is not entirely to blame.
    d. Mothers are naturally better parents than fathers.

22. American women have fewer children than in the past. One repercussion of this is that:
   a. men are putting more time into child-rearing.
   b. fewer women are entering the workforce.
   c. institutionalized day-care use is on the decline.
   d. women are able to invest more heavily in their children's development.

23. Which statement most accurately describes what the research has learned about the role of mothers?
   a. Most women expect motherhood to be happy and fulfilling, and in reality they do find it to be rewarding.
   b. Most women expect motherhood to be happy and fulfilling, but in reality motherhood has been accorded low prestige in our society.
   c. Most women expect motherhood to be a low prestige position, and that is the reality of what they find when they become mothers.
   d. Most women expect motherhood to be a low prestige position, but in reality they find it rewarding and fulfilling.

24. During America's colonial period, the father's position was that of:
   a. moral teacher.
   b. absentee bread-winner.
   c. family nurturer.
   d. nurturing guide.

25. Which of the following couples is most likely to get divorced?
   a. Elaine and Alan, whose marriage in their late 40s was the first for both
   b. Ivana and Edward, whose joint annual income exceeds $1,000,000
   c. Sandra and Joel, who got married their senior year of high school when they learned Sandra was pregnant
   d. Jennifer and Burt, who both have Ph.D.s

26. Divorced men and women have higher rates of all of the following except:
   a. clinical depression.
   b. alcoholism.
   c. sleep disturbances.
   d. immunity to disease.

27. According to Erik Erikson, if individuals are unable to develop intimacy in early adulthood, they are left with feelings of:
   a. despair
   b. stagnation.
   c. isolation.
   d. confusion.

28. Partners who have stressful intimate interactions often have:
   a. an isolated style relationship.
   b. a stereotyped style relationship.
   c. a pseudointimate style relationship.
   d. a preintimate style relationship.

29. Which of the following would White et al. (1987) consider to have the most mature relationship?
   a. Jennifer and Joe, whose perspective on their relationship is concerned with how it affects each of them individually
   b. Andrew and Sarah, who see each other as individuals within their social roles
   c. Jerry and Peggy, who understand themselves and offer each other emotional support
   d. Judith and Daniel, who take on the battles of the world together as a team

30. Jean Baker Miller (1986) believes women will gain greater power in American society:
   a. when the feminist movement becomes more fully operative.
   b. through women's increased self-determination, coupled with already developed relationship skills.
   c. once men realize that women add an important dimension to the business world.
   d. once men realize they will be healthier and live longer by sharing power.

31. In her research on intimate relationships, Harriet Lerner (1989) has found that:
   a. many men distance themselves from their partner when the going gets rough, rather than work on the relationship.
   b. once a person has reached their early 20s, it is nearly impossible to learn to move differently in our key relationships.
   c. to improve connectedness with others, we need to give up our sense of self.
   d. the future well-being of the world rests on women improving their relationships, and men improving their self-development.

32. According to Pleck's role-strain view:
    a. men need to allow women into the workforce to alleviate men's burden.
    b. the male role is contradictory and inconsistent.
    c. men have become workaholics out of their macho need to provide for their families.
    d. men's work habits are causing them to die earlier.

33. To reconstruct masculinity to be more positive, Ron Levant (1995) believes men should do all of the following *except*:
    a. reexamine their beliefs about manhood.
    b. separate out and keep the valuable aspects of the male role.
    c. connect with their feminine side.
    d. get rid of the destructive parts of the masculine role.

34. Which of the following is **most** accurate concerning the stability of personality over time?
    a. As Freud argued, our personality as adults is virtually cast in stone by the time we are 5 years of age.
    b. Later experiences in early adulthood have a greater effect in determining what the individual is like as an adult than do early childhood experiences.
    c. It is our biological heritage that determines most strongly who we become as adults.
    d. Adult personality development is greatly affected by both Freud's infant determinism and the contextual approach that tends to emphasize adult experiences.

35. *The Dance of Intimacy* argues that competent relationships are those in which:
    a. separateness and connectedness strike a balance.
    b. the intimacy versus isolation conflict is resolved.
    c. self-determination is sacrificed for intimacy with others.
    d. individuality is sacrificed for the good of the relationships.

36. Which of the following lonely individuals is probably taking the most effective steps to overcome loneliness?
    a. Pauline, who calls her parents long-distance every night
    b. Cynthia, who reads every self-help book she can find
    c. Sally, who has volunteered at her church to help feed the poor and homeless
    d. Althea, who has invested herself in her home-based computer business

Self-Test B: Matching

Match the individuals in the left column with the appropriate descriptors in the right column.

f 1. Ellen Berscheid   a. proposed the triangular theory of love
a 2. Robert Sternberg   b. developed a model of relationship maturity
h 3. Jean Baker Miller   c. classified five styles of intimacy
d 4. Harriet Lerner   d. says women must bring strong, assertive, authentic selves to relationships
b 5. Kathleen White   e. believes the contradictory, inconsistent male role creates role-strain
g 6. Jeffrey Larson   f. claimed that romantic love is 90% sexual desire
e 7. Joseph Pleck   g. found college students were grossly misinformed about marriage
c 8. Jacob Orlofsky   h. believes the study of women's psychological development opens the paths to understanding male and female development

Self-Test C: Matching Love and Intimacy Styles

Match the styles of love and intimacy in the left column with some of their descriptions in the right column.

k 1. friendship
f 2. romantic love
a 3. affectionate love
b 4. infatuation
c 5. fatuous love
d 6. consummate love
j 7. intimate
i 8. preintimate
e 9. stereotyped
h 10. pseudointimate
g 11. isolated

a. individuals desire to have the other person near; deep caring affection
b. passion is high, intimacy & commitment are low or absent
c. passion & commitment present, but intimacy is not
d. passion, intimacy, & commitment are all present
e. superficial relationship dominated by same-sex, not opposite-sex, friendships
f. strong sexual & infatuation components; often predominates early relationship
g. withdrawal from social encounters; little attachment to others
h. long-lasting sexual attachment; little or no depth or closeness
i. mixed emotions about commitment; love without obligation
j. deep & long-lasting love relationship
k. involves enjoyment, acceptance, trust, respect, mutual assistance, confiding, understanding, & spontaneity

Self-Test D: Matching Principles of Family Life Cycle

Match the stages in the left column with their descriptions in the right column.

d 1. leaving home
f 2. the new couple
e 3. becoming parents
b 4. family with adolescents
a 5. family at midlife
c 6. family in later life

a. accepting exits from/entries into family system
b. increasing flexibility of family boundaries
c. accepting the shifting of generational roles
d. accepting emotional & financial responsibility for self
e. accepting new members into the system
f. commitment to new system

Essay Questions:

1. You have been asked to address your local community on developing meaningful relationships in young adulthood. Among the topics you have been asked to discuss are: developmental norms in young adulthood; ways to recognize healthy and unhealthy relationships; and how to create healthy relationships. What will you tell these people?

2. You have been caught in the middle of an on-going argument between the men and women in your family. Each group says the other is to blame for marital dissatisfaction. They have asked for your wise input to help them deal more effectively with each other. How can you help them?

Key to Self Test A:

1.	b	p. 414	19.	d p. 421
2.	d	p. 414	20.	b p. 421
3.	c	p. 414	21.	c p. 421-422
4.	a	p. 414	22.	a p. 422
5.	c	p. 414	23.	b p. 422
6.	d	p. 414-415	24.	a p. 422
7.	a	p. 415	25.	c p. 424
8.	a	p. 415	26.	d p. 424
9.	a	p. 415	27.	c p. 425
10.	d	p. 416	28.	a p. 425
11.	a	p. 416	29.	c p. 425
12.	a	p. 416	30.	b p. 426
13.	b	p. 417	31.	a p. 427
14.	c	p. 418	32.	b p. 427
15.	a	p. 419	33.	c p. 429
16.	a	p. 420	34.	d p. 429
17.	p. a	p. 420	35.	a p. 426-427
18.	b	p. 421	36.	c p. 431

Key to Self Test B:

1.	f	5.	b
2.	a	6.	g
3.	h	7.	e
4.	d	8.	c

Key to Self Test C:

1.	k	7.	j
2.	f	8.	i
3.	a	9.	e
4.	b	10.	h
5.	c	11.	g
6.	d		

Key to Self Test D:

1.	d	4.	b
2.	f	5.	a
3.	e	6.	c

Key to Essay Questions:

1. You need to discuss the transition from identity vs. confusion to intimacy vs. isolation, as well as the interaction between independence and intimacy, for both men and women; also include at least the first two stages of the family life cycle. You will then need to discuss the different theories of relationships and intimacy suggested by Berscheid, Sternberg, and Orlofsky and relate them to the research on health. While discussing health and relationships also be sure to look at the single adult. Finally, present what the research (e.g., Lerner, Baker) has indicated about developing healthy relationships for both men and women, as well as the marital and parental myths that were discussed in the chapter.

2. You will need to explore the relationships among gender, gender and parental roles, intimacy, and family work; women's and men's development and gender issues (e.g., male role strain); and how men and women understand the world and communicate differently (e.g., Lerner's and Tannen's separate sections). Then, note what Miller says about how by understanding women better we will also come to understand men better, and what Levant says about reconstructing masculinity to be more positive. Add your own thoughts on how to improve communication and interactions between men and women, and how to reduce the blaming that often comes from these disagreements.

Research Project 1: Types of Love, Styles of Intimacy

This project will assist you in understanding the descriptions in the text of the different types of love and styles of intimacy. As objectively as you can, observe your own relationships (friendships and romantic) as well as the relationships of other people you know. Based on these observations, for each relationship indicate on the chart below the classification of the relationship according to Berscheid and Sternberg, Orlofsky's style of intimate interaction, as well as the behaviors that lead you to classify the relationship in that way.

Relationship	Berscheid's Classification	Sternberg's Classification	Orlofsky's Intimacy Style	Telling Behaviors
Self+				
Self+				

1. What similarities did you notice in terms of Berscheid's, Sternberg's, and Orlofsky's classifications for each relationship?
2. What differences did you notice in terms of Berscheid's, Sternberg's, and Orlofsky's classifications for each relationship?
3. What patterns did you notice when comparing relationships in terms of these different classifications?
4. Were your observations consistent with what you might expect from the research described? Explain your response.
5. What might you conclude about relationships and the development of relationships based on your observations?

Research Project 2: Improving Male/Female Relationships

Based on what you have learned in this chapter, make a chart to help you look at the differences that men and women have in terms of relating to each other, dealing with other relationships, dealing with family matters, dealing with work, etc. Then state ways that you believe would help them improve their relationships and their lives.

Research Project 3: Checking Out the Myths

Interview other college students to assess their beliefs about marriage and parenting. Develop a questionnaire that first asks how they define "love," then reword the myths about marriage and parenting so you can assess how much they actually know about these two topics. Record your respondents' sex and age and any other demographic information you consider to be relevant (e.g., educational level, ethnicity). Classify each participant's definition of love using one of the systems discussed in the text (e.g., Berscheid, Sternberg), which will help you determine whether they have a romantic view of love; then indicate which myths they believed.

1. Looking at the results of your interviews, what patterns did you notice?
2. Were your observations consistent with what you might expect from the research described? Explain your response.
3. Based on your observations, what might you conclude about college students' beliefs and knowledge about marriage and parenting?

Chapter 16 Physical and Cognitive Development in Middle Adulthood

Learning Objectives

1.   Give examples of the physical changes that occur as an individual enters his or her forties.

2.   Identify the most common health problems associated with middle age.

3.   Describe evidence for biological and behavioral pathways that link stress and illness.

4.   Define Type A behavior pattern and state its link to coronary disease.

5.   Define Type C behavior and indicate its significance.

6.   Describe the biological changes affecting sexuality that occur in both men and women during middle adulthood.

7.   Indicate which cognitive abilities decline during middle adulthood and explain what can be done to eliminate or compensate for some of the decrements.

8.   Discuss age-related trends in job satisfaction.

9.   Indicate what career ladders are, and be able to describe how they are affected by both gender and increasing age.

10. Compare and contrast the continuity of work pathways among men and women.

11. Characterize the extent of religion's influence on adult Americans' lives.

Explain the changes in
"middle age" from the time of
Freud & Jung to the
present.

What is the Type C behavior
pattern?
How does it relate to cancer?

Define the term
"middle adulthood."

Explain the concept
of hardiness.

Describe the primary physical
changes that typically
take place
during middle adulthood.

What kinds of
sexual changes take place
during middle adulthood?

Which diseases are the
number one and number two
killers during
middle adulthood?

What is menopause?
When does it typically
occur?

Describe the biological and
behavioral pathways
that are thought to link
stress and illness.

Explain the benefits
and risks of
estrogen replacement therapy

What is the link between
cardiovascular disease
and the Type A
behavior pattern?

What hormonal changes
do middle-aged men
experience?

Type C behavior: refers to the cancer prone personality, which consists of being inhibited, uptight, emotionally inexpressive, & otherwise constrained; this type of individual is more likely to develop cancer than are more expressive people

Freud & Jung studied midlife transitions around 1900, when average life expectancy was 47, & 3% of the population lived past 65; today average life expectancy is 75, & 12% of the population is over 65.
While "middle age" statistically would be about 38, we now consider "middle age" to be somewhere between 40 and 60 to 65.

Hardiness: a personality style characterized by a sense of commitment (rather than alienation), control (rather than powerlessness), and a perception of problems as challenges (rather than threats)
Kobasa, Maddi, & Kahn (1982) found the combination of hardiness, exercise, & social support best buffered against ill effects of stress.

Middle adulthood: the developmental period that begins approximately 35 to 45 years of age and extends into the 60s

Sexual changes in middle adulthood: menopause for women, modest decline in sexual potency for men, with hormonal changes in 50s & 60s (testosterone production declines about 1%/year), increase in erectile dysfunctions (often attributed to smoking, diabetes, hypertension, & elevated cholesterol); reduced sexual activity for both men & women

Physical changes in middle adulthood: visually, accomodation of the eye declines sharply between 40-59, with difficulty seeing close objects, & in 50s-60s eye's blood supply diminishes; hearing starts to decline about 40, with sensitivity to high pitches first; muscles weaken, back weakens, disks in spine move closer to each other & person begins to shrink

Menopause: the time in middle age, usually in the late 40s or early 50s, when a woman's menstrual periods cease completely; dramatic decline in estrogen production; average age for last period is 52; 10% of women go through menopause before age 40; contrary to popular opinion, most women view it positively

Cardiovascular disease is the number one killer in the United States.
Cancer is the number two killer in the United States, with lung cancer from smoking often surfacing for the first time in middle age.
(**Obesity** is also a problem.)

Estrogen replacement therapy: benefits include reduction of menopausal symptoms (e.g., hot flashes, sweating), help prevent or reduce osteoporosis, & reduce the risk of coronary disease; risks include higher risk for breast cancer; aerobic exercises may alleviate menopausal symptoms for women who are & are not on estrogen replacement therapy.

Biological pathways linking stress & illness: acute stressors can produce immunological changes; chronic stressors (e.g., smog, failure of close relationships) are associated with downturn in immune system responsiveness
Behavioral pathways: stress can affect eating patterns; self-medication with alcohol/other drugs

Hormonal changes for middle-aged men: modest decline in sexual potency for men, with hormonal changes in 50s & 60s (testosterone production declines about 1%/year), increase in erectile dysfunctions (which are often attributed to smoking, diabetes, hypertension, & elevated cholesterol)

Type A behavior pattern: a cluster of characteristics (excessively competitive, hard-driven, impatient, & hostile) thought to be related to the incidence of heart disease (Friedman & Rosenman, 1974); further research: people who are hostile or consistently turn anger inward are more at risk ("hot reactors": intense physiological reactions to stress could lead to heart disease)

What changes are noticeable in cognitive development during middle adulthood?

What is the relation between religion and the ability to cope with stress?

Describe the career patterns for people in middle adulthood.

Describe the adaptive skills in middle age.

Describe the pattern of moving up the career ladder.

List the guidelines set by the federal government and the Society for Public Health Education for living healthier lives.

Describe the four career patterns of professional women.

Explain the relationship between leisure and well-being.

Describe the role of religion in adult development.

Some psychologists consider prayer & religious commitment forms of defensive coping strategies (less effective in helping people cope than life-skills & problem-solving strategies); recently researchers found some styles of religious coping associated with high levels of personal initiative & competence; found more competent women & men more likely to have religious affiliation

Cognitive changes in middle adulthood: Memory decline is more likely for long-term than short-term memory; this can be improved by using memory strategies (lists, mnemonic devices, etc.); more difficulty recalling information that is recently acquired or not used often; recall is more difficult than recognition; memory decline affected by poor health & negative attitude

Adaptive skills in middle age: maintain a healthy lifestyle; cope effectively with stress; keep anger toned down; stay cognitively active; balance work & leisure; think about the meaning of life

Career patterns: satisfaction increases at least to age 60 for men & women, with & without college education, greater commitment to job, lower rates of avoidable absenteeism; about 10% change careers; most common male path: work continuously from early adulthood to retirement; female path: work until children are born, then return to work part-time when children are older, when children leave she goes back to school to update skills/retrain, take full-time paid job in 40s/50s

Guidelines for healthier living: develop preventive services targeting life threatening diseases; health promotion, including behavior modification & health education; cleaner air & water; improve workplace safety; meet health needs of special populations, e.g., better understanding of disease prevention in minority groups

Moving up the career ladder: college degree is associated with earlier & greater career advancement; individuals promoted early go further up the career ladder than those promoted late; most career advancement occurs early in adult lives--by 40-45 most of us have gone as far as we will up the career ladder

Career patterns among professional women: regular: education, training, continuous work with minimal/no interruption; interrupted career: began in regular pattern, interrupted for several years, then back to full time; second career: professional training started when children leave home or after divorce; modified second career: started training when children still home, started working (possibly part-time) until last child leaves, then shift to full-time career (Rosenbaum, 1984)

Leisure: the pleasant times after work when individuals are free to pursue activities & interests of their own choosing, e.g., hobbies, sports, or reading; constructive & fulfilling leisure activities in middle adulthood help prepare adults financially & psychologically for retirement & may make the transition from work to retirement less stressful

Religion in adult development: religion is a powerful influence in some adults' lives, may play little/no role in others'; Clausen (1993) found some adults become more religious as they age, others become less religious; 95% of Americans say they believe in God or a universal spirit & 60% attend religious services, but there is a move away from mainstream religion

Self-Test A: Multiple Choice

1. According to our author, and as reflected in Jim Croce's song, *Time in a Bottle*, our perception of time depends on:
   a. how full our lives are.
   b. where we are in the life span.
   c. our personal experiences.
   d. how many deadlines we have to meet.

2. From the time that Freud and Jung studied midlife transitions, around 1900, and now, the boundaries of middle age have:
   a. moved downward.
   b. moved upward.
   c. become relatively indistinct.
   d. stayed the same, but apply to more people.

3. A person between the ages of 40 and 59 is going to have most difficulty:
   a. reading a wall chart at the eye-care professional's office.
   b. reading street signs.
   c. reading a newspaper.
   d. watching television at a distance.

4. What changes are noticed in an adult's height as that person ages?
   a. It increases.
   b. It decreases.
   c. Unless there is illness, there is no noticeable change.
   d. The findings are contradictory--some people get taller, others get shorter.

5. The leading cause of death in the United States is:
   a. cancer.
   b. accidents.
   c. obesity.
   d. cardiovascular disease.

6. Obesity has been linked to:
   a. hypertension and digestive disorders.
   b. cancer.
   c. early visible signs of aging.
   d. prostate disorders in men.

7. Which of the following is most accurate concerning perceptions of gender differences in aging in the United States?
   a. Some aspects of aging in middle adulthood are taken as signs of attactiveness in men, but similar signs may be perceived as unattractive in women.
   b. Some aspects of aging in middle adulthood are taken as signs of attactiveness in women, but similar signs may be perceived as unattractive in men.
   c. Signs of aging in men and women are perceived as unattractive in our culture.
   d. Signs of aging in men and women typically elicit greater respect from people in our culture.

8. In the Ni-Hon-San Study of Japanese men, those living in _____ had the highest rate of coronary heart disease.
   a. Hiroshima
   b. Nagasaki
   c. Honolulu
   d. San Francisco

9. Japanese men in California have much lower rates of cerebrovascular disease (stroke) than Japanese men living in Japan, because:
   a. the diets of those living in California are more well-rounded.
   b. the Japanese men living in California have a more relaxed lifestyle.
   c. businessmen in Japan tend to drink a lot of alcohol and to chain-smoke.
   d. of the residual effects from the bombing of Hiroshima and Nagasaki during World War II.

10. Which of the following occupations is least likely to attract people with Type A personalities?
    a. lawyers
    b. bank executives
    c. college professors
    d. novelists

11. Which factor of the Type A personality is most related to coronary heart disease?
    a. excessive competition
    b. being hard-driven
    c. impatience
    d. hostility

12. One way to promote access to health care for Hispanic Americans would be to:
    a. print information about health care in Spanish.
    b. desegregate clinics for ethnic minorities.
    c. teach Hispanic Americans not to use medical care as a "quick fix."
    d. use Hispanic Americans' belief in the supernatural in treatment.

13. Linda is controlled, committed, and sees problems as challenges. She will most likely:
    a. remain healthy.
    b. develop heart disease.
    c. develop breast cancer.
    d. become obese.

14. In an extensive survey of women who had experienced menopause, most reported that menopause was a _____ experience.
    a. negative
    b. positive
    c. neutral tending toward positive
    d. neutral tending toward negative

15. What is the basis of erroneous beliefs about menopause?
    a. A majority of women experience them.
    b. The beliefs conform well with gender-typed beliefs about middle-age women.
    c. Badly controlled research supports them.
    d. Physicians promote them to guard against use of estrogen therapy.

16. The American Geriatrics Association recommends that:
    a. all women should consider estrogen replacement therapy.
    b. women who have had hysterectomies should avoid estrogen replacement therapy.
    c. the benefits of estrogen replacement therapy outweigh the risks in women who are at increased risk for breast cancer.
    d. women need to rely heavily on their doctor's advice when deciding whether they should use estrogen replacement therapy.

17. When compared to that in early adulthood, sexual activity during middle adulthood is:
    a. more frequent.
    b. less frequent.
    c. more dependent on physical activity.
    d. about the same.

18. Which of the following memory tasks would be the most difficult for an individual in the middle adult period?
    a. remembering a phone number long enough to dial it
    b. remembering a grocery list being given over the phone
    c. remembering the date of a son-in-law's birthday
    d. remembering the name of someone you just met so you can introduce him or her to your spouse

19. Job satisfaction increases with age for all of the following reasons *except*:
    a. higher pay.
    b. job security.
    c. higher positions within the company.
    d. less need for intense commitment.

20. Boris is 45 years old. He is most likely to:
    a. continue up the corporate ladder.
    b. remain at his present level in the corporation.
    c. change jobs.
    d. increase his savings for retirement.

21. According to the research, about ____% of Americans change jobs in midlife.
    a. 10
    b. 15
    c. 22
    d. 48

22. How do work pathways of men differ from those of women?
    a. Men are more likely than women to switch from one job to another.
    b. Men are more likely than women to work continuously from early adulthood until they retire.
    c. Women are more likely than men to work continuously from early adulthood until they retire.
    d. The pathways do not differ greatly; they are actually quite similar.

23. Upon finishing undergraduate school, Joan enrolls in the Metropolitan School of Law. According to Golan she is in the _____ career pattern.
    a. regular
    b. interrupted
    c. second
    d. modified second

24. All of the following have been noted to be reasons that middle-aged women enter the labor force, *except*:
    a. the need to support themselves and their family.
    b. boredom and loneliness.
    c. the desire for new interests.
    d. a need to overcome domination by men.

25. What was Aristotle's view of leisure?
    a. It is a waste of time.
    b. It is harmful.
    c. It is unnecessary.
    d. It is important in life.

26. Leisure is particularly important during middle adulthood because it:
    a. improves the nation's economy.
    b. helps adults narrow their interests.
    c. eases the transition from work to retirement.
    d. allows grandparents to babysit their grandchildren.

27. The percentage of Americans who believe in God is _____ the percentage who attend religious services.
    a. less than
    b. greater than
    c. equal to
    d. changing in comparison to

28. While Americans generally show a strong interest in religion and believe in God, they also reveal:
    a. a declining faith in mainstream religious institutions.
    b. an increasing faith in mainstream religious institutions.
    c. less faith in mainstream religious institutions, but increased faith in religious leaders.
    d. no change in terms of their faith in mainstream religious institutions, but great disappointment with religious leaders.

29. The strongest statement we can make about the relationship between involvement in religion and happiness is that:
    a. involvement in religion causes people to be happy.
    b. happiness leads people to become involved in religion.
    c. there is no meaningful relationship between religion and happiness.
    d. people who are involved in religion tend to be happy.

30. All of the following are adaptive skills in middle age *except*:
    a. maintain a healthy lifestyle.
    b. cope effectively with stress.
    c. express your anger .
    d. think about the meaning of life.

31. Which of the following is the best example of the next step toward improved health among people in middle adulthood?
    a. Cures will be found for heart disease and cancer.
    b. The federal government will develop an effective national insurance plan.
    c. Corporations will help ethnic minorities gain access to the medical system.
    d. More effective ways to help people stop smoking will be found.

Self Test B: Matching

Match the individuals in the left column with the appropriate descriptors in the right column.

1. Meyer Friedman
2. Daniel Levinson
3. Ray Rosenman
4. John Clausen
5. Gail Sheehy
6. Laurence Levine
7. Raymond Paloutzian

a. wrote about the frustrations & stigma of menopausal women
b. defensive religious strategies sometimes set the stage for effective coping
c. found smoking, diabetes, & hypertension cause erectile problems for men
d. first in the pair of researchers who invented type a personality classification
e. described mid-life career-change experience as a turning point in adulthood
f. second in pair of researchers who invented type a personality classification
g. found that competent men and women are involved in religion

Self Test C: Matching Professional Women's Career Paths

Match the career path in the left column with some of their descriptions in the right column.

1. regular
2. interrupted
3. second
4. modified second

a. professional training pursued after graduation, continuos work thereafter
b. started training while children home, then began work
c. started professional training when children left home or after divorce
d. professional training after graduation, then work/stopped/returned to work

Essay Questions:

1. Your next door neighbors are a lovely couple whom you like very much. One day they both confide you that they are fast approaching middle age and are really dreading it. They have heard that once you turn 40, everything begins to fall apart, including your sex life. What would you tell them to help them through this crisis?

2. Your best friend in college is a lovely woman who has told you about her plans for career, marriage, and family. She seems very career-minded and wants to get to the top of her field, and also wants to have a traditional family where her husband has a career he enjoys that will allow her to stay home and rear the children while they are young. But she tells you about her concerns that if she follows this plan, she will not be able to get to the top of her field. What can you tell her?

Key to Self Test A:

1.	b p. 439	17.	b p. 445
2.	b p. 439	18.	c p. 446
3.	c p. 440	19.	d p. 446
4.	b p. 440	20.	b p. 447
5.	d p. 440	21.	a p. 447
6.	a p. 440	22.	b p. 448
7.	a p. 441	23.	a p. 448
8.	d p. 442	24.	d p. 449
9.	c p. 442	25.	d p. 449
10.	d p. 442-443	26.	c p. 450
11.	d p. 443	27.	b p. 451
12.	a p. 443	28.	a p. 451
13.	a p. 444	29.	d p. 452
14.	b p. 444	30.	c p. 451
15.	c p. 444	31.	d p. 453
16.	a p. 445		

Key to Self-Test B:

1. d
2. e
3. f
4. g

5. a
6. c
7. b

Key to Self-Test C:

1. a
2. d
3. c
4. b

Key to Essay Questions:

1. Describe the specific physical changes (e.g., vision, hearing, wrinkles) and the changes in sexuality, noting that most women actually have a positive attitude toward menopause. Discuss, too, the role that cultural attitudes play in how we feel about aging physically, and the differences in perception between signs of aging in men and in women. Be sure to explain the health issues, and the health practices that will allow them to remain vital and active (e.g., don't smoke, stay cognitively active, balance work and leisure, eat a nutritious diet).

2. Explain the research concerning job satisfaction and career ladders, but stress here the four patterns of career paths for women.

Research Project 1: Balancing Work, Family, Leisure, and School

The author states that "Most of us would like to balance work, family, and leisure activities in some fashion. Clearly, though, some individuals give priority to one or two of these to the exclusion of the other or others" (p. 451). He suggests you think about how balanced or unbalanced these factors are in your own life, and asks if (and how) you think your commitment to each of these areas of your life will change. Using the chart below, indicate whether each has a high, low, or medium priority in your life right now, and the priority you anticipate each will have in the future (state the approximate date). (I have added school, since that is also an important factor in your life at this time.) Then, consider the effect that the priority you place on each of these factors is currently affecting your life.

Factor	Current Priority	Future Priority (Date:)	How It's Affecting My Life
Work			
Family			
Leisure			
School			

1. What did you notice concerning the balance of these priorities in your life?
2. What did you notice about how these priorities affect your life?
3. How do your current priorities differ from your future priorities? What effect do you think that will have on your life?
4. What patterns did you notice when looking at these four factors in terms of the material discussed in this chapter?
5. Were your observations consistent with what you might expect from the research described? Explain your response.
6. What might you conclude about your own personal development based on these observations?
7. What plan might you make for balancing each of these factors in your life to ensure you stay as healthy as possible?

Research Project 2: Community Health Project

Conduct a needs assessment evaluation in your community to see what types of health issues are important (both to the community members and the health professionals in your area) and to determine the nature of ethnic/racial/religious diversity that exists. Considering the information in this chapter, work together with local health officials to plan an intervention that would promote healthy behaviors (e.g., strategies for lowering blood pressure, get people to stop smoking, etc.). In terms of the diversity that does or does not exist in your community, what types of issues must you consider in addition to the physical and psychological health concerns?

Chapter 17 Socioemotional Development in Middle Adulthood

Learning Objectives

1. Indicate evidence for age and sex differences in satisfying love relationships.

2. Describe how children leaving home affects marital satisfaction and be able to identify the factors that may cause adult children to return home.

3. Contrast Erikson's, Gould's, Levinson's, and Vaillant's stage theories of adulthood.

4. Discuss both sides of the claim that most adults do not experience a midlife crisis.

5. Describe the criticisms concerning gender issues that have been launched against the adult stage theories.

6. Describe the life-events approach and be able to give examples of its application.

7. Summarize the findings concerning adult personality using results from the four major longitudinal studies.

8. Show how the lives of Richard Alpert and Jerry Rubin illustrate continuities in personality development.

Describe the changes in romantic love and affectionate love as we move from early adulthood to middle adulthood.

What are the typical differences in perspectives between the person initiating a divorce and the divorced partner during middle adulthood?

Explain the process of mutuality in the maturity of relationships.

Describe the "empty nest syndrome." What have been the findings concerning its prediction?

Describe the development of relationships presented in the text between two unrelated persons.

In which areas are parent-child similarities most noticeable? In which areas are parent-child similarities least noticeable?

What major differences did Reedy, Birren, & Schaie (1981) find in happily married couples over the course of adulthood?

Describe the gender differences that are typically seen with regard to intergenerational relationships.

What similarities did Reedy, Birren, & Schaie (1981) find in happily married couples over the course of adulthood?

Describe the significant issue in life that Erikson believed is faced by middle-aged adults.

Explain how Campbell's (1980) stage of stability is reached in marriage during middle adulthood.

How did Roger Gould view the developmental transformation in midlife?

Divorcer: may see the situation as an escape from an untenable relationship
Divorced partner: usually sees it as betrayal, the ending of a relationship built up over many years & that involved a great deal of commitment & trust

Romantic love is strong in early adulthood. **Affectionate or companionate love** increases during middle adulthood; i.e., physical attraction, romance, & passion are more important in new relationships; security, loyalty, & mutual emotional interest become more important as relationships mature

The empty nest syndrome: marital satisfaction decreases because parents derive considerable satisfaction from their children & the children's departure leaves parents with empty feelings; may be so for parents living vicariously through their children, but for most, marital satisfaction increases--partners have time to pursue career interests & have more time for each other

Mutuality occurs when partners share knowledge with each other, assume responsibility for each other's satisfaction, & share private information that governs their relationship (Levinger, 1974); it plays a key role in the maturity of relationships

Parent-child similarity: most noticeable in religious & political areas; least in gender roles, lifestyle, & work orientation; children whose parents had a high degree of marital conflict & who were unaffectionate subsequently had tension in their own marriages & were ineffective in disciplining their own children (Elder, Caspi, & Downey, 1986)

Development of relationships: the relationship begins at a zero point of contact between two people to an awareness by one person of the other, gradually moves from a surface relationship into more intense, mutual interaction, increasingly sharing oneself with the other; at final stage (major intersection) experience affectionate love

Gender differences in intergenerational relationships: mothers & daughters had closer relationships during adult years than mothers & sons, fathers & sons, fathers & daughters (Rossi, 1989); married men more involved with wife's families than their own; maternal grandmothers/ aunts rated most important/loved relatives twice as often as paternal counterparts

Reedy, Birren, & Schaie (1981): passion & sexual intimacy were more important in early adulthood; affection & loyalty were more important later; communication of love was more characteristic of relationships for young adult lovers than for older adult lovers; women considered emotional security to be more important in love than did men

Erikson's 7th stage: generativity versus stagnation; generativity: plans for what adults hope to do to leave legacy to next generation, enabling them to have a kind of immortality; stagnation develops when adults sense they have done nothing for next generation
Forms of generativity: biological (have children), parental (nurture children), work (develop/pass on skills), cultural (create, change, save some aspect of culture that ultimately survives

Reedy, Birren, & Schaie (1981): similarities were that emotional security was the most important factor in love, followed by respect, communication, help and play behaviors, sexual intimacy, & loyalty

Roger Gould: links stage & crisis in developmental transformations in seven stages; emphasizes that midlife is as turbulent as adolescence; in 20s assume new roles, in 30s feel stuck with responsibilities, in 40s feel sense of urgency that life is speeding by; handling midlife crisis & accepting sense of urgency as natural helps keep us on path of adult maturity

Stability is accomplished when spouses have progressed through the romance and power-struggle stages to a point of finally accepting the relationship with all of its pluses & minuses; conflict patterns become more familiar, predictable, & comfortable, less threatening & catastrophic; the couple's expectations are more realistic

Describe the periods in
Daniel Levinson's
seasons of a man's life.

Explain how the findings of
Michael Farrell &
Stanley Rosenberg (1981) differed
from research in adult development
that describes the universals

What are the four
major conflicts Daniel Levinson
believes must be
resolved by men
during their midlife transition?

What did Bernice Neugarten
(1964) conclude in the Kansas
City Study about
continuity & change in
personality over time?

Explain George Vaillant's (1977)
expansion on Erikson's theory
by incorporating the stages of
career consolidation &
keeping the meaning versus rigidity.

Describe the findings of
Paul Costa and R. R. McRae's (1980,
1989) Baltimore Study
with respect to
changes in personality
over time

Explain Neugarten's notion
of the social clock and
how that is affected by
the social environment.

State what the Berkeley
longitudinal studies
conclude about the
stability-change issue
over the course of
adult development.

Describe the
major criticisms
of stage theories of
adult development.

Describe the three groups studied
by Ravenna Helson et al. (1997) in
the Mills College Study.
What were the findings of
that study?

Explain the contemporary
life-events approach
for interpreting adult
developmental change.

Explain what a life review is
and the benefits
that may be derived
from using this technique.

Stage theories (Erikson, Gould, Levinson, & Vaillant) attempt to describe universals, not individual variations; Farrell & Rosenberg (1981) concluded that extensive individual variation characterizes adults; the individual is an active agent who interprets, shapes, alters, & gives meaning to his or her life

Levinson: early adult transition (17-22); entry life structure for early adulthood (22-28); age 30 transition (28-33); culminating life structure for early adulthood (33-40); middle adult transition (40-45); entry life structure for middle adulthood (45-50); age 50 transition (50-55); culminating life structure for middle adulthood (55-40); late life transition (60-65); era of late adulthood (60+)

Neugarten's Kansas City Study (1964): there are both continuity & change in personality over time; adaptive characteristics (coping, attaining life satisfaction, strength of goal-directed behavior) are most stable; inner versus outer orientation, active versus passive mastery changed (i.e., from active to passive mastery)

Levinson's major conflicts in change to middle adulthood: (existing since adolescence) being young versus being old; being destructive versus being constructive; being masculine versus being feminine; & being attached to others versus being separate from them; 70-80% of those interviewed found midlife transition tumultuous & psychologically painful

Costa & McRae's Baltimore study (1980, 1989): found stability in their "big five" dimensions of personality: emotional stability (e.g., calm & secure versus anxious & insecure); extraversion (e.g., sociable versus retiring); openness (imaginative versus practical); agreeableness (e.g., soft-hearted versus ruthless); conscientiousness (e.g., organized versus disorganized)

Vaillant's expansion: Career consolidation: from about 23-35, a period when an individual's career becomes more stable & coherent; *keeping the meaning versus rigidity*: from about 45-55, a time when adults feel more relaxed if they have met their goals; if not, they accept that fact; concerned with extracting meaning from life & fight against falling into rigid orientation

Berkeley longitudinal studies: some stability exists over the long course of adult development, but adults are capable of change; dimensions directly concerned with self are more consistent than dimensions concerned with interpersonal relationships

Social clock: timetable according to which individuals are expected to accomplish life's tasks, e.g., getting married, having children, establishing a career; individuals whose lives are not in synch with social clock experience more stress; social environments of a particular age group can alter the social clock & today there is less agreement about right age or sequence

Helson's Mills College study (1997): despite different college profiles & diverging life paths (family-oriented, career-oriented, neither), the women experienced some similar psychological changes in adults years; women in "neither" group changed less than other two; between 27-early 40s, shift toward less traditional feminine attitudes; in 40s developed midlife consciousness

Criticisms of stage theories: they have a male bias by emphasizing career choice & achievement; do not adequately address women's concerns about relationships, interdependence, caring; assume a normative sequence of development, but as women's roles become more varied & complex, it is difficult to determine what is normative

Life review: the process of reviewing one's life; taking a look at how things are going & how they got there can help individuals work toward the future; identifying areas of life & writing down perspectives about the past, present, & future prospects of each can offer broader view on life that is put together in a meaningful picture

The contemporary life-events approach emphasizes that how life events influence the individual's development depends not only on the life event, but also on mediating factors (e.g., physical health, family supports), the life-stage context, and the sociohistorical context.

Self-Test A: Multiple Choice

1. During the middle years, _____ love increases.
   - (a) affectionate or companionate
   - b. romantic or passionate
   - c. intimate
   - d. committed

2. Satisfying relationships in early adulthood and middle adulthood share all of the following characteristics *except*:
   - a. emotional security.
   - (b) passion.
   - c. sexual intimacy.
   - d. respect.

3. After 25 years of marriage, Andrew and Sarah have decided to divorce now that their daughters have left home. According to the research, we might expect their divorce to be more positive than a couple who divorces in early adulthood, because:
   - a. they have greater resources, so both will be able to take what they need to set up their separate households.
   - b. their children no longer have any influence in what their parents decide.
   - (c) they may understand themselves better and may be searching for changes in their lives.
   - d. they have fewer resources after paying for their daughters' college educations and weddings, so there are fewer resources to split up.

4. The empty nest syndrome predicts that parents experience decreased marital satisfaction when the children leave home. Research has found that:
   - a. marital satisfaction actually increases.
   - (b) marital satisfaction does, in fact, decrease.
   - c. there is actually increased conflict between adult siblings.
   - d. there is actually decreased conflict between adult siblings.

5. The majority of adult sibling relationships in adulthood have been found to be:
   - a. apathetic.
   - (b) close.
   - c. rivalrous.
   - d. full of conflict.

6. Anita and Larry were always very close as children. Now that they are in middle adulthood, we would expect that they would:
   - (a) still be very close.
   - b. be less close, particularly if they live in different parts of the country.
   - c. be less close no matter where they live.
   - d. be able to count on each other in times of crisis, but otherwise not maintain much contact.

7. Parents and their adult children are most likely to disagree about:
   - (a) choice of lifestyle.
   - b. church attendance.
   - c. political party.
   - d. abortion.

8. According to research by Berquist, Greenberg, & Klaum (1993), when middle-aged parents mention disappointment regarding their adult children's development, they often say:
   - a. they should have been more strict with them.
   - (b) they wish they had spent more time with them.
   - c. it is basically the children's fault for the parents' disappointment.
   - d. they should have been less punitive.

9. Sidney and Diane have been married for 20 years. We would expect them to spend more time with:
   - (a) Diane's relatives than Sidney's relatives.
   - b. Sidney's relatives than Diane's relatives.
   - c. Sidney's paternal grandparents than with his maternal grandparents.
   - d. Sidney's parents than with Diane's parents.

10. Hyun-Joo experiences great satisfaction through nurturing, guiding, and teaching skills to her children. According to Erik Erikson, Hyun-Joo is dealing successfully with which psychological task?
    - a. initiative versus guilt
    - b. industry versus inferiority
    - c. identity versus role confusion
    - (d) generativity versus stagnation

11. An adult who has successfully resolved the conflicts of the generativity versus stagnation psychosocial stage is most likely to:
    a. donate money to a scholarship fund.
    b. buy a piece of a football franchise.
    c. spend time and money on exercise programs.
    d. hire consultants to teach junior executives the finer points of business management.

12. According to Roger Gould (1978), midlife is:
    a. less turbulent than adolescence.
    b. more turbulent than adolescence.
    c. as turbulent as adolescence.
    d. the most fulfilling of the adult life stages.

13. According to Daniel Levinson, the major issue that a middle-aged man must face is:
    a. mortality versus immortality.
    b. sexual and physical decline.
    c. empty nest syndrome.
    d. industry versus inferiority.

14. According to Daniel Levinson, the success of the midlife transition is dependent upon how effectively the individual:
    a. accepts polarities of the conflicts as an integral part of his or her being.
    b. chooses the most troublesome conflict and resolves it.
    c. learns to pay more attention to the needs of others than to his or her own needs.
    d. realizes the sense of urgency in his or her life and comes to terms with it.

15. According to George Vaillant, the stage of development that occurs from approximately 23 to 35 years of age, in which careers become more stable and coherent, is:
    a. settling down; accepting one's own life.
    b. generativity versus stagnation.
    c. career consolidation.
    d. goal realization.

16. Stage theories of adult development have been criticized for all of the following reasons *except*:
    a. the research is based largely on male samples, ignoring women's experiences.
    b. the tendency is to see stages of development as crises.
    c. life events may be more important than stages in development.
    d. the investigators' questionable skills.

17. Evidence from an accumulation of studies indicates that the midlife crisis is:
    a. a universal phenomenon.
    b. present in a majority of individuals but not all.
    c. dependent on the cohort that is currently middle-aged.
    d. nonexistent.

18. A distinctly feminist critique of stage theories of adult development is that such theories:
    a. place too little stress on similarities in women's and men's development.
    b. neglect the complexity of women's lives.
    c. disregard personality variation in favor of personality continuity.
    d. focus too much on crisis at the expense of adaptation.

19. The "social clock," as described by Neugarten (1986), is a:
    a. timetable for accomplishing life's tasks.
    b. way to assess how extraverted or introverted an individual is.
    c. way to assess how extraverted or introverted a couple is.
    d. biological timetable that guides certain of life's tasks such as bearing children.

20. When women in nonindustrialized countries reach middle age, their status improves for all of the following reasons *except*:
    a. they are freed from cumbersome restrictions placed on them when they were younger.
    b. they have authority over younger relatives.
    c. they have opportunities to gain status outside the home that younger women do not have.
    d. they are no longer able to bear children.

21. According to the life-events approach, individuals may differ in the way they deal with divorce for all of the following reasons *except*:
    a. the status of their health.
    b. their previously established coping mechanisms.
    c. their developmental stage.
    d. societal acceptance of the divorce.

22. The group most often citing body-weight and health-status concerns as frequent daily hassles (Kanner et al., 1981) was:
    a. college students.
    b. middle-aged adults.
    c. divorcees.
    d. adults experiencing the empty nest syndrome.

23. Regarding age changes in personality, Bernice Neugarten in the Kansas City Study found that:
    a. personality remains fairly constant, but age changes do exist.
    b. significant gender differences in personality were present, but mostly at younger ages.
    c. neurosis increases with age, but social inhibitions in personality decline.
    d. depression increases with age, but only in the personality of elderly who are widowed.

24. Paul Costa and R. R. McRae determined that the "big five" personality factors:
    a. showed different patterns of development during middle adulthood.
    b. became the "big three" as adults matured.
    c. go through a series of developmental stages.
    d. remain relatively stable during the middle adult years.

25. All of the following are examples of planful competence except:
    a. self-concept.
    b. dependability.
    c. high intelligence.
    d. intellectual investment.

26. John Clausen (1993), a researcher in the Berkeley longitudinal studies, believes:
    a. not enough attention has been given to the role of discontinuity in adult development.
    b. the experience of recurrent crises and change is a universal factor in adult development.
    c. some people experience recurrent crises and change, while others have more stable, continuous lives.
    d. the overall pattern of development during the lifecourse is one of stability rather than change.

27. Ravenna Helson described an awareness of limitations and death as a midlife:
    a. consciousness.
    b. stage.
    c. crisis.
    d. transformation.

28. The lives of Ram Dass (Richard Alpert) and Jerry Rubin tend to support which theory of personality?
    a. change
    b. stability
    c. introversion/extraversion
    d. neuroticism/openness

29. The text suggests several strategies for developing adaptive midlife socioemotional competencies. These include all of the following except:
    a. having a satisfying love relationship.
    b. becoming more selective in friendships.
    c. being generative.
    d. evaluating the kind of person you want to be.

30. Which research reported in the text best supports the idea that there are seasons in a woman's life?
    a. Neugarten's Kansas City study
    b. Costa and McRae's Baltimore study
    c. the Berkeley longitudinal studies
    d. Helson's Mills College study

31. A major benefit of a life review is to:
    a. see where you went wrong during your life course.
    b. understand the relationships in your life.
    c. help you start over so you can "do it right."
    d. gain a broader view on life that is put together in a meaningful picture.

Self Test B: Matching

Match the individuals in the left column with the appropriate descriptors in the right column.

1. Erick Erikson
2. Roger Gould
3. Danien Levinson
4. George Vaillant
5. Bernice Neugarten
6. Judith Brown
7. Ravenna Helson
8. William James

9. Paul Costa & R. R. McRae

a. found evidence for stability in the "big five" personality factors
b. found midlife consciousness, rather than crisis, in Mills college alumnae
c. American psychologist who said personality is solidly set by age 30
d. believes an age group's social environment can alter its social clock
e. believes that only a minority of adults experience a midlife crisis
f. added two stages to Erikson's theory of personality development
g. believes that only a minority of adults experience a midlife crisis
h. sees development as a series of crises to be resolved throughout life
i. anthropologist who believes middle age has many advantages for women in nonindustrialized societies

Essay Questions:

1. You have found yourself stuck in the middle of an argument between your two best friends. One says that people never change, they're the same way they are at 50 as they were at 15; the other says that people are constantly changing—look at all the famous musicians who have moved on from folk, to Rock'n'Roll, to Rhythm & Blues, to Country—even Pat Boone went from Bobby Sox music to Heavy Metal. How would you mediate between these two positions, based on what you have learned from this chapter?

2. Your cousin is about to turn 40, and has confided in you his conccern about going through the midlife crisis. He is also concerned that his wife, who will be 40 next year, will have a similar crisis. He wants to know all that you know about what will and will not predict a crisis for both of them. What will you tell him, and what will you conlude in light of the research that has been conducted?

Key to Self Test A:

1.	a	457		17.	c	466
2.	b	457		18.	b	466-467
3.	c	458		19.	a	466
4.	b	459		20.	d	468
5.	b	459		21.	c	469
6.	a	459		22.	b	470
7.	a	459		23.	a	471
8.	b	460		24.	d	471
9.	a	459		25.	c	471
10.	d	461		26.	c	471
11.	a	461		27.	a	471
12.	c	462		28.	b	472
13.	a	463		29.	b	472
14.	a	463		30.	d	471
15.	c	464		31.	d	473
16.	d	464				

Key to Self-Test B:

1. h
2. g
3. e
4. f
5. d

6. i
7. b
8. c
9. a

Key to Essay Questions:

1. Here you will need to examine all of the personality studies (e.g., Neugarten's Kansas City study, Costa and McRae's Baltimore study [remember the "big five"], the Berkeley longitudinal study, and Helson's Mills College study). Indicate what each study says about what does and does not change; then, based on the evidence presented, come to a conclusion about change over the life span.

2. To answer this question you will need to address all of the theories presented about adult development (e.g., Erikson's, Levinson's, the life-events approach) to discuss their different positions on whether a crisis is experienced by all, some, or no adults. Be sure to address gender differences and cultural differences in answering this question.

Research Project 1: Restructuring Perceptions of Parents

This project will assist you in understanding the relationship between parents and their children across the lifespan. Refer back to *Explorations in Life-Span Development: Restructuring Our Relationships with and Conceptions of Our Parents* on page 460. Develop a questionnaire that will assess your respondents' perceptions of their parents (feel free to answer the questions yourself, as well). Some questions are used to introduce this "exploration," and you may gather others from looking at the research studies discussed (i.e., Berquist, Greenberg, & Klaum, 1993; Josselson, 1996 [also look at her book, *Finding Herself: Pathways to Identity Development in Women*, 1987]; Labouvie-Vief, 1995, 1996); and, of course, you may develop your own questions. Gather demographic data, such as age, sex, cultural background, and other information you think will be important to understand your findings. Create a chart to assist you in assessing the similarities and differences in the ways that adolescents, early adults, and middle adults view their parents and their relationships with their parents. On the basis of your findings, answer the following questions.

1. What similarities did you notice among adolescents, early adults, and middle adults in terms of how they perceive their parents and their relationships with their parents?
2. What differences did you notice among adolescents, early adults, and middle adults in terms of how they perceive their parents and their relationships with their parents?
3. What patterns of development did you notice when comparing the three groups in terms of the material discussed in this chapter?
4. Were your observations consistent with what you might expect from the research described? Explain your response.
5. What might you conclude about the development of relationships between children and their parents based on your observations?

Research Project 2: Assessing the Social Clock

Figure 17.5 in the text presents a comparison of "Individuals' Conceptions of the Right Age for Major Life Events and Achievements: Late 1950s and Late 1970s." Using the questions in that figure, survey college students as well as other members of your family and community, being sure to record age and gender. Calculate and chart the percentage of male and female respondents who agree with the suggested times for those activities/events (look at the ages of your respondents to determine if there is any major difference from one age category to another--if there is, use that as an additional variable in your chart). Compare the responses with those given in the late '50s and late '70s.

Activity/Event	Appropriate age range	% Agreeing (late '50s study)		% Agreeing (late '70s study)		% Agreeing (current study)	
		Men	Women	Men	Women	Men	Women
Best age for man to marry	20-25						
Best age for woman to marry	19-24						
When most people should become grandparents	45-50						
Best age to finish school & go to work	20-22						
When men should be settled on a career	24-26						
When most men hold their top jobs	45-50						
When most people should be ready to retire	60-65						
When a man has the most responsibilities	35-50						
When a man accomplishes the most	40-50						
The prime of life for a man	35-50						
When a woman has the most responsibilities	25-40						
When a woman accomplishes the most	30-45						

1. What similarities did you notice across the different studies?
2. What differences did you notice across the different studies?
3. What gender similarities and differences did you notice in all three time periods? What might you conclude about how men and women view activities/events within the context of social clocks?
4. What patterns did you notice when comparing the three time periods in terms of the material discussed in this chapter?
5. Were your observations consistent with what you might expect from the research described? Explain your response.
6. What might you conclude about changes in attitudes about social clocks and the time frame within which society believes certain activities or events must take place, based on your observations?

Research Project 3: Engaging in a Life Review

Refer to page 475, *Life-Span Health and Well-Being: Engaging in a Life Review*. Using the chart in that section, replicated below, or creating your own format, consider your own life (even if you have not yet reached middle age). As described in that section, consider every aspect of your life using the questions suggested, e.g., "What was most important about your childhood?" "What major events have changed your family?" "What aspects of your family life are you most and least satisfied with right now?" "How would you like to see your family life in the future, and what can you do to bring it there?" "How did you get into the work you are currently in?" "How far along have you progressed with respect to your personal goals?" "What can you do to progress along as you have wished?" "Do you need to adjust your goals for the future?" Add other questions concerning your education plans, travel, financial security, religious/spiritual side, and don't forget about the fun stuff. Also, you may wish to encourage other people you know (young and old) to do a life review as well.

Life Review Chart				
Aspects of Life	**Past**	**Present**	**Future**	**What I Need to Change**
Family				
Friends				
Education				
Career				
Travel				
Financial Security				
Religious/Spiritual				
Fun Stuff				

1. What have you learned about yourself, your goals, and how you have been achieving your goals from reviewing your life so far?
2. How can looking at your life help you understand how things are going, how they got there, and how you can get where you want to go?
3. Is there another method that would be more helpful to you in looking at who you are, where you've been, where you're at right now, and where you want to be in the future? Explain; then use that approach.
4. What has been the most useful outcome of doing a life review?

Section IX Late Adulthood

Chapter 18 Physical Development in Late Adulthood

Learning Objectives

1. Define and distinguish between life span and life expectancy, and indicate Americans' current life expectancy.

2. Sketch characteristics of the oldest old.

3. Compare the microbiological and macrobiological theories of aging.

4. Describe how the brain and sensory systems change with increasing age.

5. Indicate how sexual performance and sexual attitudes are affected by increasing age.

6. Identify the most common chronic health problems experienced by older adults and the most common causes of death.

7. Indicate the health-care and nursing home costs for elderly adults and discuss how health costs are and could be met by present and new government programs.

8. Indicate evidence for the claim that feelings of control and self-determination are good for nursing home patients' health and survival.

What is "life span" and
how has it changed over
the centuries?

What are the three
primary explanations of why
we age according to
microbiological theories
of aging?

What is "life expectancy" and
how has it changed over
the centuries?

Explain the
cellular clock theory.
How has that theory been
recently extended?

Describe the major
predictors of longevity
Explain the sex differences
that are seen in terms of
longevity.

Describe the free-radical
theory of aging.

What outcome with respect
to life expectancy for women
would be predicted in terms of
work stress?
Has that been the case?

How does the caramelization
theory explain
the process of aging?

Distinguish among the
young old, the old old, and
the oldest old.
What characteristics other than
age are noted among the oldest old?

How do macrobiological
theories explain
the process of aging?

Define the theories
that underlie the two basic levels
of biological explanations
of aging.

What changes
are typically seen
in the aging brain?

Three microbiological theories of aging: cellular clock theory, free radical theory, & caramelization theory

Life span: the upper boundary of life, the maximum number of years an individual can live; maximum life span of human beings is approximately 120 years of age
The life span has remained virtually unchanged since the beginning of recorded history.

Cellular clock theory: cells can divide a maximum of about 100 times; as we age, our cells become increasingly less capable of dividing (Leonard Hayflick, 1977)
Scientists have recently noted the tips of chromosomes (telomeres), DNA sequences that protect chromosomes, become increasingly shorter and can replicate only about 100 times.

Life expectancy: the number of years that will probably be lived by the average person born in a particular year
Improvements in medicine, nutrition, exercise, & lifestyle have increased life expectancy an average of 30 additional years since 1900.
Life expectancy of women born today is 80; for men born today it is 73.

Free-radical theory: people age because inside their cells normal metabolism produces unstable oxygen molecules known as free radicals; these molecules ricochet around the cells, damaging DNA & other cellular structures

Major predictors of longevity: heredity & family history, health (weight, diet, smoking, exercise), education, personality, & lifestyle
Beginning at age 25 females outnumber males; by age 75 over 61% of the population is female; factors include lifestyle & biology (women have more resistance to infections & degenerative diseases, perhaps because of X chromosome)

Caramelization theory: excess sugars bind with proteins to form a sticky, weblike coating that, over time, can build up & stiffen joints, block arteries, & cloud tissue

If life expectancy is influenced by stress of work, the sex difference should be narrowing (i.e., women dieing earlier) because more women are entering the labor force, but the opposite is occurring, perhaps because self-esteem & work satisfaction are outweighing the stress of work.

Macrobiological theories of aging: focus at levels of organization higher than cellular level, such as hormones (e.g., testosterone, human growth hormone, DHEA, melatonin; NIA suggests **not** taking hormone supplements), the immune system (e.g., thymus gland), & internal homeostasis (body's ability to restore homeostasis & repair declines beginning at age 30)

Young old/old age: 65-74 years of age
Old old/late old age: 75 years & older
Oldest old: 85 years & older
The **oldest old** are more likely to be female, have a much higher morbidity rate, & greater incidence of disability; more likely to be in institutions, less likely to be married, & more likely to have less education

Changes in the aging brain: brain occupies about 90% of cranial cavity from age 20-50, progressively less after 50; volume of cerebrospinal fluid begins increasing about age 40 & speeds up after 60; possible deficit in cholinergic activity & norepinephrine in older adults; loss of neurons, which may be from 15-57%; however, aging brain retains much plasticity & adaptiveness

Microbiological theories of aging: look within the body's cells to explain aging; the label "micro" is used because a cell is a very small unit of analysis
Macrobiological theories of aging: examine life at a more global level of analysis than the cell; "macro" refers to a larger, more global level of analysis

Explain the significance
of the nuns' study by Snowden
(1995, 1997).

What is arthritis and
what parts of the body
does it affect?

Describe the sensory
changes that take place
in late adulthood.

Describe osteoporosis and
the populations it
most commonly affects.
How can it be prevented?

What changes take place
in the circulatory
and respiratory systems
during late adulthood?

Describe the characteristics
of the robust
oldest old.

Describe the changes
in human sexual performance
related to aging.

Explain the three kinds of
services or levels offered
in nursing homes.

What are the
major health problems and
causes of death
in old age?

Describe how providing options
for control and teaching
coping skills
are related to health in
nursing homes.

What are
chronic disorders?

Describe the rules of thumb
for elderly people to cope
effectively with their
health problems.

Arthritis: an inflammation of the joints accompanied by pain, stiffness, & movement problems; especially common in older adults There is no known cure, but symptoms can be reduced by drugs (e.g., aspirin), range-of-motion exercises, weight reduction, & replacement of crippled joints with prostheses

The nuns are the largest group of brain donors in the world--by examining their brains, & others, neuroscientists have learned of the brain's remarkable capacity to change & grow, even in old age; looking at the brains of the intellectually stimulated nuns, researchers have found that stimulating the brain with mental exercises may cause neurons to increase dendritic branching

Osteoporosis: an aging disorder involving an extensive loss of bone tissue & the main reason many older adults walk with a marked stoop; women are especially vulnerable to osteoporosis, the leading cause of broken bones in women; more common in white, thin, small-framed women over age 60
Prevention: young/middle-aged women: eat calcium-rich foods, get lots of exercise (e.g., weight lifting), avoid smoking; estrogen replacement therapy after menopause

Sensory changes in late adulthood: vision (e.g., decreased night vision, slower dark adaptation, reduced peripheral vision, need for larger print), hearing, taste, smell, & pain (decreased sensitivity to/less likely to suffer from pain); sensory acuity may be related to behaviors such as bathing, grooming, doing household chores, intellectual activities, tv viewing

Robust oldest old: 33% of adults over 80 in one sample were classified robust based on: no difficulty walking 1/4 mile, stooping, crouching, kneeling, lifting 10 lbs, walking up 10 steps without resting; 3/4 of robust elders had no hospitalizations & fewer than six doctor visits in previous 12 months

Circulatory system: blood pressure may rise due to illness, obesity, anxiety, stiffening of blood vessels, lack of exercise; for healthy heart, amount of blood pumped stays the same or may even increase; **Respiratory system**: lung capacity drops 40% from age 20 to 80; lungs lose elasticity, chest shrinks, diaphragm weakens; these can be improved

Three levels of nursing care: skilled nursing facility (most extensive, carefully reviewed & monitored by federal & state governments); in intermediate or ordinary nursing facilities care is less extensive; residential nursing care is mainly routine maintenance & personal assistance in meeting day-to-day needs, but may include some rehabilitation

Sexual performance: greater change in male than in female: orgasms less frequent, need more direct stimulation to produce an erection Absent disease & the belief that old people are or should be asexual, sexuality can be lifelong. Even without intercourse, closeness, sensuality, & being valued persist in relationships.

Giving options for control/teaching coping skills: Individuals who believe they have high degree of control are more likely to feel their actions affect their lives, thus more likely to take better care of themselves (Rodin, 1990); perception of control reduces stress & stress-related illnesses; learning assertiveness & time management reduces cortisol

Health problems: heart conditions, diabetes, asthma, & arthritis; low income is strongly related to health problems in late adulthood

Causes of death: heart disease, cancer, cerebrovascular disease (stroke), chronic lung diseases, pneumonia, influenza, diabetes, & accidents

Rules of thumb for dealing with health problems: speak up (ask for explanations, bring Rx drugs to exams for doctor to see); question assertions based solely on age; get the family involved (let them know your wishes ahead of time); decide now instead of waiting for a crisis (e.g., fill out a living will)

Chronic disorders: characterized by a slow onset and a long duration; chronic disorders are rare in early adulthood, increase during middle adulthood, & become common in late adulthood

Self-Test A: Multiple Choice

1. In the "Images of Life-Span Development" section, the author relates a story about 85-year-old Sadie Halperin. To what does she attribute her increased vitality?
   a. better medical treatment
   b. improved nutrition
   c. exercise
   d. her state of mind

2. With improvements in medicine, nutrition, exercise, and lifestyle, our life:
   a. span has increased.
   b. expectancy has increased.
   c. expectancy has stayed the same, but our lives are healthier.
   d. expectancy has dropped, but the quality of life has improved.

3. What factor was found to be the best predictor of longevity in the Duke Longitudinal Study?
   a. health
   b. not smoking
   c. education
   d. happiness

4. Women outlive men for all but which of the following reasons?
   a. financial status
   b. health attitudes
   c. occupations
   d. lifestyle

5. The second X chromosome that women have appears to give them a health advantage over men in that it may:
   a. counteract the negative effects of free radicals.
   b. be associated with production of more antibodies to fight disease.
   c. offer greater resistance for dealing with stress.
   d. protect women against lung cancer, a leading cause of death in men.

6. Who would be classified as the "oldest old"?
   a. Methusaleh, who is 78
   b. Eve, who is 83
   c. Noah, who is 88
   d. all three are among the oldest old

7. Marisol is 35 years old and has never been married. She has an 88-year-old grandmother, but never met her other grandparents because they died before she was born. She exercises daily, does not smoke, and is a practical woman who works as a patent attorney in a large, well-respected law firm. What might we predict about her life expectancy?
   a. Her grandmother's long life would predict long life for Marisol.
   b. Being single at 35 and having three grandparents who died early would predict a shorter-than-average life expectancy.
   c. Her education, occupation, and lifestyle would predict a longer-than-average life expectancy.
   d. There is not enough information to predict her life expectancy.

8. As more information is gathered concerning the life and abilities of individuals over age 85, a more _____ picture is beginning to emerge.
   a. optimistic
   b. homogeneous
   c. depressing
   d. psychopathic

9. All of the following are microbiological theories of aging *except* the _____ theory.
   a. lifespan
   b. cellular clock
   c. free-radical
   d. caramelization

10. Microbiological theories of aging:
    a. take a broad perspective to explain the aging process.
    b. look within the body's cells to explain aging.
    c. assume an interaction between genetics and the environment.
    d. predict that we could, under special conditions, live for 200 years.

11. Macrobiological theories of aging focus on:
    a. the cell.
    b. genetics.
    c. systems within the body.
    d. cellular interaction.

12. Leonard Hayflick found that cells can divide a maximum of about _____ times.
    a. 50
    b. 100
    c. 500
    d. 1,000

13. A recent extension to Hayflick's cellular clock theory suggests that cells die because:
    a. they disintegrate over time.
    b. they become too large and are no longer able to sustain themselves, thus they explode and leave harmful waste.
    c. the telomeres, or DNA sequences that cap the chromosomes, become shorter over time.
    d. the RNA in our bodies is programmed to stop sending nutrients to the cells over time.

14. Jeremy has read that by taking testosterone supplements he will maintain muscle and increase his energy and sex drive, so he is willing to pay the $100 each month for a testosterone patch. If 70-year-old Jeremy is aging normally, without any illnesses or unhealthful habits, we might expect his reputable doctor to:
    a. encourage him to use the patch because it will make life happier for Jeremy and his wife.
    b. discourage him from using the patch because at his age he should be slowing down his sex drive to maintain his health.
    c. discourage him from using the patch because it's unnecessary in terms of normal sex drive and can trigger prostate tumors and increase risk of stroke.
    d. suggest a penile implant instead.

15. Which hormone has been claimed to improve sleep, protect cells from free-radical damage, strengthen immunity, and prevent cancer, but the NIA suggests not taking it due to potential risks?
    a. testosterone
    b. human growth hormone (HGH)
    c. dehydroepiandrosterone (DHEA)
    d. melatonin

16. In the aging brain, it appears that:
    a. dendritic expansion compensates for neural loss.
    b. neural cell size is compensated for by myelin loss.
    c. neural efficiency is compensated for by neural size.
    d. neural transmitter production increases as neural numbers are lost.

17. Which of the following *is not* a normal decline in vision due to aging?
    a. diminished tolerance for glare that reduces night vision
    b. slower dark adaptation, taking longer to recover vision when going from light to dark areas
    c. lower ability to detect events in the center of the visual field
    d. reduction in the quality or intensity of light reaching the retina

18. Sixty-five-year-old Julia does not hear high-frequency sounds quite as well as she did at 25. Regarding this change in hearing:
    a. she would be a good candidate for two hearing aids, which would correct each ear separately.
    b. she is typical of her age group.
    c. people should speak more loudly to her.
    d. she will find reading more enjoyable than watching television.

19. Eighty-year-old Ethel noticed she cut her foot, although she didn't feel any great pain when she did it. Since it is normal for older adults to be less sensitive to pain, Ethel:
    a. should consider herself lucky it didn't hurt.
    b. shouldn't worry about it one way or another, just bandage her foot.
    c. needs to be aware of this since not feeling pain may mask injury or illness that needs treatment.
    d. should be concerned that while it may be "normal," it may also indicate some other underlying disease process.

20. All of the following changes normally take place in the respiratory system between ages 20 and 80 *except*:
    a. lung capacity drops 40%.
    b. lungs lose elasticity.
    c. the chest expands.
    d. diaphragm weakens.

21. Physiological changes that affect sexual behavior:
    a. are more prevalent in men than in women.
    b. are more prevalent in women than in men.
    c. cannot be corrected in men and limit their sexual activity.
    d. cannot be corrected in women and limit their sexual activity.

22. A study by Matthias et al. (1997) of more than 1,200 adults with a mean age of 77 found:
    a. over half of them had participated in sexual activity in the past month.
    b. two-thirds were satisfied with their current level of sexual activity.
    c. almost 75% of them had discontinued having sex within the past five years.
    d. the men were more sexually active than the women.

23. The most common chronic disorder in late adulthood is:
    a. hypertension.
    b. arthritis.
    c. diabetes.
    d. heart condition.

24. The chronic illness that puts the greatest limitation on work is:
    a. asthma.
    b. arthritis.
    c. a heart condition.
    d. diabetes.

25. The leading cause of death among the elderly is:
    a. heart disease.
    b. cancer.
    c. stroke.
    d. influenza.

26. The decline in strokes over the last several decades is due to all of the following *except*:
    a. a decrease in smoking.
    b. improved treatment of high blood pressure.
    c. better diet.
    d. less overexertion.

27. An aging disorder that is associated with calcium and vitamin D deficiencies, estrogen depletion, and lack of exercise is:
    a. arthritis.
    b. osteoporosis.
    c. pernicious anemia.
    d. depression.

28. To prevent osteoporosis, young and middle-aged women should do all of the following *except*:
    a. avoid weight-bearing exercises.
    b. eat foods rich in calcium.
    c. avoid smoking.
    d. subscribe to estrogen replacement therapy.

29. Compared to younger persons, elderly adult accident victims are likely to spend more time in the hospital because:
    a. recovery is often complicated by mental depression.
    b. Medicare focuses mainly on long-term treatments.
    c. healing rates are slower in older adults.
    d. family members feel the older adult is safer in the hospital.

30. Edith is 82 years old. She walks a mile a day, exercises with 10-lb weights, can stoop, crouch, and kneel, and walks the two flights of stairs to her apartment rather than take the elevator. She would be considered among the _____ oldest old.
    a. majority of the
    b. robust
    c. exceptional
    d. typical

31. Approximately ___% of adults over 65 reside in nursing homes, compared with over ___% of those over 85.
    a. 5; 20
    b. 5; 50
    c. 10; 20
    d. 10; 50

32. In a residential nursing facility:
    a. personal care is given to meet day-to-day needs.
    b. medical care is extensive and closely monitored.
    c. nursing care is moderate.
    d. patients care for themselves and meet for meals.

33. Bill's adult children realize that he needs some nursing assistance in meeting daily needs and require only a least restrictive nursing facility. They should look for which of the following type of nursing homes?
   a. skilled
   b. intermediate
   c. residential
   d. practical

34. Alternatives to nursing homes include all of the following *except*:
   a. home health care.
   b. day care centers.
   c. long-term care facilities.
   d. preventive medicine clinics.

35. Judith Rodin and Ellen Langer found that nursing home patients who were given some responsibility and control over their lives became:
   a. more difficult to manage.
   b. more likely to want to return home.
   c. healthier.
   d. happier, but lived no longer than those individuals who were given no responsibility and self-control.

36. In comparing physician responsiveness to older versus younger patients, Green et al. (1987) found that physicians were:
   a. more responsive to older patients.
   b. more responsive to younger patients.
   c. equally responsive to patients of both age groups.
   d. more responsive to those with more severe illnesses, despite their age.

37. Blumenthal et al. (1989) found that older adults who were _____ experienced significant improvement in cardiovascular fitness.
   a. in a yoga class
   b. taught transcendental meditation
   c. in an aerobic exercise group
   d. on a weight-loss program

38. Older adults who subscribe to a low-calorie diet:
   a. have been shown to live substantially longer than those who do not.
   b. are likely to die sooner than those who do not.
   c. may be risking their health, because not much is known about the long-term effects of low-calorie diets.
   d. should be on high-protein diets with vitamin supplements.

39. The vitamin supplements called antioxidants may affect health by counteracting the effects of:
   a. white corpuscles.
   b. DNA changes.
   c. free radicals.
   d. cholesterol.

40. Which statement concerning health care and the elderly is true?
   a. Elderly individuals are least likely to be given prescription drugs.
   b. Elderly individuals are often excluded from research to cure ailments that are common to their age group.
   c. Women over age 65 are least likely to get breast cancer and the most likely to be treated for it.
   d. Elderly people tend to overreport vision and hearing ailments because they believe such problems are normal.

Self Test B: Matching

Match the individuals in the left column with the appropriate descriptors in the right column.

1. Leonard Hayflick
2. Stanley Rapaport
3. Judith Rodin
4. Ellen Langer
5. William Ershler
6. Richard Schultz
7. Francis Bacon
8. Linus Pauling

a. showed that nursing home residents who controlled visits were healthier
b. says that perception of control may reduce stress & related hormones
c. first author to recommend scientific evaluation of diet and longevity
d. says older adults may respond better to treatment for many types of tumors
e. found that old brains rewired themselves to compensate for losses
f. believes there are biological clocks in our cells that cause us to age
g. argued that vitamin C slowed the aging process
h. argued the importance of older adults understanding they can choose what they think

Essay Questions:

1. Your next door neighbor is an eighty-year-old woman who knows you have been taking this class in life span development. She confides in you that she feels she is slowing down and can't quite do the things she used to do. Also, she feels that none of her doctors takes the time to listen to her, they just say "Norma, you're in great shape for a woman your age." Knowing she's an intelligent woman who practiced law for fifty years, what would you tell her about the aging process, how to keep healthy, and how to get the best possible medical assistance?

2. You have been asked by your local Rotary Club to design a program for their older members to help them stay in optimum health. What areas would you focus on, and what kinds of activities would you suggest for them?

Key to Self Test A:

1.	c	p.	483	21. a	p.	493
2.	b	p.	484	22. b	p.	493
3.	a	p.	484	23. b	p.	493
4.	a	p.	484	24. c	p.	493
5.	b	p.	484	25. a	p.	493
6.	c	p.	485	26. d	p.	493
7.	d	p.	486	27. b	p.	494
8.	a	p.	487	28. a	p.	494-495
9.	a	p.	487-488	29. c	p.	496
10.	b	p.	487	30. b	p.	496
11.	c	p.	488	31. a	p.	496-497
12.	b	p.	487	32. a	p.	497
13.	c	p.	488	33. c	p.	497
14.	c	p.	488	34. c	p.	497
15.	d	p.	489	35. c	p.	497-498
16.	a	p.	490	36. b	p.	498-499
17.	c	p.	491	37. c	p.	499
18.	b	p.	492	38. c	p.	500
19.	c	p.	492	39. c	p.	501
20.	c	p.	493	40. b	p.	503

Key to Self-Test B:

1. f   5. d
2. e   6. a
3. b   7. c
4. h   8. g

Key to Essay Questions:

1. To answer this question you would basically summarize everything in this chapter including age changes in the brain, the sensory, circulatory, and respiratory systems, and you might also let her know there is no need to expect a reduction in her sexual activity; then let her know about the various health issues including the diseases that are common and what she can do to reduce her risk factors (e.g., estrogen replacement therapy, taking calcium, exercising), while letting her know what has and has not yet been determined about use of supplements (yes on calcium and anti-oxidants, but either too little is known about some of the others or they pose potential risks). Finally, help her develop techniques to talk effectively with her physicians, pharmacist, and family members about her health needs and how to find the types of information and health care that are appropriate for her. Do be sure to let her know about the research by Langer, Rodin, and Schulz about the importance of maintaining control (or, at least, the perception of control) for living a longer, healthier life.

2. Here you would first need to address the basic issues of aging--what can be expected to change (e.g., vision, hearing) and what can be done to avoid problems (e.g., don't smoke, do exercise). Then discuss what kinds of things you believe (in light of this chapter) would be appropriate for helping seniors maintain a long, healthy life. Be sure to include exercise and nutrition as well as assertiveness training.

Research Project 1: The Nuns' Study

As our author notes, the Nuns' study is an intriguing investigation of Alzheimer's disease; it is one that I discuss with my students that offers great potential for understanding the disease and learning about its precursors and how to forestall its onset. Although space did not allow for a greater discussion of this study, you may wish to pursue it further because of the implications it may have in terms of prolonging mental acuity. To do so, you may wish to explore the research further by reading what David Snowden has written about his investigation so far--you can find articles in the library (see the Reference section of the text for the three listed on page 491); check out the Internet; or even write to Professor Snowden at the University of Kentucky. Also, there are videotapes about this research--the one I use in my classes was from Nightline with Ted Koppel a few years back and is obtainable from ABC News (*Beating Alzheimer's — The Nuns' Gift*). One thing you will note as you delve further into this topic is that remaining active does not necessarily **prevent** Alzheimer's, but it does appear to delay the onset. What advantage would you see to that? Another thing you'll find is that early life experiences and abilities seem to be connected to later life lucidity, on the one hand, but on the other hand, keeping your mind and body challenged acts as a buffer. As you read more about this topic, consider what you have read in Chapter 18.

1. What did you notice in your reading about the Nuns' study that was consistent with what you read in the chapter?
2. What differences did you notice between your reading about the Nuns' study and what you read in the chapter? How would you explain those differences (if there were any)?
3. What patterns of development did you notice when learning more about the research on Alzheimer's in terms of the material discussed in this chapter?
4. What might you conclude about cognitive changes with age based on your reading?

Research Project 2: Centenarians View Life

Consider the thoughts of the centenarians presented on page 488 ("Through the Eyes of Adults"). While you may not know anyone who is 100 years old or older, do your own interviews of elderly people you do know and compare them with the comments made by the five representatives of Segerberg's (1982) sample.

1. What similarities did you notice when comparing the comments of the five people from Segerberg's sample? What similarities did you notice when comparing the comments of the people you interviewed with those from Segerberg's sample?
2. What differences did you notice when comparing the comments of the five people from Segerberg's sample? What differences did you notice when comparing the comments of the people you interviewed with those from Segerberg's sample?
3. What patterns of development did you notice when looking at the comments, both from Segerberg's study and from your own interviews in terms of the material discussed in this chapter?
4. Were your observations consistent with what you might expect from the research described? Explain your response.
5. What might you conclude about development in old age based on your observations?

Research Project 3: Can You Live to Be 100?

Take the test in Table 18.1 for predicting your longevity, noting the additional instructions in the introductory paragraph (e.g., if you are in your 50s or 60s add ten years). Adding and subtracting the points in each category, determine your life expectancy total and compare it with the basic life expectancy (73 for males, 80 for females). Where do you rank? Give the test to family members and friends to see where they rank. How does your score compare with theirs and with the scores of your classmates? What steps could you take at this point in your life to extend your life expectancy?

Chapter 19 Cognitive Development in Late Adulthood

Learning Objectives

1. Compare Horn's position on intelligence with Baltes' and Schaie's positions.

2. Define and distinguish between cognitive mechanics and cognitive pragmatics.

3. Use the information on education, work, and health to explain why cohort effects need to be taken into account in studying the cognitive functioning of older adults.

4. Indicate how speed of processing, memory, and wisdom change with increasing age.

5. Indicate which cognitive skills are trainable and which ones are not.

6. Describe the trends in part-time employment and the age of retirement for people in the late adulthood period.

7. Understand the stages of retirement.

8. Describe the rate, causes, and symptoms of depression and Alzheimer's disease in older adults.

9. Discuss the significance of religion in people's lives during late adulthood.

Contrast crystallized intelligence with fluid intelligence.	Describe what happens to speed of processing information in late adulthood & how older adults compensate.
Explain the problems that K. Warner Schaie (1983) found with Horn's research on intellectual decline.	Describe episodic memory.
How does Paul Baltes recast the issue of cognitive decline?	Describe semantic memory.
Explain the computer analogy of cognitive mechanics.	Explain the concept of working memory.
Explain the computer analogy of cognitive pragmatics.	Explain the concept of perceptual speed.
What does sensory functioning predict in late life?	Which noncognitive factors influence an older adult's performance on memory tasks?

Speed of processing declines in late adulthood, but there is much individual variation; also, while reactions may be slower, adults may compensate for loss of speed in other ways--e.g., the older typists who physically typed more slowly but compensated by looking farther ahead to see the characters that were coming up & thus typed as fast as the younger typists

Crystallized intelligence: an individual's accumulated information & verbal skills, increases with age
Fluid intelligence: one's ability to reason abstractly, steadily declines from middle adulthood

Episodic memory: the retention of information about the where and when of life's happenings (e.g., what it was like when a younger sibling was born, what happened on your first date); younger adults have better episodic memory than older adults--older adults remember older events better than more recent events; the older the memory, the less accurate it is

Schaie (1983) argued that because Horn's data were cross-sectional, they can lead to erroneous conclusions; particularly, any differences that are found from one age group to another might be due to cohort effects involving educational differences rather than to age.

Semantic memory: knowledge about the world; including one's fields of expertise (e.g., knowledge of chess for a skilled chess player); general academic knowledge as that learned in school (e.g., geometry); and "everyday knowledge" about meanings of words, famous people, important places, common things; it is independent of one's personal identity with the past

Baltes (e.g., 1995) noted cohort effects in intelligence are important but smaller than originally assumed; recast the issue in terms of (1) the multidimensional, multidirectional nature of intelligence; and (2) the concept that with increasing age, more & more resources need to be invested in maintenance or repair.

Working memory: the concept currently used to describe short-term memory as a place for mental work; working memory is like a mental "workbench" that allows individuals to manipulate and assemble information when making decisions, solving problems, & comprehending written & spoken language

Cognitive mechanics: the hardware of the mind; they reflect the neurophysiological architecture of the brain developed through evolution; at the operational level, cognitive mechanics involve the speed & accuracy of the processes involving sensory input, visual & motor memory, discrimination, comparison, & categorization

Perceptual speed: a cognitive resource; the ability to perform simple perceptual-motor tasks such as deciding whether pairs of two-digit or two-letter strings are the same or different; shows considerable decline in late adulthood & is strongly linked with decline in working memory

Cognitive pragmatics: the culture-based software programs of the mind; at the operational level, cognitive pragmatics include reading & writing skills, language comprehension, educational qualifications, professional skills, & the type of knowledge about the self and life skills that help us to master or cope with life

Noncognitive factors that influence older adults' performance on memory tasks: health, education, & socioeconomic status; also, the testing situation

Sensory functioning is a strong late-life predictor of individual differences in intelligence;.

What is wisdom?
What categories are used to assess wisdom?

What are the seven phases of retirement?

How does Timothy Salthouse's conclusion about the link between health and cognitive performance differ from public opinion?

State the primary factors that predict who will adjust best to retirement.

Explain the terminal drop hypothesis.

What is major depression? What are the most common predictors of major depression?

What are the two main conclusions that have been derived from the research on declining cognitive skills in adulthood?

Define the term "dementia." How many types have been identified?

What are mnemonics & how are they used to improve older adults' cognitive skills?

What is Alzheimer's disease?

Explain the essence of the Age Discrimination Act of 1967.

What have the researchers found concerning religion and spirituality in old age?

Phases of retirement: remote (little is done to prepare for retirement); near (begin to participate in preretirement program); honeymoon (many people feel euphoric); disenchantment (recognize that preretirement fantasies about retirement were unrealistic); reorientation (take stock, pull self together, develop more realistic alternatives); stability (criteria set to evaluate choices in retirement & how to perform once choices made); termination (sick/dependent)

Wisdom: expert knowledge about the practical aspects of life that permits excellent judgment about important matters
Categories used to assess wisdom: basic factual knowledge; procedural knowledge; life-span context; value relativism; recognition & management of uncertainty

Predictors of who adjust best to retirement: those who adjust best are healthy, have adequate income, are active & better educated, have an extended social network including friends & family, & usually were satisfied with their lives before retirement

Salthouse (1992) concluded that, contrary to intuition & public opinion, there is little evidence that declines in cognitive performance are mediated by declines in health status.
In contrast, others such as Schaie conclude that some diseases--heart disease, diabetes, high blood pressure--are linked to cognitive dropoffs due to lifestyle (e.g., overeating, inactivity, stress.

Major depression: a mood disorder in which the individual is deeply unhappy, demoralzied, self-derogatory, & bored; individuals with major depression do not feel well, lose stamina easily, have poor appetite, & are listless & unmotivated
Common predictors: earlier depressive symptoms, poor health, loss events, low social support

Terminal drop hypothesis states that death is preceded by a decrease in cognitive functioning over approximately a 5-year period prior to death.

Dementia: a global term for any neurological disorder in which the primary symptoms involve a deterioration of mental functioning; among the most complex & debilitating of mental disorders among the elderly
Over 70 types or causes of dementia have been identified.

Two main conclusions about atrophying of cognitive skills in late adulthood: (1) there is plasticity, & training can improve the cognitive skills of many older adults; & (2) there is some loss in plasticity in late adulthood (Baltes, 1995)

Alzheimer's disease: a progressive, irreversible brain disorder (first diagnosed in 1906) that is characterized by gradual deterioration of memory, reasoning, language, & eventually physical functioning; the most common & possibly most serious type of dementia

Mnemonics: techniques designed to make memory more efficient; by teaching the elderly mnemonic techniques (e.g., method of loci, chunking), they are able to improve their memory

Religion in late adulthood: individuals over 65 are more likely than younger people to say religious faith is the most significant influence in their lives, they try to practice their faith, & they attend religious services; they are more likely to pray & be interested in spirituality; & religion appears to be related to a sense of well-being & life satisfaction in old age

Age Discrimination Act of 1967: became federal policy to prohibit the firing of employees due to their age before reaching mandatory retirement age; in 1978, Congress extended age from 65 to 70 for business, industry, & the federal government; in 1986, Congress banned mandatory retirement except where safety is an issue

Self-Test A: Multiple Choice

1. Lisa finds that as she enters middle adulthood, her ability to reason abstractly is declining. This decline is occurring in:
   a. crystallized intelligence.
   b. fluid intelligence.
   c. creative intelligence.
   d. abstract intelligence.

2. Which task requires crystallized intelligence?
   a. doing algebra problems
   b. interpreting metaphors
   c. writing a short story
   d. proving a theorem in geometry

3. John Horn says _____ increases with age.
   a. fluid intelligence
   b. crystallized intelligence
   c. chunking of information
   d. long-term memory

4. Which type of study shows general intellectual decline associated with age?
   a. cross-sectional
   b. longitudinal
   c. sequential
   d. quasi-experimental

5. K. Warner Schaie argues that cross-sectional studies of intelligence in late adulthood:
   a. can lead to erroneous conclusions due to problems associated with mortality.
   b. can lead to erroneous conclusions due to cohort differences.
   c. are the most relevant because they show the greatest difference in intellectual change over time.
   d. are not significantly different from longitudinal studies of intelligence in late adulthood.

6. Which factor plays the biggest role in determining the pattern of cognitive pragmatics in adulthood?
   a. evolution
   b. culture
   c. early neural development
   d. inheritance

7. In older adulthood:
   a. cognitive pragmatics can be more important to performance than cognitive mechanics.
   b. cognitive mechanics can be more important to performance than cognitive pragmatics.
   c. the relative influences of cognitive pragmatics and mechanics on performance may be virtually identical.
   d. any of the above may be correct.

8. Which of the following tasks will be most difficult for older adults?
   a. problem solving in a natural setting
   b. problem solving in a laboratory setting
   c. speeded tasks in a laboratory setting
   d. speeded tasks in a natural setting

9. In a study of younger and older typists, Salthouse (1984) found that:
   a. younger typists consistently outperformed the older typists.
   b. older typists consistently outperformed the younger typists.
   c. when older typists could look ahead, they typed as fast as younger typists.
   d. when the number of characters that the typists could look ahead at was limited, the younger typists slowed considerably.

10. Older subjects are brought into the laboratory and given a list of nonsense syllables to remember. They are then given a list of groceries to pick up at the store and their ability to remember the items is recorded. Research on memory ability in older adults would predict that their memory of the nonsense syllables will be _____ their memory of the grocery items.
    a. about the same as
    b. better than
    c. worse than
    d. poor, but better than

11. Evelyn is 101 years old, is active in her community, and continues to play the piano at social gatherings. She loves to tell stories about when she was a little girl. Based on the research on memory and aging, we could expect that:
    a. she believes her memory to be accurate, but in reality it has become increasingly inaccurate as she has aged.
    b. her memory of the events is accurate, and she is telling the stories as they happened.
    c. her memory of the events is accurate, but she is probably adding a lot to her stories that didn't happen.
    d. she can no longer remember these events very well, but she wants to entertain her audience, so she pretends it is good.

12. As we proceed into late adulthood, we can normally expect declines in all aspects of memory *except*:
    a. episodic memory.
    b. working memory.
    c. semantic memory.
    d. perceptual speed.

13. Expert knowledge about the practical aspects of life is known as:
    a. the stability phase.
    b. fluid intelligence.
    c. crystallized intelligence.
    d. wisdom.

14. Which task would require wisdom?
    a. remembering a grocery list
    b. braking when a pedestrian steps out in front of your car
    c. helping a son keep his marriage from falling apart
    d. helping a granddaughter with her algebra

15. When investigating real-world problem solving, Denny (1986) found all of the following *except*:
    a. practical problem-solving ability increased through the forties and fifties.
    b. 70-year-olds performed as well as 20-year-olds.
    c. 20-year-olds and 70-year-olds performed the task quite well.
    d. subjects of all ages did quite well on the task, but 20-year-olds did substantially better than subjects in the other age groups.

16. Which of the following characteristics is positively correlated with IQ scores?
    a. introversion
    b. well-rounded personality
    c. job experience
    d. educational experience

17. The text has noted that older adults return to school because they:
    a. become obsolete due to technological advances.
    b. want to learn more about aging.
    c. have a desire to learn more effective cognitive and social-coping skills.
    d. all of the above are correct.

18. Clarkson-Smith and Hartley (1989), in their study of the effects of exercise on cognitive functioning, found that:
    a. vigorous exercisers showed greater improvement than low exercisers.
    b. both vigorous and low exercisers showed similar improvement.
    c. there was improvement in the elderly, but not in the other age groups.
    d. only those in good health showed improvement.

19. The terminal drop hypothesis claims that death is preceded by a decrease in:
    a. physical functioning.
    b. cognitive functioning.
    c. social interaction.
    d. emotional attachment.

20. Which statement is most accurate concerning cognitive skills in the elderly?
    a. Training has little effect on slowing declines.
    b. An increasing number of developmentalists have found the elderly can be retrained.
    c. Memory is the only cognitive skill that can be improved by training.
    d. A shift from factual knowledge to wisdom occurs in most elderly adults.

21. The mnemonic being used when an item to be remembered is paired with a location is:
    a. chunking.
    b. story-telling.
    c. rehearsing.
    d. the method of loci.

22. All of the following are true when older workers are compared with younger workers *except*:
    a. older workers have better attendance records.
    b. older workers have fewer accidents.
    c. older workers have more disabling injuries.
    d. older workers are more productive.

23. The decline in the percentage of men over the age of 65 who continue to work full time is due to:
    a. age discrimination against the elderly.
    b. better retirement plans for the elderly.
    c. an increase in part-time work by the elderly.
    d. an inability to compete effectively with younger workers.

24. The 1986 United States ban on any type of age-related mandatory retirement would not apply to:
    a. Harpo, who was the president of 3-M.
    b. Groucho, who was a college professor.
    c. Chico, who was a mail carrier.
    d. Zeppo, who was a fire fighter.

25. In Europe:
    a. many of the capitalist countries are attempting to encourage early retirement, while the former communist countries are trying to encourage older adults to continue working.
    b. many of the former communist countries are attempting to encourage early retirement, while the capitalist countries are trying to encourage older adults to continue working.
    c. many capitalist and former communist countries are attempting to encourage early retirement.
    d. many capitalist and former communist countries are attempting to encourage older adults to continue working.

26. In which of Robert Atchley's (1976) retirement phases do workers begin attending pre-retirement seminars?
    a. honeymoon
    b. near
    c. remote
    d. stability

27. In the reorientation phase of retirement, individuals:
    a. develop realistic life alternatives for how to spend their time.
    b. adjust to engaging in all of the activities they eagerly anticipated when they were working.
    c. adjust to the many illnesses that accompany increasing age.
    d. begin to look forward to retirement with eager anticipation.

28. Who *is not* exhibiting a symptom of major depression?
    a. Ariel, who is making self-derogatory comments
    b. Belle, who has recurring nightmares
    c. Cathy, who is not eating
    d. Darlene, who is completely unmotivated

29. _____ *is not* a part of the definition of Alzheimer's disease.
    a. Irreversibility
    b. Genetically based
    c. Brain disorder
    d. Deterioration of memory and physical functioning

30. In the 1970s, a deficiency of acetylcholine, which plays an important part in memory, was discovered to occur in:
    a. major depression.
    b. Alzheimer's disease.
    c. arteriosclerosis.
    d. multi-infarct dementia.

31. Older adults may feel more vulnerable to crime due to:
    a. physical declines.
    b. inability to crime-proof their homes.
    c. the fact that most neighborhoods they live in have deteriorated and become high-crime areas.
    d. large amounts of cash kept at home due to their general distrust of banks.

32. When compared with younger adults, adults over the age of 65 receive _____ of psychological services.
    a. more than their share
    b. less than their share
    c. about the same amount
    d. substantially more than their share

33. Psychotherapists have been accused of failing to accept many older adult clients because:
    a. they believe the prognosis for the older adult is poor.
    b. fewer techniques for treating mental problems among older adults exist.
    c. older clients, compared to younger clients, are less likely to pay the therapists for services rendered.
    d. older clients typically forget appointments.

34. Which of the following would be most consistent with the research on religion and aging?
    a. Rivka, an 84-year-old widow who considers her religious faith to be extremely significant in her life, expresses a sense of well-being.
    b. Avram, a 75-year-old man who practices his religion faithfully, lacks a sense of satisfaction with his life.
    c. Malka, an 86-year-old housewife who has begun to doubt whether there is a god, is satisfied with her life as it is.
    d. Mort, an 80-year-old retiree who no longer practices his faith, expresses a sense of satisfaction with his life.

35. As noted in the text, religion can provide important psychological needs in older adults, including all of the following *except*:
    a. assistance in finding and maintaining a sense of meaningfulness and significance in life.
    b. the ability to accept impending death and the inevitable losses of old age.
    c. social activities and social support.
    d. assistance with psychological problems, such as depression.

36. Maria is attending a university program that will train her as a clinical psychologist who specializes in aging and working with the elderly. This is the _____ program.
    a. gerontology
    b. clinical geropsychology
    c. adulthood and aging
    d. clinical aging

37. According to Martha Storandt (1996), there is a lack of assessment instruments for use with older adults particularly in the areas of:
    a. Alzheimer's disease and myocardial infarction.
    b. Alzheimer's disease, affective disorders, and insomnia.
    c. senile dementia, hypersomnia, and schizophrenia.
    d. affective disorders, schizophrenia, and Alzheimer's disease.

38. Margaret Gatz argues that one step that should be taken in order for the current health-care system to meet the needs of older adults with mental disorders is to:
    a. allow physicians to provide prescriptions over the phone.
    b. consider limiting the types of psychological care covered by Medicare.
    c. create elder care centers in the workplace.
    d. put subtle pressure on the elderly to get help for their psychological problems.

Self-Test B: Matching

Match the individuals in the left column with the appropriate descriptors in the right column.

1. John Horn
2. K. Warner Schaie
3. Paul Baltes
4. Nancy Denny
5. Timothy Salthouse
6. Sherry Willis
7. Robert Atchley
8. Martha Storandt
9. Margaret Gatz

a. troubled by lack of coordination among components of health-care systems
b. gerontologist who described the seven phases of retirement
c. investigated the effects of training on cognitive skills of the elderly
d. distinguished between cognitive mechanisms and cognitive pragmatics
e. argues that fluid intelligence declines steadily from middle adulthood
f. described the state of assessment & treatment in clinical geropsychology
g. found people in their 20s & 70s equally good at practical problem solving
h. found age-related cognitive declines are independent of health
i. concludes that until late in life, intelligence remains stable

Self-Test C: Matching Phases of Retirement

Match the phases of retirement in the left column with the descriptions in the right column.

1. remote
2. near
3. honeymoon
4. disenchantment
5. reorientation
6. stability
7. termination

a. a time when retirees feel euphoric
b. retirement role replaced by sick/dependent role
c. begin to participate in preretirement programs
d. take stock, pull oneself together, develop more realistic life alternatives
e. individuals do little by way of preparing for retirement
f. recognize that preretirement fantasies about retirement were unrealistic
g. decide on set of criteria for evaluating retirement choices & how to perform once the choices are made

Essay Questions:

1. Your parents have started worrying about getting older and the effect that will have on their ability to take care of themselves and retain their cognitive functioning. Already they notice that they are forgetting more than they did even a year or two ago. What can you tell them about cognitive changes in late adulthood and how best to hold onto their mental faculties?

2. Your mother is CEO of a large corporation that offers an excellent retirement package. However, after evaluating a survey conducted of the employees, she is now concerned that relatively few employees have made any plans for their retirement. Because you are taking this Life-Span Development class, she has asked you to address her employees about retirement, their need to plan for the future (including both continuing work and retirement), and what they can expect once they do decide to retire. What will you tell them?

Key to Self Test A:

1.	b.	p.	507	20.	b	p.	513
2.	c	p.	507	21.	d	p.	513
3.	b	p.	507	22.	c	p.	515
4.	a	p.	507	23.	c	p.	515
5.	b	p.	507	24.	d	p.	515
6.	b	p.	509	25.	c	p.	515
7.	d	p.	509	26.	b	p.	516
8.	c	p.	509	27.	a	p.	516
9.	c	p.	509-510	28.	b	p.	517
10.	c	p.	510	29.	b	p.	518
11.	a	p.	510	30.	b	p.	518
12.	c	p.	510	31.	a	p.	519
13.	d	p.	511	32.	b	p.	519
14.	c	p.	511	33.	a	p.	519
15.	d	p.	511	34.	a	p.	519, 521
16.	d	p.	512	35.	d	p.	521
17.	d	p.	512	36.	b	p.	520
18.	a	p.	513	37.	b	p.	520
19.	b	p.	513	38.	c	p.	523

Key to Self Test B:

1.	e		6.	c
2.	i		7.	b
3.	d		8.	f
4.	g		9.	a
5.	h			

Key to Self Test C:

1.	e		5.	d
2.	c		6.	g
3.	a		7.	b
4.	f			

Key to Essay Question:

1. To answer this question you will need to discuss the differences among the researchers (e.g., John Horn, K. Warner Schaie, Paul Baltes) in terms of what type(s) of decline might or might not be expected (e.g., crystallized versus fluid; cognitive mechanics versus cognitive pragmatics) and what would affect whether a decline is or is not seen. You might also reassure them in terms of the method of research study, so that cross-sectional studies more likely reflect cohort differences rather than actual decline, which is less evident in longitudinal studies. Also address the issues of sensory/motor and speed of processing, and what has been concluded about the various memory systems (e.g., declines are seen in episodic and working memory, not in semantic memory); the relationship between health and cognitive aging; and look at the different factors involved in the terminal drop hypothesis. Then end with the good news by Nancy Denny (in solving practical problems) and Sherry Willis, K. Warner Schaie, and Carolyn Nesselroade about the effects of teaching memory strategies (e.g., mnemonics) and retraining.

2. First you would need to address changes in work patterns since the turn of the century, and look at how many older adults are now continuing to work either full-time or part-time, noting that as the Age Discrimination Act now stands, unless there is an issue of safety (e.g., fire or police departments), employers are prohibited from firing older workers. Then go into Atchley's phases of retirement, noting that young people who believe themselves to be far from retirement tend not to be thinking or planning, however, that is the best time to start. Finally, address the issue of who adjusts best to retirement, pointing out ways to retain their sense of control and self-determination, which are so important for their continued health and well-being--something they are sure to want when they finally have time to enjoy life.

Research Project 1: Retirement Planning

First, consider your own present situation with regard to career planning and retirement planning in light of the material presented in the text. Which phase are you in? Then, interview people of different ages, asking them about the type of job they currently hold or if they are currently retired, the type of career path they see for themselves or they followed while employed, the plans they have made for their retirement (whether still working or retired), and what they expect they will be doing or expected they would be doing upon retirement. For those who are already retired, ask what they are currently doing with their time and if that is consistent with what they anticipated. Based on your interviews, can you chart these findings in a way that would reflect Atchley's phases of retirement? Were your findings consistent with what you might expect from the text (e.g., people who are further away from retirement have not yet begun to plan)? What have you learned in terms of your own retirement plans from doing this?

1. What similarities did you notice among your respondents in terms of how they have planned for retirement? Was age a predictive variable?
2. What differences did you notice among your respondents in terms of how they have planned for retirement? Was age a predictive variable?
3. What patterns of development did you notice when looking at people's retirement plans in terms of the material discussed in this chapter?
4. Were your observations consistent with what you might expect from the research described? Explain your response.
5. What might you conclude about retirement planning based on your observations?

Research Project 2: Maintaining a Challenging Life in Old Age

Visit local senior centers, including nursing homes, senior day care, and centers for active older adults. Notice the people who are active and involved as compared with those who seem isolated and withdrawn. Get permission to interview some of these elderly people--those who are active as well as those who are more isolated. Determine from them what it is that they believe keeps them active or withdrawn, involved or isolated, happy or unhappy, etc. Note what the text says about keeping mentally active, staying physically healthy, reducing cognitive decline, adapting to work and retirement, maintaining good mental health, and having an interest in religion or the meaning of life. Combining what you find from these observations and interviews with the information in the text, design two programs: (1) one to help younger adults develop the types of skills they will need to remain challenged and happy with their lives; and (2) one to help older adults maximize and enjoy their lives by remaining as active and involved as their health allows.

1. While interviewing your respondents, did you notice that some of the people who have a sense of well-being may have more physical handicaps and chronic health problems than some who seem unhappy? What would account for this?
2. What part does religion play in your respondents' sense of well-being and satisfaction with life?
3. Is what you learned from these interviews consistent with what you read in the text? Explain.
4. What might you conclude about maintaining a challenging life in old age based on your observations?

Chapter 20 Socioemotional Development in Late Adulthood

Learning Objectives

1. Compare and contrast the three major social theories of aging.

2. Evaluate the claim that old people are an economic burden on society because they suffer poor health and do not work.

3. Describe income levels and living arrangement options for older adults.

4. Explain the double jeopardy faced by aging ethnic minority individuals and aging women.

5. Describe the importance of friendship among older adults.

6. Compare and contrast various adaptations of married versus single old people.

7. Explain what it means to be a grandparent, what the most common grandparenting styles are, and how they differ across gender and for blended families.

8. Compare Erikson's and Peck's characterizations of personality in late adulthood.

9. Identify the factors that predict life satisfaction for older adults.

11. Summarize the bases of successful aging.

Explain the basic
concepts of
disengagement theory.

What is eldercare?
What important issue does
it raise?

Explain the basic
concepts of
activity theory.

Discuss the policy issue
of
generational inequity.

Explain the basic
concepts of
social breakdown-reconstruction
theory.

What special concerns
do the elderly have
about income?

What is ageism?
What are the consequences
of ageism?

Discuss the various forms
of living arrangements
commonly seen among
the elderly.

What are the seven
stereotypes of the elderly that
Hummert et al. (1994) found
consistently among young,
middle-aged, and elderly adults?

What are the roles of
ethnicity and gender
in aging?

Describe the policy issues that an
aging society and older persons'
status in society raise
with regard to the well-being
of older adults.

What factors are associated with
whether the elderly are
accorded a position of high status
in a culture?

Eldercare: the physical & emotional caretaking of older members of the family, whether that care is day-to-day physical assistance or responsibility for arranging & overseeing such care

Important issue: how it can best be provided

Disengagement theory: argues that as older adults slow down, they gradually withdraw from society; disengagement is a mutual activity--the older adult not only disengages from society, but society disengages from the older adult, who develops an increasing self-preoccupation, lessens emotional ties, & shows decreasing interest in society's affairs

Generational inequity: states that an aging society is being unfair to its younger members because older adults pile up advantages by receiving an inequitably large allocation of resources
Raises questions about whether the young should be required to pay for the old

Activity theory: the more active & involved older adults are, the more likely they are to be satisfied with their lives; individuals should continue their middle adult roles through late adulthood; if the roles are taken away (e.g., through retirement), they need to find substitute roles that keep them active & involved in society's activities

Elderly concerns about income: overall number of older people in poverty has declined since the 1960s & has consistently been between 10-12% since early 1980s; more than 25% of older women who live alone live in poverty (60% for older African American women & 50% for older Latina women); rates for ethnic minorities are 2-3 times higher than for Whites; oldest old most vulnerable

Social breakdown-reconstruction theory: argues that aging is promoted through negative psychological functioning brought about by negative societal views of older adults & inadequate provision of services for them; social reconstruction can occur by changing society's view of older adults & providing adequate support systems for them

Living arrangements for the elderly: nearly 95% live in the community, not institutions; almost 2/3 live with family members (e.g., spouse, child), almost 1/3 live alone--of those, a majority are widowed; 5% of adults 65 & older live in institutions, 23% of those over 85 live in institutions

Ageism: prejudice against others because of their age, especially prejudice against older adults
Consequences: older adults may not be hired for new jobs or may be eased out of old jobs; they may be shunned socially; perceived as children; edged out of family life; perceived as incapable of thinking clearly, learning new things, enjoying sex, contributing to the community, holding jobs

Ethnicity/gender: older minority individuals face problems of ageism & racism; their wealth & health decrease faster than for Whites; more likely to become ill/less likely to get treatment; less education, more unemployment, worse housing, shorter life expectancy; poverty rate for elderly females is twice that of elderly males; older ethnic females face *triple* jeopardy

Stereotypes of the elderly held by young, middle-aged, & elderly adults: perfect grandmother, golden ager, John Wayne conservative, severely impaired, shrew/curmudgeon, despondent, & recluse

7 factors that predict status for the elderly in a culture: elders have valuable knowledge; they control key family/community resources; they are permitted to engage in useful/valued functions; role continuity through life span; role changes involve greater responsibility/authority/ advisory capacity; extended family is common; culture is more collectivistic than individualistic

Policy issues in an aging society: the status of the economy & the viability of the Social Security system; the provision of health care; supports for families who care for elderly adults; & generation inequity

Discuss the research findings concerning marriage in late adulthood.

Describe Robert Peck's (1968) developmental task of body transcendence versus body preoccupation.

Describe the meaning of the grandparent role.

Describe Robert Peck's (1968) developmental task of ego transcendence versus ego preoccupation.

Describe the three styles of grandparent-grandchild interaction found by Neugarten & Weinstein (1964).

Explain the process of life review.

Discuss the five types of intergenerational family structures presented in the text.

What is life satisfaction? What dimensions of life satisfaction have been investigated?

Define Erik Erikson's final stage of psychosocial development.

Describe the factors that go into successful aging.

Describe Robert Peck's (1968) developmental task of differentiation versus role preoccupation.

Explain the selective optimization with compensation model.

Body transcendence versus body preoccupation: Peck's (1968) developmental task in which older adults must cope with declining physical well-being; aging may bring chronic illness/deterioration in physical capabilities; many adults are able to enjoy life through human relationships that allow them to go beyond preoccupation with aging body

Marriage in late adulthood: married individuals live longer than those whose marriage broke up; those who were married continuously lived longer than those who were married but previously divorced; 8% of those who reach 65 have never been married & they have least difficulty coping with loneliness; with or without marriage, friendships are important for well-being

Ego transcendence versus ego preoccupation: Peck's (1968) developmental task in which older adults must recognize that while death is inevitable and probably not too far away, they feel at ease with themselves by realizing that they have contributed to the future through the competent rearing of their children or through their vocation & ideas

Role of grandparenting: about 75% of adults over age 65 have at least one grandchild; most have regular contact with grandchildren; 80% are happy with relationships with grandchildren; majority say grandparenting is easier than parenthood/they enjoy it more, grandfathers are less satisfied than grandmothers; middle-aged grandparents more willing to give advice & assume responsibility for grandchildren than older grandparents

Life review: a common theme in theories of personality development in late adulthood; life review involves looking back at one's life experiencs, evaluating them, interpreting them, & often reinterpreting them; reorganization of past may provide new & significant meaning to one's life & prepare the individual for death (Butler, 1966, 1975)

Grandparent styles: (1) for some, it is a source of biological reward & continuity with feelings of renewal or extension of self/family into the future; (2) for others, it is a source of emotional self-fulfillment, with feelings of companionship & satisfaction missing from earlier adult-child relationships; (3) for still others, it is not very important & may be experienced as a remote role

Life satisfaction: psychological well-being in general or satisfaction with life as a whole; a widely used index of psychological well-being in older adults; may include: zest versus apathy, relation between desired goals & achieved goals, self-esteem, & mood tone; associated with income, health, active lifestyle, network of friends & family

Intergenerational relationships/diversity in family structure/roles: age-condensed (teen pregnancies reduce age distance between generations/blurs boundaries); age-gapped (delayed child-bearing--creates strains & reduces pool of caregivers for aging parents); truncated (childless; establish bonds with extended family); matrilineal (out-of-wedlock births cause grandmother to be "other parent"); stepfamily (elderly parents must reconstitute intergenerational family)

Successful aging: associated with proper diet, exercise, mental stimulation, good social relationships & support, & absence of disease; requires effort & coping skills

Erikson's 8ᵗʰ stage: late adulthood is characterized by integrity versus despair; the later years are a time to look back at what we have done; if this produces a picture of a life well spent, the elder will be satisfied (integrity); if previous crises resolved in negative way, retrospective glances may reveal doubt, gloom, despair over the worth of one's life

Selective optimization with compensation model: successful aging is related to: selection (reduced capacity/ loss of functioning require reduction of performance in most domains), optimization (practice & use of new technologies allow us to maintain performance in some areas), compensation (when life tasks require level of capacity beyond current level)

Differentiation versus role preoccupation: Peck's (1968) developmental task in which older adults must redefine their worth in terms of something other than work roles; need to pursue a set of valued activities so time previously spent with children/work can be filled

Self-Test A: Multiple Choice

1. Those who adopt a disengagement theory of aging believe that:
   a. as older adults slow down, they gradually withdraw from society.
   b. the more active adults are, the less likely they will age.
   c. the more active adults are, the more satisfied they will be.
   d. reduced social interaction leads to decreased satisfaction with life.

2. When Sarah sold her business and retired, she gradually became less active and began to withdraw from society. This is an example of the _____ theory of aging.
   a. activity
   b. life review
   c. life satisfaction
   d. disengagement

3. Omar, an older retired adult who maintains his interest in friends, gold, and the stock market, illustrates the _____ theory of aging.
   a. engagement
   b. disengagement
   c. activity
   d. social construction

4. According to activity theory, when one of an older person's roles is taken away, the individual should:
   a. withdraw from society.
   b. become self-preoccupied.
   c. lessen emotional ties with others.
   d. find a replacement role.

5. Margaret finds that reaching old age is made more stressful by the general impatience and disregard society displays toward her. She best illustrates the _____ theory of aging.
   a. social breakdown-reconstruction
   b. disengagement
   c. activity
   d. generational disparity

6. According to the social breakdown-reconstruction theory of aging, when society views the elderly as incompetent, the elderly:
   a. fight back by proving their competence.
   b. label themselves as incompetent.
   c. label themselves as competent.
   d. must improve their coping skills.

7. _____ is a term that is defined as negative social stereotyping of older adults.
   a. Scapegoating
   b. Ageism
   c. Generation gap
   d. Senility

8. All of the following are examples of ageism *except*:
   a. mandatory retirement ages.
   b. when older couples holding hands are labeled as "cute"..
   c. when older adults are asked to serve as "grandparents" for teenage parents.
   d. letting employees go because they reach a certain age.

9. People over 65 make up about 12% of the population and account for _____ percent of the total health-care bill in the United States.
   a. about 12
   b. over 25
   c. over 30
   d. over 50

10. One philosophical concern over the current medical system is that it is:
    a. "care"-oriented, while most elderly health problems are chronic.
    b. "care"-oriented, while most elderly health problems are acute.
    c. "cure"-oriented, while most elderly health problems are chronic.
    d. "cure"-oriented, while most elderly health problems are acute.

11. Due to the increase in chronic illnesses as people age, many older people are cared for in their homes. This necessitates:
    a. more Medicare assistance.
    b. cooperation among health-care professionals, patients, and family members.
    c. that doctors return to the practice of making house calls.
    d. improved facilities for placing elders so their adult children can live their lives.

12. Problems with eldercare include all of the following *except* the:
    a. age of the persons giving the care.
    b. increasing number of women in the job market.
    c. uncooperativeness of the medical profession.
    d. costs.

13. A policy issue that focuses on the greater amount of resources received by the elderly compared to those received by younger adults is referred to as:
    a. generational inequity.
    b. eldercare.
    c. ageism.
    d. role preoccupation.

14. In stating that it is a disgrace to an affluent society such as ours that we have such large numbers of poor children, Bernice Neugarten (1988) stresses:
    a. we must reassess the sums of money going to the elderly, and reallocate some of those funds to children.
    b. the only way to meet the needs of both our youth and our elders is to reallocate funds from other social programs.
    c. the elderly have already lived their lives; it is the children who need the funds to have a better chance to succeed.
    d. the problem should not be viewed as one of generational equity, but a shortcoming in our economic and social policies.

15. The average income of retired Americans is:
    a. approximately 80% of what they earned at the time they retired.
    b. about half of what they earned when they were fully employed.
    c. greater than what they earned while working once we consider they have fewer work-related expenses such as meals, work clothes, travel, etc.
    d. about the same as what they earned while working once we consider they have fewer work-related expenses such as meals, work clothes, travel, etc.

16. Most elderly adults prefer to live:
    a. alone or with spouses.
    b. with an adult child or relatives.
    c. in a retirement community.
    d. in the Sunbelt.

17. During the 1970s and 1980s, poverty among both elderly and nonelderly adults:
    a. rose sharply.
    b. rose slightly.
    c. did not change.
    d. declined.

18. Sixty-year-old Anna is single and living alone. If she is typical of single, elderly females, it is most likely that Anna is:
    a. emotionally depressed.
    b. among the physically disabled population.
    c. poor.
    d. more in control of her life.

19. Within the United States, which of the following groups would be the poorest?
    a. African American females over 70
    b. the so-called "hidden poor"
    c. Asian Americans with severe physical disabilities
    d. ethnic American males who must depend on churches for assistance

20. Who is the best example of the concept of "triple jeopardy"?
    a. Maximilian, who is 75 years old, poor, White, and male
    b. Mattia, who is 75 years old, poor, Black, and female
    c. Carlos, who is 15 years old, poor, Hispanic, and male
    d. Yeh, who is 15 years old, poor, Asian, and female

21. All of the following support systems help older American minority women cope with their triple jeopardy *except* their:
    a. husbands.
    b. churches.
    c. families.
    d. neighbors.

22. Traditionally, Americans have associated the high status for the elderly with _____ cultures.
    a. our own
    b. Asian
    c. Eastern European
    d. South American

23. Which 72-year-old has a characteristic that *is not* typically associated with elevating the status of elderly individuals within a culture?
    a. Uri, who, like most people in his country, will live to be about 90
    b. Henry, who controls his family's wealth
    c. Haing, who possesses information valuable to the welfare of his country
    d. James, who is given promotions and more authority in his company based on performance and time on the job

24. Eula is typical of elderly African American women in cities. Consequently, we would expect her to value all of the following *except*.
    a. solitude.
    b. her family.
    c. the American work ethic.
    d. her religion.

25. Retirement seems to lead to greatest changes in a:
    a. "traditional" family with a working male and homemaking female.
    b. family where both spouses work and retire at the same time.
    c. family in which both parents work, but retire at different times.
    d. single-parent household.

26. The traditional older couple adjusts best to retirement when:
    a. the husband gets a part-time job.
    b. the wife gets a part-time job.
    c. both members of the couple become more expressive.
    d. both members of the couple become more independent.

27. Laura, an elderly woman, will be most content if she:
    a. continues to make new friends.
    b. has at least one close person in her network.
    c. has at least three close people in her network.
    d. remarries after her divorce.

28. Which of the following facts about grandparents *is true*?
    a. Grandfathers are more satisfied with the grandparenting role than grandmothers.
    b. Younger grandparents are less willing to care for grandchildren than older grandparents.
    c. Paternal grandparents spend less time with their grandchildren than maternal grandparents.
    d. About 50% of grandparents say they are happy with their relationship with their grandchildren.

29. Regarding their relationship with grandchildren, most grandparents report that:
    a. grandchildren these days show little respect for their elders.
    b. grandfathers are more satisfied than grandmothers.
    c. older grandparents, compared with younger grandparents, are more likely to be strict with their grandchildren.
    d. grandparenting is less difficult than parenting.

30. In the _____ style, according to Neugarten and Weinstein (1964), grandchildren are a source of leisure activity, and mutual satisfaction was emphasized.
    a. formal
    b. fun-seeking
    c. distant
    d. nurturant

31. Which of the following grandparents is *least likely* to display a formal style of interaction?
    a. one under 65 who lives near grandchildren
    b. one over 65 who lives near grandchildren
    c. one over 75 who lives near grandchildren
    d. one over 65 who lives far away from grandchildren

32. Erik Erikson believed that which final life-cycle stage characterizes late adulthood?
    a. integrity versus despair
    b. trust versus mistrust
    c. generativity versus stagnation
    d. intimacy versus isolation

33. Which of the following developmental tasks, according to Robert Peck, requires older adults to face and accept the reality of death and the value of their lives?
   a. life review versus life satisfaction
   b. differentation versus role preoccupation
   c. body transcendence versus body preoccupation
   d. ego transcendence versus ego preoccupation

34. Older adults who have derived part of their identity from their physical appearance are going to have the most difficult time with Peck's _____ developmental stage.
   a. differentiation versus role preoccupation
   b. ego transcendence versus ego preoccupation
   c. keeping the meaning versus rigidity
   d. body transcendence versus body preoccupation

35. Life review can produce all of the following *except*:
   a. increased fear of death.
   b. the discovery of the meaning of one's life.
   c. a new sense of self.
   d. an opportunity to share insights with significant others.

36. The concept of _____ in late adulthood is most closely analogous to the concept of self-esteem in adolescence.
   a. self-efficacy
   b. life satisfaction
   c. self-definition
   d. life orientation

37. All of the following are adaptive socioemotional skills suggested in the text *except*:
   a. narrow close relationships to a few of the most important people in your life.
   b. stay connected in positive ways with children and grandchildren.
   c. engage in a life review.
   d. know the factors involved in successful aging and incorporate them into your life.

38. According to the optimization component of the selective optimization with compensation model, a 70-year-old secretary who complains about her poor eyesight interfering with her proofreading skills should:
   a. buy a computer with a built-in grammar and spell checker.
   b. just accept the fact that she cannot perform the way she used to.
   c. practice grammar and spell-checking during her off-time.
   d. quit her job.

39. Social support in the elderly is associated with:
   a. higher levels of depression.
   b. rejecting assistance from formal support services.
   c. higher immune responses for caregivers.
   d. more effective coping skills.

Self-Test B: Matching

Match the individuals in the left column with the appropriate descriptors in the right column.

1. Bernice Neugarten
2. Laura Carstensen
3. Sigmund Freud
4. Carl Jung
5. Erik Erikson
6. Robert Peck
7. Robert Butler
8. Paul Baltes
9. Carol Ryff
10. Janice Kiecolt-Glaser

a. believed in old age we return to narcissistic interest of early childhood
b. believes late adulthood is characterized by integrity versus despair
c. suggests thinking what a positive spirit of aging would mean to America
d. believes life review is set in motion by looking forward to death
e. successful aging is related to selection, optimization, & compensation
f. found long-term caregivers are at risk for clinical depression
g. said that in old age little contact with reality was possible
h. said adults who have at least 3 close people in their network seem content
i. believes older adults must pursue a set of valued activities
j. older adults link well-being with good health & ability to accept change

Essay Questions:

1. Your local senior citizens center has asked you to talk to its patrons about patterns of aging and how to "stay young longer." Of special concern are issues of ageism, retirement, relationships, and health. What would you tell them?

2. The City Council in your city has approached you because the population seems to be split between the young adults and old adults. There is a concern that problems may arise as limited resources must be allocated that would affect each of these groups. What issues would you tell them to consider, and how would you suggest the matter be resolved?

Key to Self Test A:

1.	a	p.	525	21.	a	p.	532
2.	d	p.	527	22.	b	p.	531
3.	c	p.	527	23.	d	p.	532
4.	d	o.	527	24.	a	p.	532
5.	a	p.	527-528	25.	a	p.	533
6.	b	p.	528	26.	c	p.	533
7.	b	p.	528	27.	c	p.	534
8.	c	p.	528	28.	c	p.	535
9.	c	p.	529	29.	d	p.	535
10.	c	p.	529	30.	b	p.	535-536
11.	b	p.	529	31.	a	p.	536
12.	c	p.	529	32.	a	p.	537
13.	a	p.	529-530	33.	d	p.	538
14.	d	p.	530	34.	d	p.	537
15.	b	p.	530	35.	a	p.	538-539
16.	a	p.	530	36.	b	p.	539
17.	d	p.	530	37.	a	p.	539
18.	c	p.	531	38.	a	p.	540
19.	a	p.	532	39.	d	p.	543
20.	b	p.	530				

Key to Self Test B:

1.	c	6.	i	
2.	h	7.	d	
3.	a	8.	e	
4.	g	9.	j	
5.	b	10.	f	

Key to Essay Question:

1. You should address the three different social theories of aging, noting that older adults' active participation in society is beneficial; discuss ageism, its causes and consequences, and efforts to improve the status of the elderly, but don't neglect the issue of generational inequity; discuss the impact that health, income, gender, culture, and relationships have on an elderly person's well-being; then address the personality factors noted by Erickson and Peck. It would be appropriate for you to discuss the importance of a life review and the strategies presented for successful aging (e.g., Baltes' selective optimization with compensation model.) Be sure to underscore the importance of relationships and support systems in maintaining optimum life satisfaction and well-being.

2. Perhaps the most important issue to discuss here is generational inequity--what it is, how it came to be, and what are its consequences--and then present what Neugarten says about the problem (i.e., the real issue is one of shortcomings of our broad economic and social policies). Looking at the cultural factors associated with whether the elderly are accorded a position of high status, suggest how the younger and older people can work together for the common good of the whole community.

Research Project 1: Life Review--A Reprise

Note that in Chapter 17 of this Study Guide, Research Project 3 suggested you address the topic of life reviews. That project is repeated in this chapter with some revisions. Using the chart below, creating your own format, or using a basic interview format, interview an older adult. Ask your respondent to consider every aspect of her or his life using the questions suggested, e.g., "What was most important about your childhood?" "What major events have changed your family?" "What aspects of your family life are you most and least satisfied with right now?" "How would you like to see your family life in the future, and what can you do to bring it there?" "How did you get into the work you are currently in?" "How far along have you progressed with respect to your personal goals?" "What can you do to progress along as you have wished?" "Do you need to adjust your goals for the future?" Add other questions concerning education, travel, financial security, religious/spiritual side, leisure, and ask if there are other things the respondent considers to be important or relevant.

Life Review Chart				
Aspects of Life	**Past**	**Present**	**Future**	**Consequences of Review**
Family				
Friends				
Education				
Career				
Travel				
Financial Security				
Religious/Spiritual				
Leisure				

1. What did you learn about your respondent's goals, and whether those goals have been achieved?
2. How can looking at one's life help that person understand how things are going, how they got there, and how they can get where they want to go?
3. Is there another method that would be more helpful fpr looking at these issues? Explain; then use that approach.
4. What has been the most useful outcome of doing a life review?
5. What has been the most harmful outcome of doing a life review?
6. Butler (1996) noted that "as the past marches in review, the older adult surveys it, observes it, and reflects on it." Did you find this to be so in evaluating your respondent's life review? Explain.
7. Butler (1996) also noted that "this reorganization of the past may provide a more valid picture for the individual, providing new and significant meaning to . . . life. It may also help prepare the individual for death, in the process, reducing fear." Did you find this to be so in evaluating your respondent's life review? Explain.
8. What might you conclude about development in late adulthood based on your interview and your respondent's life review?

Research Project 2: Dealing with Diversity

As pointed out throughout this chapter, and elsewhere throughout the text, being female, ethnic, and old places women at high risk for all of the problems associated with poverty and aging. Consider the various factors that may put these women at risk (e.g., low educational level, prejudice) and the potential consequences that each may have (e.g., inability to access services); then consider the strengths that have been noted that these women often have (e.g., family support) and the consequences that these may have (e.g., caregiving support). (You should gather ideas from throughout the entire chapter, especially the "Sociocultural Worlds of Development" section, and also use your own observations and ideas.) Chart these factors and consequences, then answer the questions that follow.

Risk Factors	Potential Consequences
Women's role is unimportant	
Low income	

Strengths	Potential Consequences
Family support	
Religious	

1. What did you notice about the risk factors and their potential consequences?
2. What did you notice about the strengths and their potential consequences?
3. What patterns did you notice when comparing these risk factors and strengths with the information discussed in this chapter?
4. Were these patterns consistent with what you might expect from the research described? Explain your response.
5. What might you conclude about the issues that older women (particularly minority women) face based on what you have observed?
6. Based on your observations here, what type of interventions (individual, community, federal, etc.) would you suggest for alleviating the problem of double- and/or triple-jeopardy that these women experience?

Section X   Death and Dying

Chapter 21 Death and Dying

Learning Objectives

1.   Define brain death and indicate controversies concerning its definition.

2.   Define and distinguish between living wills and durable powers of attorney.

3.   Define euthanasia and distinguish between active euthanasia and passive euthanasia.

4.   Compare and contrast the meaning and experience of death in several cultures.

5.   Indicate the typical causes of death during the major life periods.

6.   Describe and compare attitudes toward death typical of children, adolescents, and adults.

7.   Define and distinguish among Elisabeth Kübler-Ross's denial and isolation, anger, bargaining, depression, and acceptance stages of dying.

8.   Compare and contrast hospitals, homes, and hospices as places in which people die.

9.   List recommendations about how to converse with a dying individual.

10. Define grief, and distinguish among the shock, despair, and recovery stages of grief as applied to the death of another.

11. Indicate the factors associated with optimal adjustment to a partner's death.

12. Define suttee and sketch cultural variations in mourning practices.

Explain the controversy
surrounding
Dr. Jack Kevorkian.

What historical changes
involving death
are discussed in the text?

Define the process
of brain death.

How does the notion of
death differ between the
United States and other
cultures?

What is the purpose
of a
living will?

Explain the various
forms of denial evident
in the way death is perceived
in the United States.

Explain the purpose
of a
durable power of attorney.

What is
Sudden Infant Death Syndrome
(SIDS)?

Differentiate between
active euthanasia and
passive euthanasia.

What are the major
causes of death
in childhood and adolescence?

What are the text's
suggestions for
avoiding pain at the
end of life?

How does the perception of
death change during childhood?
How do psychologists suggest
discussing death with children?

Historical changes involving death in U.S.: complexity of determining when someone is dead; the age group it strikes most often--200 years ago almost 50% of children died before age 10 & 1 parent died before children grew up; now death occurs mostly among the elderly; now more than 80% of deaths occur in institutions, away from family, minimizing our exposure to death

Dr. Jack Kevorkian, the "suicide doctor," encourages physician-assisted suicide; our society & our health-care system struggle with assisted suicide, although it is legal in the Netherlands if a person is terminally ill & has requested to terminate life--but even there some people oppose assisted suicide for personal or moral reasons

Cultural differences: Americans are conditioned early to live as though they are immortal & may reach adulthood without seeing someone die; in other societies death is seen daily--children die of malnutrition/disease, mothers lose as many babies as survive; in peasant areas people die at home, attend large funerals, have daily contact with aging adults, which prepares them for death

Brain death: a neurological definition of death that states a person is brain dead when all electrical activity of the brain has ceased for a specified period of time; a flat EEG (electro-encephalogram) recording for a specified period of time is one criterion of brain death; since higher portions of the brain often die before lower portions, breathing & heartbeat may continue

Denial of death in the U.S.: funeral industry glosses over death, fashioning lifelike qualities in the dead; euphemistic language for death; persistent search for fountain of youth; rejection/isolation of the aged, who remind us of death; belief in pleasant afterlife, suggesting immortality; medical community's emphasis on prolonging biological life, not end to suffering

Living will: a document that ensures the right of individuals to choose whether heroic measures will be used to sustain their lives; it permits individual to decide how, when, & under what circumstances life-sustaining treatment will be used or withheld; establishes a contract with the person, medical community, & close relatives

Sudden infant death syndrome (SIDS): the sudden death of an apparently healthy infant; SIDS occurs most often between 2 & 4 months of age; the immediate cause is that the infant stops breathing, but the underlying cause is not yet known

Durable power of attorney: specifies a surrogate person (e.g., lawyer, physician, relative, friend) as the legal designate who can make health-care decisions if the individual becomes incapacitated

Major causes of death in childhood: accidents (e.g., automobile accident, drowning, poisoning, fire, fall from a high place); illness (e.g., heart disease, cancer, birth defects)
Major causes of death in adolescence: suicide, motor vehicle accidents (often alcohol-related), & homicide

Euthanasia: painlessly putting to death persons who are suffering from an incurable disease or severe disability; sometimes it is called "mercy killing"; **Active euthanasia**: death is induced deliberately (e.g., injection of lethal dose of a drug); **Passive euthanasia**: a person is allowed to die by withholding an available treatment (e.g., withdrawing life-sustaining device)

Perception of death: infants experience loss or separation with accompanying anxiety, but have no concept of death; 3-5 years old confuse death with sleep, see it as reversible, only bad/careless people die; by 9 recognize its finality; Kastenbaum says they try to understand it
Discussing death: be honest, do *not* treat it as unmentionable

There are few fail-safe measures to avoid pain at end of life, but: make a living will & be sure someone will bring it to doctor's attention; give power of attorney to someone who knows your wishes about medical care; give doctors specific instructions ("DNR"); tell family & doctor if you want to die at home; check to see if your insurance covers home/hospice care

Explain the typical
adolescent perspective
on death.

What suggestions
does the text make for
conversing & communicating with a
dying individual?

How does an increase in
consciousness about death
develop?
How does this change in
old age?

Define & describe the
stages of grief.

Describe Kübler-Ross'
five stages of
dying.

What strategies does
the text suggest
for coping with
death & dying?

Explain the relevance of
perceived control and
denial for older people
who are dealing with death.

Explain the Hindu practice
of suttee.

Describe the hospice
movement.

Describe the basic
premises of
thanatologists.

Explain the reasons
that psychologists suggest
it is best for dying individuals
and their significant others
to know they are dying

How do
concepts of healthy grieving
differ cross-culturally?

Conversing with the dying: focus on person's strengths & preparation for remainder of life; establish your presence; eliminate distractions; be sensitive to the person's frailty; don't insist on acceptance or denial of death; allow expression of feelings; don't fear asking about the prognosis; make contacts for the person; encourage reminiscence; express your feelings of love

While more abstract than childhood, in adolescence the prospect of death is so remote that it has little relevance; the subject may be avoided, glossed over, kidded about, neutralized, & controlled by a spectatorlike orientation; while typical of adolescent self-conscious thought, some show concern for death, trying to fathom its meaning & confronting their own possible death

Grief: the emotional numbness, disbelief, separation anxiety, despair, sadness, & loneliness that accompany the loss of someone we love
Stages of grief: shock, despair, & recovery
or
numbness, pining, depression, & recovery

An increase in consciousness about death accompanies individuals' awareness that they are aging, which usually intensifies in middle adulthood; adults in midlife may fear death more than younger or older adults, but older adults think & talk about it more, & they have more experience with it; older adults are forced to examine the meaning of life & death

Coping with death & dying: don't sweep death & dying under the rug; record your death-related requests; recognize that there are different ways to face death psychologically; communicate effectively with a dying person; engage in healthy grieving & bereavement; recognize that coping with loneliness/managing daily tasks are difficult when bereaved; learn more about death & dying

Kübler-Ross' stages of dying: denial & isolation (the person denies death is going to occur); anger (denial can no longer be maintained & gives way to anger/rage/envy); bargaining (hope develops that death can be delayed); depression (certainty of death accepted, period of depression/ preparatory grief may appear); acceptance (peace & acceptance of one's fate develops)

Suttee: the now-outlawed Hindu practice of burning to death a dead man's widow to increase his family's prestige & firmly establish an image of her in his memory

Perceived control & denial: may work together as an adaptive strategy for elderly facing death; if they believe they can influence & control events (e.g., prolonging their lives), they may become more alert & cheerful; denial can protect against the tortuous feeling that we are going to die & can be adaptive (avoid damaging impact of shock) or maladaptive (keep from needed surgery)

Thanatologists: persons who study death & dying; they believe that death education provides a positive preparation for both dying and living; often stress that confronting one's own mortality & that of others is important for developing the mature perspective necessary for making life/death decisions

Hospice: a humanized program committed to making the end of life as free from pain, anxiety, and depression as possible; the hospice's goals contrast with those of a hospital, which are to cure illness and prolong life; a primary goal is to bring pain under control & help dying patients face death in a psychologically healthy way; tries to include the family as well

Healthy grieving cross-culturally: beliefs about breaking ties with the deceased vary: Western-- break bonds/return to autonomous life; Japan-- maintaining ties is accepted/ sustained; Hopi-- deceased quickly forgotten with breakoff between mortals & spirits; Egypt--dwell on grief at length; Bali--laugh & be joyful, not sad; Netherlands-- maintain contact with deceased

Psychologists believe it is best for dying persons to know they are dying & that significant others know as well, so they can interact & communicate with each other on the basis of this mutual knowledge; advantages: closure, complete plans/projects, reminisce, & more understanding of what is happening to their bodies & what doctors are doing to them

Self-Test A: Multiple Choice

1. Twenty-five years ago, all of the following were clear signs of death *except*:
   a. lack of breathing.
   b. rigor mortis.
   c. brain death.
   d. nonexistent blood pressure.

2. Elvira was brought into the hospital after a car accident. She has had a flat EEG for over 20 minutes and the doctors have informed her parents that there is no longer any electrical activity in her brain, and that she is brain dead. The doctors have given a _____ definition of death.
   a. psychological
   b. philosophical
   c. neurological
   d. anatomical

3. Currently, _____ states in the United States have accepted the cortical definition of death as a legal definition of death.
   a. no
   b. 2
   c. 36
   d. most

4. Dylan watched his father suffer for a year before dying of cancer. Now Dylan wants to be sure that he retains control over any decisions made concerning how, when, and under what circumstances life-sustaining treatments will be used or withheld in the case of his own final illness. To ensure this, Dylan should prepare a:
   a. living trust.
   b. living will.
   c. last will and testament.
   d. power of attorney.

5. Active euthanasia is:
   a. allowing the patients, if they so choose, to self-administer a lethal dose of drug.
   b. letting the person die naturally.
   c. the intentional administration of a lethal drug dose by medical personnel to the dying patient.
   d. allowing the dying patient to decide when painkilling drugs should be administered.

6. Most people tend to find fewer ethical problems with _____ euthanasia, especially where it involves older, terminally ill individuals.
   a. involuntary
   b. active
   c. assisted
   d. passive

7. The Institute of Medicine (1997) recently reported that death in America is:
   a. most often an easy process.
   b. often lonely, prolonged, and painful.
   c. usually made much easier through use of medication.
   d. increasingly a family-based event.

8. In the United States, about _____% of all deaths occur in institutions or hospitals.
   a. 20
   b. 50
   c. 80
   d. 90

9. Which of the following represents the predominant attitude toward death in the United States?
   a. general acceptance of the aged in our communities
   b. the medical community's general interest in reducing human suffering
   c. acceptance
   d. searching for the fountain of youth

10. Denial of death in the United States takes all of the following forms *except*:
    a. use of phrases like "passing on."
    b. the never-ending search for a fountain of youth.
    c. the emphasis on human suffering rather than on prolonging life.
    d. rejection of the elderly.

11. The view of most societies is that death is:
    a. the end of existence.
    b. a biological end to the body, but the spirit lives on.
    c. a time to celebrate the person's life.
    d. a terrifying experience.

12. One day Jennifer gets a call from her sister who informs Jennifer that her niece has died from sudden infant death syndrome (SIDS). As a physician, Jennifer realizes that while the cause of SIDS remains unknown, her niece actually died because:
    a. she had a heart attack.
    b. she stopped breathing.
    c. she had a massive cerebrovascular accident.
    d. her immune system failed.

13. Death in childhood is most often the result of:
    a. accidents or illness.
    b. SIDS.
    c. childhood diseases.
    d. cancer.

14. Death in adolescence is most likely to occur from any of the following *except*:
    a. suicide.
    b. motor vehicle accidents.
    c. homicide.
    d. cancer.

15. Older adults are more likely to die of:
    a. chronic disease.
    b. accidents.
    c. suicide.
    d. homicide.

16. Most preschool-aged children are not upset by seeing a dead animal. The most likely reason is that:
    a. the dead animal is not a pet and therefore they have not become attached to it.
    b. they have often seen dead animals and heard of death in stories and on TV.
    c. they have had little experience with death; therefore they have not learned to fear it.
    d. they believe the dead can be made alive again.

17. An individual who believes that people die because they were bad or because they wanted to die is most likely in the _____ period of development.
    a. infancy
    b. early childhood
    c. middle or late childhood
    d. adolescent

18. The individual who glosses over death and kids about it, but can also describe it in terms of darkness and nothingness is most likely in the _____ period of development.
    a. middle childhood
    b. late childhood
    c. adolescent
    d. early adulthood

19. The advantages of knowing that you are dying include all of the following *except*:
    a. being able to finish unfinished business.
    b. dying the way you want to die.
    c. having the opportunity to reminisce.
    d. the stress of knowing you are dying may speed up the process.

20. When asked how they would spend the next six months of their lives if they knew they were going to die, older adults are more likely than younger adults to want to:
    a. travel.
    b. meditate.
    c. finish a project around the house.
    d. read all of the books they never had time to read.

21. The order of the stages of dying as proposed by Elisabeth Kübler-Ross are:
    a. denial, anger, bargaining, acceptance, depression.
    b. anger, denial, bargaining, depression, acceptance.
    c. denial, anger, bargaining, depression, acceptance.
    d. anger, bargaining, acceptance, depression, denial.

22. During which stage of death is a person most likely to request to be alone?
    a. denial
    b. bargaining
    c. depression
    d. acceptance

23. A major criticism of Kübler-Ross' stages of dying is that they:
    a. don't actually form an invariant sequence.
    b. only apply to females.
    c. last much longer than she thought.
    d. only explain the pattern found in older adults.

24. Denial of death comes in all the following forms *except*:
    a. denying the facts.
    b. denying the implications of disease.
    c. denying the finality of death.
    d. denying the inevitability of death.

25. After learning she has terminal cancer, Ivana joins a wellness group and begins taking control of as many aspects of her life as she can, believing this will cause her cancer to go into remission. Based on the research, we might expect that Ivana will:
    a. die more quickly.
    b. become more alert and cheerful.
    c. become depressed if this does not work.
    d. become more serious and compulsive.

26. Which idea is in direct contrast to the underlying goals of a hospice?
    a. morphine for pain
    b. family for support
    c. cure for a disorder
    d. no intensive-care unit

27. When the terminally ill patient becomes depressed, others should:
    a. attempt to cheer up the patient.
    b. talk about anything other than death.
    c. tell the medical staff about it.
    d. accept the depression as normal.

28. John's mother recently died. He has trouble sleeping, is restless, and often longs for her. He is most likely in which stage of grief?
    a. shock
    b. numbness
    c. despair
    d. recovery

29. Grief work for a spouse is coming to an end when the mourner:
    a. begins to date again.
    b. recalls good times shared with the deceased.
    c. sells the house and moves away.
    d. stops crying and returns to work.

30. Which of Averill's stages of grief is similar to Kübler-Ross' acceptance stage for the dying person?
    a. despair
    b. shock
    c. recovery
    d. pining

31. A major problem with long-term grief is the potential for:
    a. depression and suicide.
    b. keeping one's feelings locked away.
    c. sadness turning to uncontrollable rage.
    d. internalization of feelings that leads to the breakdown of the immune system.

32. Which family is engaging in the most common postdeath group experience concerning the loss of a family member?
    a. The Cleavers, who each blame themselves for Jerry's death
    b. The Nelsons, who refuse to discuss anything about Ricky's recent death
    c. The Cartwrights, who seem to be reliving and recalling more about the last few weeks of Lorne's life
    d. The Bradys, who are thinking about only positive interactions that occurred with David before his death

33. Research by Lund (1996) found most people who suffer the loss of someone close to them:
    a. require professional help if they are to get through the bereavement successfully.
    b. are extremely resilient.
    c. have very similar feelings about the loss.
    d. soon recover from the loneliness, but have continuing problems managing the tasks of daily living.

34. _____ is an outlawed Hindu practice in which widows of deceased men were burned.
    a. Hara-kiri
    b. Mortali
    c. Suttee
    d. Matricide

35. Which practice *is not* commonly associated with Amish mourning?
    a. holding the funeral ceremony in a barn
    b. a horse and buggy "hearse"
    c. a deceased body dressed in black
    d. support for bereaved family members

36. Sydney, a thanatologist, believes:
    a. people are by nature seekers of death.
    b. learning about death causes people to consider taking their own lives.
    c. the dead are unclean and anyone who touches a dead body becomes defiled.
    d. education provides good preparation for dying and living.

Self-Test B: Matching

Match the individuals in the left column with the appropriate descriptors in the right column.

1. Jack Kevorkian
2. Robert Kastenbaum
3. Elisabeth Kübler-Ross
4. Dale Lund

a. believes that despite the stress of death, many survivors are resilient
b. proposed a five-stage process of death and dying
c. the "suicide doctor" who assists terminal patients in their suicide
d. believes very young children are acutely aware of separation and loss

Self-Test C: Matching Stages of Death and Dying/Grief

Match the stages of death & dying or grief in the left column with some of their descriptions in the right column.

1. denial
2. anger
3. bargaining
4. depression
5. acceptance
6. shock
7. despair
8. recovery

a. resolution of grief; resumption of ordinary activities, pleasant memories of deceased
b. development of hope that death can somehow be postponed or delayed
c. feeling of shock, disbelief, & numbness, often weeping or becoming easily agitated
d. development of a sense of peace, acceptance of one's fate; often desire to be alone
e. painful longing for/memories & visual images of deceased; sadness, insomnia
f. belief that death is not really going to take place
g. feelings of resentment, rage, and envy; great realization of loss
h. certainty of death is accepted & preparatory grief may appear

Essay Questions:

1. A good friend has approached you with a difficult decision--his father is in the last stages of a terminal illness and the medication he is on is not controlling the excruciating pain he experiences. Your friend tells you that his father has asked for help in dying, and your friend is torn between the anguish of watching his father suffer and his own moral reluctance to help his father die. He asks for your help in deciding what he should do. Take a totally objective perspective on this, based on what you have read in the chapter on euthanasia--discuss under what circumstances a person in the medical profession might consider terminating a patient's life, and when it would not be appropriate to do so. Include in your answer a discussion of when a person is considered "dead" from a clinical perspective, and how you might advise your friend under those circumstances. Finally, take a stand on the issue of euthanasia and support your position.

2. You have just learned from your mother that your favorite aunt is dying. Having no children of her own she has always been extremely close to you, even more so than any of her other nieces and nephews, although she considers all of you to be like her own children. Your mother says the doctor, a young oncologist, has not yet told your aunt of her diagnosis, wanting to discuss it with the family first. To achieve the best possible outcome for your aunt and for the family who love her, what should be done? Should she be told? If so, why; if not, why not? How should the rest of the family be told? How should family members deal with her and with each other? How would you expect your aunt and other members of the family to react during and after her death? Would you recommend hospice care? Explain the reason for your answer.

Key to Self Test A:

1.	c	p.	551		19.	d	p.	556
2.	c	p.	551		20.	b	p.	556
3.	a	p.	552		21.	c	p.	556-557
4.	b	p.	552		22.	c	p.	556-557
5.	c	p.	552		23.	a	p.	558
6.	d	p.	552		24.	c	p.	558
7.	b	p.	552		25.	b	p.	558
8.	c	p.	553		26.	c	p.	559
9.	d	p.	554		27.	d	p.	560
10.	c	p.	554		28.	c	p.	560
11.	b	p.	553		29.	b	p.	560
12.	b	p.	554		30.	c	p.	560
13.	a	p.	554		31.	a	p.	560-561
14.	d	p.	555		32.	c	p.	561-562
15.	a	p.	555		33.	b	p.	561
16.	d	p.	555		34.	c	p.	563
17.	b	p.	555		35.	c	p.	563
18.	c	p.	555-556		36.	d	p.	564

Key to Self Test B:

1. c
2. d
3. b
4. a

Key to Self Test C:

1.	f		5.	d
2.	g		6.	c
3.	b		7.	e
4.	h		8.	a

Key to Essay Question:

1. Whatever your personal biases for or against euthanasia, you will need to put them aside to answer this question. Explain the terms *euthanasia, passive euthanasia,* and *active euthanasia,* then explain when they are used. Address the issues of assisted suicide and Dr. Kevorkian—looking at such things as the patient's suffering, moral/ethical concerns (both sides of that issue), and legal concerns; also to be considered here is the financial, physical, and emotional drain on the family as well as their feelings about the dying patient. Then it is important to look at exactly what constitutes death—is it the cessation of breathing, brain function, etc., and discuss the issues involved in brain death. After addressing all of these issues, you may then explore your own personal feelings on the subject.

2. Here it would be important to discuss the reasons psychologists suggest it is best to tell a terminal patient of his or her impending death (e.g., putting affairs in order, making decisions regarding his or her own life and death, etc.); it is also important to be honest with other family members, taking their age into account in terms of how they are told. Family members should be encouraged to talk to each other and to her, noting the many suggestions throughout the chapter on how to communicate with someone who is dying. Then, to predict how your aunt and other family members will react, you will need to discuss Kübler-Ross' stages of dying, noting the limitations of that theory and that there is no one right way to die; and look at the two theories of grieving presented in the text (Averill's three stages, Parke's four stages). Explore the notion of hospice care--what it does and does not offer--taking into consideration your aunt's own wishes. It would also be important to discuss the issue of a living will and preparing a durable power of attorney to ensure that your aunt's wishes will be carried out.

Research Project 1: Talking About Death and Dying/Grief

Contact a local hospital, seniors citizen center, community center, hospice, or other facility that sponsors support groups for terminal patients and their families to find one that will allow you to sit in on a group meeting and talk to group members (some will, some won't--you'll have to check them out). Learn about their experiences and observe their patterns of dealing with their potential or actual loss; more importantly, observe how they have come to deal with and accept the loss--the strategies they use, the types of support system they have, etc.

On the basis of your participation and observations, answer the following questions:

1. What similarities did you notice between the terminally ill and their loved ones?
2. What differences did you notice between the terminally ill and their loved ones?
3. Were there differences in the way people dealt with these issues based on gender, age, ethnic or cultural background, marital status, support system, or religious orientation? Explain these differences and what you conclude about how each of these variables affected the individuals' ability to cope with loss.
4. What patterns did you notice for dealing with loss in terms of the material discussed in this chapter?
5. Were your observations consistent with what you might expect from the research described? Explain your response.
6. What might you conclude about coping with one's own death or the death of a loved one based on your observations?

Research Project 2: Helping Others Deal with Death, Dying, and Grief

Dying is a personal experience not only for the terminal individual, but for surviving family and friends. Taking account of individual differences (whether based on personality/temperament, cultural background, gender, age of the dying person, age of mourners, etc.), and drawing on the material presented in this chapter, design an intervention that will help the person who is dying as well as family and friends to deal with the impending death and, afterwards, for the survivors to deal with their grief. Be sure to remember that even people from the same family may deal with their grief differently--there is no one "right way" to do it. When you have designed your program, present it to a local hospice, hospital, religious center, or other appropriate organization for feedback and implementation. What types of interventions would you use? How do your strategies differ, depending on the different variables involved? Report what you learn about using such a program--did you get constructive feedback on how to improve it? Was your intervention well received? If it was utilized, what types of comments did you get in terms of how helpful it was for those involved? How did you feel about creating the program and implementing it?

A variation on this project might be specifically to target children--both in terms of children who are terminally ill as well as children who have experienced the loss of a loved one. How would your intervention differ for them, as opposed to dealing with adults? What types of strategies would you use for children that you might not use for adults? Would it be easier or more difficult to work with children? Explain.

Having designed and implemented (or attempted to implement) your death and dying/grief intervention, answer the following questions:

1. What similarities did you notice between the terminally ill and their loved ones in the way they responded to the intervention?
2. What differences did you notice between the terminally ill and their loved ones in the way they responded to the intervention?
3. Were there differences in the way people dealt with these issues based on gender, age, ethnic or cultural background, marital status, support system, or religious orientation? Explain these differences and what you conclude about how each of these variables affected the individuals' ability to cope with loss.
4. What patterns did you notice for dealing with loss in terms of the material discussed in this chapter?
5. Were your observations consistent with what you might expect from the research described? Explain your response.
6. What might you conclude about coping with one's own death or the death of a loved one based on your observations?

Research Project 3: Pictorial Life Review

Note that in Chapters 17 and 20 of this Study Guide, Research Projects addressed the topic of life reviews. Those projects are repeated here with some revisions. Think about your own life and ask yourself about your life using the questions suggested, e.g., "What was most important about your childhood?" "What major events have changed your family?" "What aspects of your family life are you most and least satisfied with right now?" "How would you like to see your family life in the future, and what can you do to bring it there?" "How did you get into the work you are currently in?" "How far along have you progressed with respect to your personal goals?" "What can you do to progress along as you have wished?" "Do you need to adjust your goals for the future?" Add any other questions concerning education, travel, financial security, religious/spiritual side, leisure that you consider important or relevant.

After considering all of the issues that you feel are relevant to your life review, present those ideas pictorially. You may draw or paint your life or a self-portrait containing the answers to your questions, put together a collage, or do any other type of visual project that will assist you in seeing your own life in answer to the questions you have asked. After completing the visual project, answer the questions that follow.

1. What did you learn about your goals, and whether those goals have been achieved?
2. How can looking at your life help you to understand how things are going, how you got there, and how you can get where you want to go?
3. Is there another method that would be more helpful for looking at these issues? Explain; then use that approach.
4. What has been the most useful outcome for you in doing a life review?
5. What has been the most harmful outcome for you in doing a life review?
6. Butler (1996) noted that "as the past marches in review, the older adult surveys it, observes it, and reflects on it." Did you find this to be so in evaluating your life review? Explain.
7. Butler (1996) also noted that "this reorganization of the past may provide a more valid picture for the individual, providing new and significant meaning to . . . life. It may also help prepare the individual for death, in the process, reducing fear." Did you find this to be so in evaluating your life review? Explain
8. What might you conclude about development in late adulthood based on your life review?